Architecture from the Indonesian past

In all cities mentioned on the maps, the architecture firm Fermont-Cuypers had built one or more projects between 1927-1957 CON

Obbe Norbruis

ARCHITECHTURE FROM THE INDONESIAN PAST

Life and work of Fermont-Cuypers in the Indonesian archipelago 1927-1957

LM PUBLISHERS

CONTENTS

1 Introduction 7

2 Preface 9

Notes accompanying chapters 1 and 2 11

3 Designing in Turbulent Times 13

Notes accompanying chapter 3 71

4 List of works 77

5 Catalogue of works 79

6 The Architects 281

- Freek Dicke (1909-1985) 281
- Arnold Dikstaal (1903-1968) 281
- Arthur Fermont (1882-1967) 282
- Willem Jaski (1868-1958) 283
- Han de Jongh (1886-1965) 283
- Matthias Kaptijn (1890-1963) 284
- Laurent Logemann (1898-1954) 284
- Karel Mekel (1920-1997) 285
- Henk Roebbers (1923-1999) 285
- Thomas Nix (1904-1998) 286
- Theo J. Taen (1889-1970) 287

7 Bibliography 289

8 Index 293

9 Abbreviations 296

Jakarta, the former NITOUR building in 2013, with the bridge and the statue of Mercury in the foreground PHOTO: PETER BOSMAN CON

1 INTRODUCTION

In 1927 revolts broke out against the colonial authority in the Dutch East Indies. They were suppressed, but the fear of repetition lingered. The Netherlands suppressed that fear through the bombastic reburial of former Governor-General Van Heutsz, the man who once had the colony under control.[1] Van Heutsz belonged to another time, just as Eduard Cuypers who had died shortly before. The architecture firm he once founded with Marius Hulswit in the colony, which is written in the book *Landmarks from a bygone era*, continued under the new name 'Fermont-Cuypers' and went on to build more than ninety buildings, during a quarter of a century, most of which still exist. The story behind these buildings has remained unknown until now. In Indonesia they know nothing about it. Knowledge of colonial times in Indonesia is limited. 'The Dutch have achieved a lot and brought little' was an English journalist's answer to a question.[2] When attention was drawn to irrigation works, large ports and other infrastructure, the answer was: 'the Dutch installed them to get something', and: 'They kept the population clueless. In British India, the English built schools for the local population'. There was no indication of how untrue this was, because in the Netherlands this self-image also exists.[3] The economic crisis, in the early 1930s, meant that the Dutch government, supported by the parliament, began structurally cutting back on the construction of schools for the first time since 1901. Perhaps that was a lasting impression, but there were also other initiatives than those taken by the government. The Fermont-Cuypers firm designed and built more than twenty-five schools in ten years, thanks to the Catholic people in the Netherlands, who funded them. Twenty-five schools in a decade was barely a drop in the ocean because the population grew by more than twenty million people in the same period. You always had too few schools with such growth in the population.[4] The job was virtually beyond normal capabilities but the Netherlands did not want to acknowledge this. Fermont-Cuypers was not discouraged. The fact that their buildings did not reach the architecture trade journals in the Netherlands did not matter either. There was always little interest in terms of architecture in the Dutch East Indies. In the Netherlands, architects in the 1930s were occupied with themselves, with each other and with a directional struggle between 'modernists' and 'traditionalists', coupled with a 'left' or 'right' political conviction.

After the crisis, business began to regain confidence in the Dutch East Indies. Fermont-Cuypers designed their new head offices, robust structures in a modern business style. In January 1940 *Life* magazine published an article about the Dutch East Indies, 'This sprawling empire of 20,000 islands, covers a sea area wider than the U.S. It has 65,000,000 brown natives of 137 cultures(...) The Dutch have given every nation in the world a startling demonstration of how to get the best out of a colonial empire'.[5] The travel industry in the Dutch East Indies had faith in the future and counted on more tourists as 1940 approached. Fermont-Cuypers designed Netherlands Indies Touring's 'Nitour' office and also the Rotterdamsche Lloyd's passenger terminal in the port of Jakarta. Both buildings were designed in the optimistic 'international style'. Even after the Germans had overrun the Netherlands, the insurance company 'De Nederlanden van 1845' put its new premises in Surabaya to use. The stained-glass windows of the building designed by Fermont-Cuypers, still show that the public could insure themselves against everything. Or against almost everything, because there was no insurance against what happened shortly afterwards.

The buildings of Fermont-Cuypers are buildings from a past that was partially suppressed on both the Indonesian and the Dutch sides. Delving into the history of these buildings reveals their material and emotional value and is both amazing and admirable.

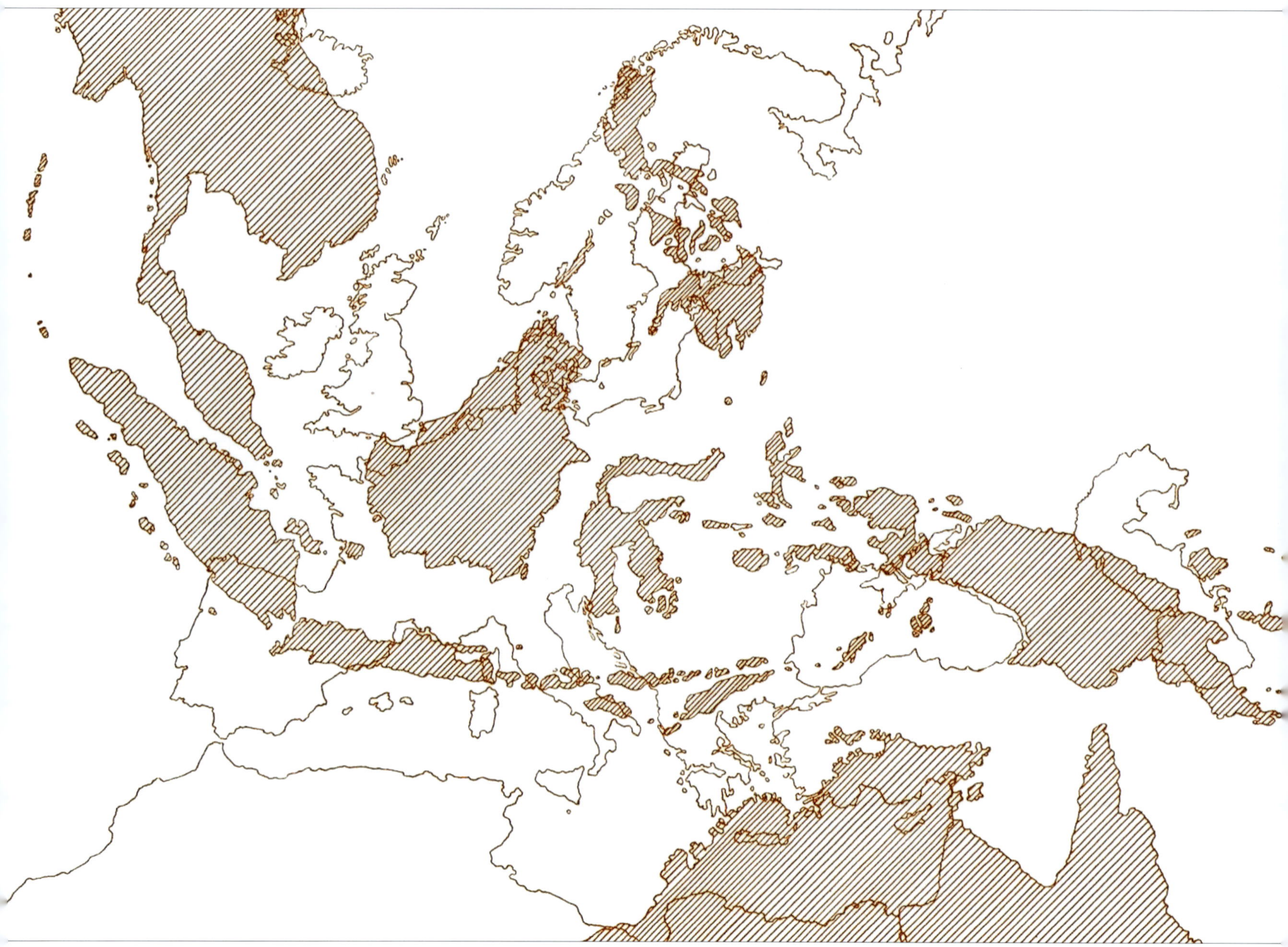

The Indonesian archipelago, superimposed on the map of Europe COLIJN 1911, P.1

2 PREFACE

Research

Various Dutch historians conducted research into the development of Indonesia under the Dutch government. Their books are often illustrated with photographs, in which buildings form the setting for the things they describe. In this book the events form the decor of the buildings and the firm that designed them. Their story has never been written down, and those who knew about it were often forced to leave Indonesia to return to the Netherlands, where no one showed interest in their stories, which were also overshadowed by the war and the Indonesian struggle for independence.[6] This book is about buildings, their architecture and the people behind them. I have deliberately refrained from judging architectural quality with the measuring rod that was provided to us in the West, with 'modernity and innovation' being important criteria. The Dutch East Indies was not the Netherlands. I have immersed myself in the architects, their lives and their ideas. All the newspapers they would read are now digitally available. These give a picture of a society that I do not judge. 'We have to assess the historical facts in the context of the time as they occurred', said Dutch historian Cees Fasseur, 'No cheaper wisdom than wisdom after the fact'.[7] Supplemented with information from archives, interviews and the discovery of a large part of the archive of the firm, I reconstructed the story of Fermont-Cuypers, including their entire works. In this story I also included the events in Asia and Europe that (potentially) influenced their thinking. In the absence of available research findings to present a complete picture, at times I had to rely on assumptions. I chose to ignore the period 1942 to 1950, in the first place because works in the office work were at a standstill, but also because the misery of the past did not cast a shadow on what had preceded it.

For whom

This book brings order to an unknown part of (architectural) history. It remained unspoken as it was shrouded in discomfort relating to what was supposed to have happened in colonial times, or what did indeed happen. This book contains information about buildings that Indonesia deals with on a daily basis. Nowadays, large Dutch architecture firms are highly successful in Asia. They, and other people who are interested in architecture can read here about how their predecessors worked in a different time and under different conditions. Most buildings that are described are used by Indonesian companies. This book is also meant for them. It corrects inaccuracies surrounding the Fermont-Cuypers firm that have been recorded in the past, often through ignorance. This book also seeks to highlight the correct facts before they take on lives of their own in the Netherlands and Indonesia. Finally, this book is for people who are interested in the 'most productive firm of architects' in pre-war Indonesia.

Method

Almost nothing is known about the people who worked at Fermont-Cuypers. I immersed myself in the books, magazines and newspapers they read, and gained therefore an understanding of colonial society in the 1930s. I have used present-day geographical names, including Jakarta (Batavia, Djakarta) and Bogor (Buitenzorg), but I do speak of the Dutch East Indies.[8] I have thoroughly explored all available sources, which predecessors have also drawn from. These searches yielded much new information from archives, libraries and newspaper articles, which are now much more accessible than in the last century.[9] Through the discovery of a large part of Fermont-Cuypers' office archive, I was able to give more content to the research than I initially dared hope for. Interviews in the Netherlands also contributed to this, as did my visits to Indonesia. Meetings with people there confirmed my suspicion that I was working from a eurocentric approach.[10] This was an inevitability as I am not an Indonesian. Nor were the people I describe.[11] The Dutch writer Hella Haasse wrote: 'I was born in the Dutch East Indies (...) and yet I was nothing more than a stranger in that country'.[12] I have nothing to add to these words. I was not even born in that country.

Sources

The fact that the Fermont-Cuypers firm is not well known is partly due to the company itself. The firm rarely published its own work. There is more written about those colleagues who did so. Those who referred to the work of Fermont-Cuypers, referred to the names of Eduard Cuypers (1859-1927) and Marius Hulswit (1862-1921). They were generally associated with exclusively nineteenth-century architecture.[13] Architectural historian Bert Gerlagh paid attention to Fermont-Cuypers for the first time in the late seventies, in a study on Eduard Cuypers.[14] His thesis provided input for the oeuvre list that others later adopted, including the inaccuracies.[15] This meant that the few sources that existed, had to be tested and recalibrated. Indonesia does not have accessible archives with building plans. The firm often worked on behalf of Catholic institutions that were accountable to their congregations in the Netherlands. This resulted in photographs, building plans, specifications and explanations in the archives of the various Catholic orders.[16] The interviews with relatives of a number of architects brought them to life. Arthur Fermont took his archive, consisting mostly of photographs, from Indonesia after the war and kept it himself. After his death in 1967, it remained in the family.

The firm

In 1927, after the death of Eduard Cuypers, the firm was renamed 'Fermont-Cuypers', and subsequently retained this name.[17] Arthur Fermont was its director.[18] He was appointed by the shareholders' meeting, which reappointed him a few times. The firm had an average of fifteen permanent employees, varying from secretary to accountant and from contractor to civil engineer.[19] Theo Taen, Han de Jongh, Matthias Kaptijn and Mrs. Ter Beeke-Heijnneman, the secretary, worked there for more than twenty years. Thomas Nix was employed for more than nine years. Nix was a good designer and left his signature on his drawings. Laurent Logemann worked for more than seven years, beginning in 1926. Both Logemann and Nix had studied architecture in the Netherlands. That did not apply to Arnold Dikstaal, who gained a few years of experience with the architect Dudok in Hilversum, before he went to the Dutch East Indies.[20] Theo Taen, who studied architecture in Germany, was ultimately responsible for the design work throughout the prewar period. No drawing went out the door without his initials. Theo Taen also designed a lot. Taen, who was the grandson of the famous Dutch architect Dr. P.J.H. Cuypers,[21] was rather modest, 'perhaps too modest', according to his family.[22] Many employees were Catholics. That was practical for Catholic clients, but they were not selected for that reason. They were certainly familiar with Catholic cultural views, and Thomas Nix followed lectures from the well-known professor Granpré Molière (1883-1972) in Delft.[23] They nonetheless followed the latest trends in European architecture. Fermont and Nix were fond of airplanes and fast cars, as is clear from their family albums. In 1942, the firm closed its doors after the Japanese invasion, reopening them six years later with much smaller team and some newly recruited employees. This group, with Henk Roebbers, in 1953 graduated from Delft, contributed to the building of Indonesia until Sukarno's 'Sinterklaas' decree of December 5, 1957 forced all Dutch people to leave the country.[24]

Architectural styles

In Indonesia, architectural styles from colonial times are regularly lumped together and are called 'empire style'.[25] Studies of the work of Fermont-Cuypers, but also of that of their colleagues, reveal a considerable differentiation. Architects in the Dutch East Indies were strongly influenced in their time by international developments, from expressionist, Art Deco, functional, modern objective and traditional styles. All movements stemmed from Western architecture. An Indonesian interpretation had to be given, because building in the tropics involved different demands than in Europe. Each movement evolved its own variation. Fermont-Cuypers often applied functionalism for schools and hospitals built in the Dutch East Indies; modern objectivity for offices and business premises; traditional for ecclesiastical institutions; and 'modern' for clients who asked for it. In the 1950s a young generation of architects worked in Indonesia, in an architecture now called 'Jengki style', inspired by post-war architecture in American suburbs. Fermont-Cuypers also participated in this. Former employee Freek Dicke, as a professor in Bandung, was one of the driving forces behind this movement.

Architecture

'Modernism', as is recognised in the Western world and also known in the Netherlands as 'Het Nieuwe Bouwen', did not lend itself to the tropics until the arrival of the air-conditioning.26 Fermont-Cuypers therefore almost always opted for the Indonesian roof and for narrow tall windows with awnings above them to keep the sun out. A modern design with a flat roof only originated from the drawing boards of Fermont-Cuypers if the client explicitly asked for this.[27] For example, the firm designed the building which the Italian consulate in Jakarta would occupy in 1934,[28] as well as some villas and the 'Nitour' building in Jakarta. Other modern-looking buildings were given a roof such as Hotel des Galeries in Jakarta and the British American Tobacco factory in Semarang.[29] The latter was built in the early 1930s as a business complex by Hollandsche Beton Maatschappij, including a flat slab floor.[30] At Fermont-Cuypers, they closely followed developments in architecture in Europe. The firm never stuck rigidly to one architecture style: "All things change, and we move with them" was the slogan of the office.[31] In order to follow the latest developments in the field of architecture, the world's exhibitions were pre-eminently suitable. The architects of Fermont-Cuypers combined a visit to the Netherlands as much as possible with one of the many exhibitions that took place in Europe between 1927 and 1940.

As author I use these exhibits with the architectural discussions in Dutch trade magazines, as a backdrop for the architectural developments at Fermont-Cuypers.

Oeuvre list

This book describes the period from 1927 to 1957, which saw the completion of almost ninety projects of Fermont-Cuypers. The number is larger, but how much greater was not possible to determine. The list was made up of information from the aforementioned sources. The projects are in the order of the year of completion, because drawings with dates are almost always missing. The description refers to the building as it was shortly after being completed. Brief reference is also made to the current state and the use of the building. Each project is accompanied by photos from the past, to do justice to the era. Because buildings appeal more when the people behind them come to life, they are consciously given a prominent place in the explanatory notes.

Author

I do not have a (family) bond with Indonesia. In the Netherlands I belong to the generation with whom there was no nuanced talk about the colonial past. In 2010 I decided to visit Indonesia. I wanted to see what had been built there in colonial times with my own eyes. Relatively little about it had been written.[32] Strange that a country such as the Netherlands, which attaches so much importance to its own building past has charted so little of the past that it shares with Indonesia. 'Most people here on land will not know much about the many works that have been built there by Dutch architects over the years', wrote an architect in 1959 with some sadness.[33] There has been little improvement since then...

Obbe H. Norbruis, Amsterdam 2020

Notes accompanying chapters 1 and 2

1 Witte (1976), p. 129.

2 Pisani (2014), p. 19.

3 Jong (1984), part 11a, p. 145. 'In comparison with the British Indies, the percentage of native children who received a form of education in the Dutch East Indies was no less'.

4 With this population growth, more than a thousand schools had to be built annually nationally.

5 Life January 22, 1940.

6 Den Doel (1996), p. 297. '...the decline of the Dutch East Indies, the Japanese occupation and war with the Republic of Indonesia have remained traumatic events for many Dutch people, (...) invariably the focus is on the imprisonment in the Japanese internment camps and the actions of the Dutch military during the so-called police actions, subjects about which much has been written.'

7 Fasseur (1995), p. 212.

8 The Dutch East Indies, I reserve the name Indonesia for the independent republic.

9 See chapter Abbreviations.

10 Doorn (2003), p. 17.

11 Doorn (2003), p. 12. 'What can also be said to the detriment of colonialism, it must primarily be understood as a route to prosperity and civilisation, a phase in history in which the more developed Western world, driven by their own interests led lesser developed societies, against their will to a better future'.

12 Haasse (2010), p. 94.

13 Akihary (1990), pp. 100-102.

14 Gerlagh (1979), pp. 87-88. Bert Gerlagh devotes some attention to his successors for the first time in his study of Eduard Cuypers in 1979.

15 Passchier (2016), p. 176. Two obvious inaccuracies that were until recently still being publicised are that Fermont died in 1954 and that the Fermont-Cuypers firm ceased to exist. A.A. Fermont died in 1967 and the Fermont-Cuypers office folded, after being seized by Indonesia in 1960.

16 Much archive material has been collected at Erfgoed Kloosterleven in St. Agatha (Netherlands).

17 The firm's name changed a few times before 1927, which caused confusion. In Amsterdam the old office changed Ed. Cuypers, after the death of its founder, to the name 'Eduard Cuypers'.

18 Gerlagh (1979), p. 87; Akihary (1990), p. 105; Passchier (2016), p. 176. All mention an incorrect year of death.

19 A short career plan has been included in this book of a number of employees working between 1927-1957.

20 Dikstaal succeeds on October 6, 1939 in Bandung for the exam as an architect.

21 P.J.H. Cuypers (1827-1921) was the architect of among others the Amsterdam Rijksmuseum and Central Station.

22 Interview with Mr. T.F.M. Taen (1924-2014) and his wife on May 21, 2014 in Nijmegen (Netherlands).

23 Molema (2010), p. 71. Molema calls the representatives of this group 'conservative and against the spirit of the times'.

24 What remained of the Fermont-Cuypers firm was nationalised on January 16, 1960.

25 Kusno (2007), p. 132.

26 Most examples of 'modernism' in the Dutch East Indies therefore arose only at the end of the 1930s into the early 1940s.

27 It seems that most other firms in the Dutch East Indies were doing the same.

28 Passchier (2016), p. 84. About the consulate: 'It is one of the few buildings in Menteng that have been built in a modernist style'.

29 For comparison: Hilversum Town Hall (W.M. Dudok, completed 1931). Rotterdam Van Nelle factory (L.C. van der Vlugt, completed 1930).

30 This construction was later also used in the Pasars in Semarang and Palembang designed by Th. Karsten.

31 The firm put this motto on a menu at a dinner celebrating the laying of a foundation stone for the Javasche Bank (now: Bank Jateng) in Semarang.

32 Leushuis (2011). This practical guide from Leushuis had not yet been published.

33 *Bouwkundig Weekblad*, March 14, 1959, p. 130, M. Westerduin.

Amsterdam, front of Palace on Dam Square, the procession for the reburial of former Governor-General Van Heutsz on June 9, 1927 CON

« Bandung, poster of the Malabar broadcasting station CON

‹ In 1927 Dutch Queen Wilhelmina used the radio to address her compatriots in the Dutch East Indies. Behind her is Princess Juliana KITLV

Jakarta, the Fermont family left for the Netherlands in 1926. Some colleagues said goodbye to them, in the back row: Laurent Logemann (with tie) and to the right Emiel Schedler. To his right with bow tie, Theo Taen and on the far right Matthias Kaptijn. Squatting on the right is Philip Wijsman and Han de Jongh with bow tie. Mr. and Mrs. Fermont are seated CFC

3 Designing in Turbulent Times

Amsterdam 1927: Everything is engineering

Less than a week after the funeral of Eduard Cuypers (1859-1927), former Governor-General Van Heutsz (1851-1924) was reburied, sparking great interest.[1] He had ensured 'peace and unity' in the colony and was a hero for many Dutch, especially those in the Dutch East Indies. Since the end of 1926, uprisings had broken out on Sumatra, spreading to Java; the establishment in the colony craved peace and order.[2] Reconstruction of those events showed that there were revolutionary plans, at least on paper, that were 'carefully thought through by a small group of Indonesians with communist sympathies'.[3] From reports found later it appears that there were calls for arson, cutting through telephone wires, the destruction of rails and railway bridges, as well as the killing of top civil servants and the liberation of prisoners. The uprisings caused a shock among the European population, who continued to believe in the role that they thought they had to play in the Dutch East Indies. The army vigorously opposed these revolts, leading to a ban on the communist party. The house of Mohammed Hatta (1902-1980), studying in the Netherlands, was thoroughly searched. He was chairman of the Perhimpoenan Indonesia association, that published the magazine *Indonesia Merdeka*, which was smuggled to the Dutch East Indies. There, Sukarno (1901-1970) founded the Perserikatan (Partai) Nasional Indonesia (PNI), a party that grew considerably.[4] The 26-year-old Sukarno, who graduated in 1926 as a civil engineer in Bandung, was chairman of the party.[5] A party that was clearly in favour of the immediate independence of Indonesia without any reservation. They founded their own schools, started peoples' universities and trade unions and mainly focused on young people. This meant that many Indonesians became more critical of the Dutch in their country, who in turn felt threatened and started to handle things more conservatively.[6] The Dutch newspaper *De Telegraaf* of September 2, 1927 devoted many words to a discussion about the expansion of the number of Indonesians in the Council of the Dutch East Indies. The Catholic Party believed that 'increasing the number of natives at the expense of the number of European members will greatly harm the prosperity and development of the Dutch East Indies.[7] Although not everyone shared that opinion in the Catholic camp, the willingness to participate in a self-government effort lost momentum. This attitude was in line with a change in European thinking where in many countries democracy was exchanged for 'strong men' and 'forms of dictatorship'. *De Telegraaf* of September 2, 1927 devoted space to a meeting of the Dutch Royal Institute of Engineers, during which the members of the annual meeting stood still at the death of members whom they had lost, including Eduard Cuypers. Then all attention went to the 'Radio Telephony' with the Dutch East Indies. 'In Kootwijk (the Netherlands) a transmitter with large electric power is now ready. It may be that the distance between the Dutch East Indies and the Netherlands has not yet structurally been overcome by plane, the ether has made the leap', according to the newspaper.[8] The time is coming of big, bigger, biggest. In Holland, the *Algemeen Handelsblad* held a survey among its readers who they considered the greatest figures of their time. In first place and third place were Edison and Marconi; Benito Mussolini came second.[9]

Under this constellation, engineers, also in the Netherlands, were given plenty of room to do 'something big'. Now known as innovation. The Zuiderzee works were in full swing and at the Philips company in Eindhoven the millionth radio was produced as a triumph of technology. The Dutch Queen Wilhelmina and Princess Juliana used it, also to speak to their subjects in the East. 'The first word, which I can address directly to the Dutch East Indies, is a greeting from heart to heart to the overseas region which, despite the distance, is so dear to me.'[10] Mr. Zeilinga (1884-1933), former director of the Javasche Bank (now: Bank Indonesia), did the same a year later. In his radio message, which was also to be heard in Jakarta, he evoked memories of his time in the Orient, in which he explicitly named Marius Hulswit (1862-1921) and the 'woodcarvers who worked under his inspiring leadership'.[11] The time of Eduard Cuypers, Hulswit and Zeilinga was a bygone era.

Jakarta, Fermont-Cuypers offices on Molenvliet Oost 30 (now: Jl. Hayam Wuruk) as it was built in 1922, according to their own design CFC

Jakarta 1927, in front of the offices is the ever busy Molenvliet canal (now: Batang Hari) CON

Jakarta 1927: Architects and Engineering Fermont-Cuypers

After the death of Eduard Cuypers, Arthur Fermont and Theo Taen continued the office under the name Fermont-Cuypers. That was good for the continuity and recognisable for the customer. Theo Taen welcomed the Cuypers name. It was his mother's maiden name. It was through her that he joined Eduard Cuypers in 1918 and ended up in the Dutch East Indies three years later. Han de Jongh and Matthias Kaptijn, who had been working for the firm for more than five years, apparently had no trouble with that name. 'Fermont-Cuypers' was applied with large letters on the façade of the building they had been occupying since 1923 on Molenvliet-Oost (now: Jl. Hayam Wuruk). Laurent Logemann (1898-1954) made a name for himself in the office. He was the son of Rotterdam's city architect.[12] After obtaining some architecture diplomas, he had left for the Dutch East Indies in 1926. Laurent was versatile and made appealing sketches. During his training he had met numerous architects with just as many views on the subject and architecture.[13] His arrival contributed to interesting discussions about the architectural viewpoint and the course of the firm.

The variation in architectural styles that had been used in the past was easy to explain. Eduard Cuypers had given strong direction to this. The firm had little time for modernism, and it was not the only one in the Dutch East Indies. What were you supposed to do in the tropics with large windows, flat roofs and the credo: 'Light, air and space'? Ideally, they built 'East Indies', that is to say in a building style developed in the tropics, called 'East Indies objective'. They displayed it again with the St. Joseph pavilion of the Borromean hospital in Bandung.[14] For buildings with an international status they used 'modern objective' style, such as the last two buildings for the Javasche Bank on Sumatra.[15] Emiel Schedler (1906-1986) and Philip Wijsman (1902-1970) produced the drawings.[16]

In Banda Aceh, in the presence of Willem Jaski, the foundation stone was laid for the new Catholic church. Jaski was the expert with experience, the contractor who built the first Eduard Cuypers project in the Dutch East Indies twenty years earlier. He once started his career with the design and construction of the first Roman Catholic church in Medan in 1904.[17] The train journey from Medan, where Jaski lived, to the capital of Aceh lasted at least two days at the time. The task was a heavy one for Jaski who suffered from eye problems.[18] Fermont came from Jakarta on the one hand to assist him, but also to obtain a commission for a Catholic hospital in Medan. That hope quickly came to nothing. Han Groenewegen (1888-1980), an architect from the Netherlands, came over on a tip from his brother-in-law, who had informed him that Catholic Medan wanted a new hospital. Groenewegen made some appealing sketches and shortly afterwards received the assignment. In the years that followed Groenewegen got a lot more work in Medan.[19] Bitter for Fermont-Cuypers. They increased the accessibility of Medan with a 'passenger terminal' in Belawan, but did not profit from it themselves. For Jaski and Fermont there was little else left for them to do in Medan other than the completion of the construction of the 'Amsterdamsche Handelsvereeniging' and laying of the first stone foundation of the Escomptobank (now: Bank Mandiri) , for which Fermont-Cuypers made the design.[20]

In Jakarta there was an assignment from the Nederlandsche Handel-Maatschappij, which wanted to build simple business premises at the port of Cirebon on the north coast of Java.[21] Apparently satisfied with the result, the Factorij ('Nederlandsche Handel Maatschappij', the Dutch Trading company) provided a new assignment shortly afterwards for a business building with office in Cilacap on the south coast of Java. In Jakarta, it was time to work on the famous Hotel des Indes. The creation of Hulswit and Ed. Cuypers was once again in need of renewal.

Banda Aceh, the builders of the church KDC TF3C9538

Banda Aceh, the new church shortly after completion in 1927 CON

That meant a thorough renovation, for which Fermont-Cuypers received the assignment. The firm had brand recognition in the hotel industry. It was approached at the end of 1926 for a new front building for the 'Oranje Hotel' (now: Majapahit Hotel) in Surabaya, an interesting job that, for unknown reasons, did not take place.[22] They were happy with the renovation of Hotel des Indes, but it would have been better if the design for the new main building had been entrusted to the firm. Earlier they had made a design proposal in 1925, for which Alfred Kreisler (1888-1980), then working at the firm, had made a promotional drawing. Eduard Cuypers was then still involved in that design process, which led to a Dutch-East-Indies-looking building with an impressive roof construction. This ensured good ventilation and a chic appearance. On Kreisler's drawing, the new building was situated in such a way that the party hall or the 'glass pendopo' of Hulswit and Ed. Cuypers from 1919, was also clearly visible from the road. In October 1927, this plan was slightly modified by Logemann in the hope that the management would grant them this assignment.[23]

Amsterdam 1928: 'The modernists on the warpath'

In 1928, the successors of Eduard Cuypers published a new magazine in Amsterdam: *Het Nederlandsche en Ned.-Indische Huis Oud en Nieuw*. The name was not original, nor was the content. The first issue was entirely dedicated to the death of Eduard and his work. The fact that he made the design for an Olympiad cup that served as a trophy at the Amsterdam Olympics that year remained unmentioned.[24] The organisation of the games had been financially dependent on fundraising activities among companies and private parties. The Dutch government did not contribute anything. A majority of parliament, consisting of liberals and confessionals, did not see sport and play as a concern for the government. This was different in countries such as the Soviet Union and Italy. This led to centrally controlled processes that had to 'uplift' the country and the people. That appealed to everyone who was in favour of innovation in Europe, including many modern-oriented architects. The Soviet Union was their favourite, because it had fundamentally broken with the past, also in architecture. In the rest of Europe, modernism had barely any impact. To stand firm in the struggle for modernism, twenty-three architects met in 1928 in La Sarraz, Switzerland.[25] They called their meeting Congrès Internationaux d'Architecture Moderne (CIAM).[26] An official statement was signed with the promise to forcefully oppose other architectural views. They consistently called them 'conservative', because in their view modernism was the only option that offered a way to the future. They thought that everything was measurable and rationally explainable. Le Corbusier accordingly looked at a building in the same way as a machine, a ship or even a human being.[27] Otherwise oriented architects felt supported by a few contemporary philosophers, including Broder Christiansen (1869-1958). He concluded: 'The modernists rationalise everything: art, labour, life and themselves'.[28] Someone like Henri Bergson (1859-1941), who received the Nobel Prize in 1927, said that there was more than reason (ratio). You also needed intuition and faith, because only that provided vitality and dynamics in life.[29] At the Technical University in Delft, modernism hardly received any attention during those years. It was regarded as something of a passing trend, 'because architecture has to look for an eternal truth in architecture by rejecting all transitory currents', according to Professor M.J. Granpré Molière.[30] He stated that 'modernism has made a deep break in our spiritual heritage'.[31] Granpré Molière said he admired modern architecture, adding that 'this movement is only focused on 'mechanical beauty' and therefore it lacks depth.[32] His words matched those of the previously mentioned Broder Christiansen.[33] These noted that modernism did not seem to need any gods and therefore modernism was free of 'carriers of belief'.[34] A dozen students, with different religious convictions, went in search of 'architecture with depth' within an Architecture Study Group they founded in Delft.[35] In their search, they discovered that it was a

Amsterdam, on the occasion of Eduard Cuypers' death, his successors in Amsterdam decided to publish *Het Nederlandsche en Ned.-Indische Huis Oud & Nieuw*. This was for three years: 1928, 1929 and 1930
CON

Cirebon, the recently opened commercial premises of the 'Nederlandsche Handelsmaatschappij' in 1927, designed by Fermont-Cuypers CFC

Amsterdam, a memorial glass for the Olympic Games in 1928, designed by Eduard Cuypers shortly before his death COF

Amsterdam, postcard showing the stadium for the Olympic Games in 1928 CON

Medan, the new Escompto bank building to the left of the Varenkamp bookshop in 1927 CON

Pontianak, opening of the Javasche Bank on May 7, 1928. Fourth from left is Arthur Fermont CFC

Malang, in December 1928 two towers were added to the church that Marius Hulswit built in 1906 CFC

matter of simple main forms, restraint, natural materials, a protective roof and small windows carefully placed in the façade. 'These designers were asked to exercise self-control in order to keep what serves the individual subordinate to what serves the general.[36] One of them was Thomas Nix, who, with a diploma under his arm, wanted to return to the Dutch East Indies, the country where he came from.[37]

Jakarta 1928: Madiun and the legacy

In May 1928 Arthur Fermont sailed to Kalimantan to attend the opening of the Javasche Bank in Pontianak. The building was technically ingenious. It stood on a floating caisson, because the swampy soil wasn't suitable for sinking foundations. The same principle they had previously applied to the Javasche Bank in Banjarmasin in 1923. Both bank buildings have disappeared now. In his opening speech, Fermont was full of enthusiasm about all the technical ingenuity that his office had applied. On July 3, 1928 he sailed to Medan to assist Jaski, whose health continued to fail. Jaski said goodbye as a municipal councillor and left the office shortly afterwards to return to the Netherlands.[38] Fermont decided to close the branch in Medan, also because Han Groenewegen had gained a firm foothold. Shortly thereafter, he would expand the Catholic church of Jaski and provide it with a tower. At Fermont-Cuypers, a much smaller church was conceived at that time, namely in Tanjung Karang on the southern tip of Sumatra. It was built with half-timbering, so that it was resistant to earthquakes. In the office in Jakarta there was another church on the drawing board, namely that for Bandung East. Architecturally, this was more prestigious. Other assignments were a building for the Javasche Bank in Kediri and a club building in Subang. However, the biggest assignment came from the new mayor of Madiun in central Java. He came as a mayor from the much larger Cirebon and wanted, before his retirement, to put his new municipality on the map.[39] He was committed to a new town hall and, with good memories of Cirebon, a beautiful bank building for Javasche Bank.[40] Shortly after his appointment as mayor, a resident miss M.E.J. Manuel, died who, to everyone's surprise, left a considerable legacy for the municipality. In her will, she had two conditions attached: the money should finance a theatre to be built on her plot on the main street. The other condition was that the entire city council had to attend her funeral. Although some council members had little to do with her, they all came, possibly at the mayor's insistence.[41] He succeeded in persuading the city council to accept the inheritance, perhaps with the addition that it was financially sensible to enlist the same architectural office for the town hall and for the theatre. Then the mayor proposed the Fermont-Cuypers firm, the 'in-house architect' of the Javasche Bank. Fermont travelled to Madiun, 700 kilometres from Jakarta. The mayor asked him to make two preliminary designs, including two global cost estimates, to which the city council had to agree.

In Jakarta, the board of directors of the Hotel des Indes, after lengthy deliberation, decided that A.I.A. architects were allowed to design its main building.[42] Probably in response to the sketches of Fermont-Cuypers, this office had presented a more modern design proposal, for which the 'glass pendopo' had to make way.[43] Fermont succeeded in winning the assignment for the management of this building. Meanwhile, in Malang a wish expressed by Marius Hulswit was posthumously fulfilled. After many years there was enough money to add two towers to the Sacred Heart Church, which would make the church a cathedral. The church board had approached Mr. A. Grünberg with the request to supervise the construction. He must have contacted the firm in Jakarta to be able to work on the basis of Hulswit's drawings.[44] Grünberg was no stranger to Fermont-Cuypers. Previously, he was a senior civil servant at the municipality of Jakarta. A little while later, the bells, which had been hanging in Hulswit's steel belfry next to the church for almost 25 years, were installed in both towers. At the end of the year the completed church was solemnly consecrated.[45]

Amsterdam 1929: Stock market crash and crisis in the Netherlands

Events in the old world were not reassuring. Mussolini, the Italian leader, concluded a concordat with the Vatican City. The treaty was considered a triumph for the Italian dictator. The Roman Catholic Church saw him as the best available alternative in Italy, despite the criticism it had of fascist violence, also against its own institutions.[46] In Germany, there were riots of left-wing radicals against the social-democratic government of the shaky Weimar Republic. The *Nationaalsocialistische Deutsche Arbeiterpartei* (NSDAP) of Adolf Hitler benefited greatly, according to results of the municipal elections. To make matters worse, the stock market crash in New York followed in October 1929. Due to a drop in the share prices, the banks were asking companies to repay their outstanding loans, resulting in an avalanche of bankruptcies. In Moscow, Communist leadership put an end to the tactics of 'a united front with the Social Democrats'. Stalin told the world that it was the 'main duty of the international working class to support the Soviet Union with all available means.' Idealists, including architects went there, partly to escape the crisis in their own country. Many would experience powerful repression and return disillusioned. In Spain, unrest arose due to major political opposition. The Netherlands wanted to be neutral and with the slogan 'Buy Dutch manufactured goods', it tried to keep its own production going. The Netherlands also wanted to count as a colonial nation. The Colonial Exhibition, which took place in Paris in 1931, offered an excellent stage for this. The organisation for the Dutch contribution was in the hands of P.A.J. Moojen (1879-1955), the man who lived in the Dutch East Indies since 1903, but barely worked as an architect since 1914.[47] Moojen had searched for the most suitable architect for the pavilion. He approached nine people who had impressed him in the past. Four of them now lived in the Netherlands.[48] Fermont-Cuypers was not on his list. He probably associated this firm with Eduard Cuypers, an architect with whom he had had serious collisions in the past. No winner emerged from the Moojen competition.[49] As a result of the crisis in the Netherlands, there was also a considerable unemployment rate in construction.[50] For architects who chose to go to the Dutch East Indies, things would go from bad to worse , because the crisis got much harder there.[51]

Jakarta 1929: 'Duo' Passenger Terminal on the Koningsplein-West

At the end of 1929, 26-year-old Arnold Dikstaal set foot in the Dutch East Indies with his wife.[52] Arnold's brother, who lived there, had convinced him to come over: 'because you can mean something for the Dutch East Indies'.[53] The Netherlands was no longer waiting for an architectural draftsman. He was welcomed at Fermont-Cuypers.[54] There were no less than nine projects in the planning. The new Catholic Church was completed in Bandung East shortly before his arrival. The construction took only four months. British American Tobacco wanted a large factory in Semarang, for which Fermont-Cuypers was commissioned. The complex, unlike in Cirebon, was outside the city centre. The firm designed a building with a modern look and a simple roof construction to control the indoor temperature. It was not designed as a 'box'. There was little enthusiasm in the Dutch East Indies for such a design, as it appeared from a discussion in some newspapers on the occasion of the opening of Rechtshoogeschool (law school; now: Kementerian Pertahan Republik Indonesia) in Jakarta. A reviewer, with a lot of affection for modern architecture, wrote in the *Javabode*: 'In its strict simplicity the new building of the Rechtshoogeschool at Koningsplein West should attract the special attention of everyone who passes through it.[55] The building has succeeded as modern architecture, in which the quiet flat layout and the horizontal band and awning decoration contribute to the individual aspect.' The *Nieuws van den Dag voor Nederlandsch-Indië* reacted strongly to this: 'instead of "strict simplicity" it would be more apt to speak of "childish building blocks."' According to the newspaper, the building did not attract 'the special attention, but the wholehearted annoyance of thinking people about bad taste. And if one soon plants some bushes and trees around it, the horrible miscarriage will not hurt the eye for long. It is the ugliest, most prosaic impulse that has ever come to our attention. The horrible Beurs of Berlage in Amsterdam is a Renaissance palace in comparison with this building.[56] And now all kinds of "artistic" buffoons say of course: "Yes, but this is modern architecture now. And you do not understand that!" But I answer: "It's a litter box!"'[57]

Jakarta, sketch of the front building for Duo passenger terminal, as included in the bid book that won Fermont-Cuypers the commission in 1929. The drawing is by Laurent Logemann. The building is now being used by the Ministry of Human Development and Culture CFC

Jakarta, the new building of the Rechtshoogeschool (now in use; Ministry of Defence) designed by M.B.T. Tideman (BOW) as it was completed in 1929. It was considered 'beautiful' by some, whilst others described the building as a 'hideous litter box' CON

Fermont-Cuypers worked on Duo Passenger Building, which also came to Koningsplein-West (now: Medean Merdeka Barat). Stoomvaart Maatschappij Nederland and the Rotterdamsche Lloyd wrote a project proposal for this one year earlier under the name N.V. Duo. Fermont-Cuypers won, with the commitment on their part that they could complete the project in record time.[58] Laurent Logemann made the presentation drawing. It was a sleek, stylish building in a 'Dutch East Indies commercial' style. This connected with many other buildings around the Koningsplein, except for 'the litter box'.

In May 1929 Fermont left for Kediri for the opening of the Javasche Bank.[59] It meant travelling over more than 700 kilometres, but the Javasche Bank was a customer who appreciated his presence at openings. The more than 150 attendees heard him say: 'This is the eighteenth bank building that we have been allowed to build for the Javasche Bank (now: Bank Indonesia) and I hereby express my great thanks for the trust you have placed in us'. During one of his trips to Madiun, Fermont made a stop in Ambarawa a few times, to discuss a new school building there. Shortly afterwards, Madiun's city council gave the green light. For the first time at Fermont-Cuypers, a town hall and a theatre would take concrete shape. The first sketch by Logemann for the town hall shows a romantic, almost endearing building. The plan eventually became more business-like, possibly at the instigation of Thomas Karsten (1884-1945), who at that time acted as advisor to the municipality of Madiun.[60]

Amsterdam 1930: 'Modernism departed from the foggy countries'

In Antwerp there were again a great many pavilions in Art-Deco style at the World Exhibitions for Colonies. They were more sober and more cubic compared to previous exhibitions. The Dutch pavilion was an example of this: a box with a monumental character, with some sculptural towers protruding high and angled to attract attention.[61] The building did not want to be overshadowed by the English pavilion, which as a colonial power radiated power with its more classical architecture. The architecture of modernism was the great absentee. The Soviet Union, of which this style of architecture was to be expected, was not present at this exhibition.[62] Countries, where modernism had played a role until recently, started to rediscover their taste for decorations and ornaments.[63] Only in Italy did modernism play a significant role. At the opening of a building by Giuseppe Terragni (1904-1943) in Como it was written: 'The new architecture continue to move on, it left the foggy countries of the north and arrived in Italy'.[64] The group of archi-

Antwerp, Dutch pavilion in 1930, designed by H.Th.Wijdeveld (1885-1985) *TROPISCH NEDERLAND* AUGUST 11, 1934

tects who sympathised with modern architecture in Italy did not want to break with tradition. They wanted to 'connect in an abstract way to a sober functionality from old times'.[65] There was plenty of work in Italy, both from individuals and from the regime, which set up numerous projects.[66] Italian fascism presented itself with modernism as a youthful and revolutionary movement.[67] Italy showed the world that it believed in the future, although that was not apparent from the architecture of its pavilion in Antwerp with a dome, Ionic columns and some statues from Roman times.

Jakarta 1930: 'Continue to build for education'

Due to the rumours that the National Party (PNI) was considering a coup on January 1, 1930, the police in Bandung searched the houses of all leaders and 'propagandists' of this movement. Several hundred were detained, including Sukarno. Shortly after, everyone was released, with the exception of Sukarno and three fellow board members. The land council accused them of 'inciting resistance against colonial authority'. Sukarno's punishment was the most severe with four years of imprisonment.[68]

For Fermont-Cuypers, the year started with the completion of the new building for the Canisius College in Jakarta.[69] The firm designed a large cluster of buildings in an 'Indies functional' style. At the opening, the mayor said it was unfortunate that nothing of the new building was visible from the public road.[70] Two old villas blocked the view of all renovation because it had not been possible to buy them. That would happen later. Laurent Logemann drew three proposals for a new Javasche Bank in Semarang in February, which the management could choose from. They opted for the design that most closely matched the new zeitgeist in Europe: the 'monumental era'.[71] Despite the simple main form, the building did not come across as modern due to the heavy vertical lines and the blunt tower. The bank decided to postpone construction due to the crisis. For the next phase of the Vincentius hospital in Surabaya, years of saving had raised sufficient funds. A final building plan was made by Fermont-Cuypers. It was a different story for the Theresia Church in Jakarta, where funds were still being raised. The office had been hoping for an assignment for the church and the presbytery since 1926. Several design proposals had already been made for both projects. Eduard Cuypers may even have been involved with this project shortly before his death.

Madiun, town hall shortly after its completion in 1930

KERCHMAN (1930) P. 437

Madiun, the theatre shortly after completion in 1930 CFC

Madiun, council chamber in the town hall with the portrait of Queen Wilhelmina on the back wall *LOCALE TECHNIEK* JANUARY 1933, PP. 1-9

Jakarta, Duo passenger terminal on Koningsplein-West (now: Jl. Medan Merdeka Barat) shortly after completion in 1930. The building is now being used by the Ministry of Human Development and Culture CFC

Jakarta, sketch of the front building of Duo passenger terminal, made by Lauren Logemann in 1929 CFC

Eventually there was enough money for the presbytery. For the church, the bureau again made a sketch design, which was printed on a postcard. Sales of these cards also had to generate money. The campaign did not have much success, it would take at least four years before the church was completed, a different one than on the postcard. At companies, banks and the government it was clearly noticeable that the Dutch East Indies almost exclusively produced raw materials. The country was hit by the crisis even more than other countries. Of the approximately fifty thousand Europeans who worked in the private sector in 1930, a fifth were unemployed six years later, while more than four hundred thousand Indonesians lost their jobs in the same period.[72] The firm's order book dried up. It was decided to create more advertising. An advertisement appeared in the book *De Koloniale Roeping van Nederland*, which came out in 1930 and now appears to the reader as one big hymn to the work of the engineers in the Dutch East Indies.[73] However, a lot changed. Projects at distant locations were no longer accepted by most architectural firms, unless there were several of them at once. Fermont-Cuypers went to work with a few orders on the island of Banka, namely a school in Belinyu, a convent, a school and a small church in Muntok as well as a school complex in Pangkal Pinang. The firm developed building systems, with which, depending on the task-setting budget, a smaller or larger building plan could be realised. In 1930, a compact church was erected in Purwokerto based on such a construction system.[74] Inside, the church breathed a cubist modernity, visible in its furniture, columns, capitals and a light ceiling frame with rectangular and square plates.

In Madiun, the town hall and the theatre were nearing completion. Due to setbacks during construction, Fermont asked the municipality to pay for the additional costs, but the mayor did not agree. There were no words about it at the openings of both buildings. The Dutch red-white-blue flags hung on August 1, 1930, and tribute was paid to the architects, the builders and the officials involved. The mayor expressed the wish that the construction of the town hall would stimulate others to build new buildings, thereby referring subtly to the Javasche Bank.[75] Then a portrait of the Dutch queen was unveiled in the council chamber. It had arrived from Amsterdam shortly before. After the unveiling, a suppressed chuckle went through the Council chamber. The image did not look very much like her majesty. In the evenings, the guests were seated at the new theatre, where they could laugh freely at a stage setting. From outside this setting would later become the typical 1930s style. In the hall hung a picture of Miss Manuel, the generous donor who had made the building possible.

Although the Escomptobank (now: Bank Mandiri) was also affected by the recession, Fermont-Cuypers received two assignments from them in 1930, namely for a building in Banjarmasin on Kalimantan and in Padang on Sumatra. The designs of both buildings shared the same simplicity. The bank in Padang was larger but had to miss the luxury of previously completed bank buildings. As far as the buildings are concerned there was similarity in the proportions, the symmetry in the façade and the roof with the expressive 'diadem' with vertical flagstaff.

After a discussion over the direction of the Indische Katholieke Partij (the Catholic party in the Netherlands East Indies), Matthias Kaptijn left municipal politics in Jakarta.[76] He then took over a number of organisational tasks from Fermont, who was therefore able to travel to his family in Europe more often. Theo Taen did not aspire to a leading role. He continued to coordinate the design work with pleasure. The Duo passage building at Koningsplein-West (now: Medean Merdeka Barat) was festively opened in 1930. 'It has become a beautiful building in all its simplicity', according to the *Nieuws van den Dag voor Nederlandsch-Indië*.[77] Two days before the opening, there was tumult on the other side of the Koningsplein in the Volksraad (The People's Council). The national group demanded under the leadership of M.H. Thamrin (1894-1941) 'independence from Indonesia as soon as possible'. Thamrin wanted to achieve this by 'political reforms and the aim to eliminate all colonial antitheses and by all appropriate legitimate means'.[78] His demand reached the Governor-General, who referred it to the Netherlands, knowing that little would happen. The Netherlands was mainly concerned with itself. It seemed that Dutch East Indies, since the crisis, only functioned as a cash cow for the homeland. The irritation about the Dutch position was so great that the Europeans in the Dutch East Indies thought that 'their country' should become more independent.[79] To promote the Dutch East Indies abroad, the 'Handbook of the Netherlands East Indies', published by the Department of Economic Affairs, was published in 1930, containing five photographs of buildings designed by Fermont-Cuypers and their predecessors.[80] The depression caused the government to cut sharply in the budgets for education in the Dutch East Indies.[81] The firm only designed school concepts that could be developed in phases. In itself that was not unusual, they had been working in this fashion for years on hospital projects, such as the 'Carolus' in Jakarta where they designed a new main building as well as a convent and a chapel, which were built consecutively. When it appeared that for the project in Pangkal Pinang the budget only covered a 'half boarding school', it was decided to complete half of it. Despite the economic crisis, Thomas Nix was allowed to expand staff numbers in Jakarta in November 1930. He was a year younger than Arnold Dikstaal. He had completed his studies at the Technical University in Delft, after which he married Lies and they had a son. Now he had returned with his family to the Dutch East Indies, his native country. Thomas sketched a lot, gladly and easily, mostly pen drawings with the most diverse subjects, but especially of people going about their daily activities.

Amsterdam 1931: 'More distance between east and west'

In the year in which National Socialists strengthened their grip on power in Germany: Hitler became a German citizen; the Spanish king fled his country; Japan conquered large parts of China; and a National Crisis Committee was established in the Netherlands - the Colonial World Exhibition took place in Paris.[82] Arthur Fermont, on leave in Europe, visited this Exhibition. Once inside, there were tall, free-standing columns and light poles bordering a wide entrance lane with a modern-looking reception building. At night, spotlights illuminated the pavilions, most of which had a classic feel, often with high pillars reaching up to the eaves. Countries showed off replicas of buildings from their overseas territories. Although the Dutch preparatory committee did not want a replica, the Dutch pavilion looked like a monumental Balinese temple. P.A.J. Moojen had made the design more or less himself.[83] Moojen, was the man who had worked against Eduard Cuypers for twenty years, in his preparations for a comparable exhibition, in what he called the 'exhibition building'. He arranged for the Dutch department to be able to extend over a wide area, where everything was displayed as in a museum. Most of the objects had been loaned by the 'Koninklijk Bataviaasch Genootschap' in Batavia. (now: Museum Nasional)[84] Other countries emphasised the latest techniques. In that respect, the illuminated maps with the shipping lines of, among others, the Rotterdamsche Lloyd and the 'Koninklijke Pakketvaart Maatschappij' were doing well. Most western countries emphasised the latest techniques. The same was true for the eye-catching luminous lines of the weekly KLM (Royal Dutch Airlines) flights with small moving airplanes. The European visitors of 1931 wanted sensation above information and walked excitedly through the light shows, water theatres and totem fountains. The comparatively tame Dutch pavilion unintentionally caused sensation, because it burned down to the ground on June 28, 1931. The *Algemeen Handelsblad* enumerated all the valuables that were lost and concluded: 'our people can no longer buy a ticket to Paris to see what we do in the Dutch East Indies [...] it is a national disaster and we must actually express our condolences towards our entire people'.[85] It was decided to build a new pavilion to be opened 17 August.[86] Both in the first and the second building, the contributions showed unwittingly that the gulf between the culture of the indigenous population and that of the West was only widening. This certainly compared with the exhibition in 1910 in Brussels, for which Eduard Cuypers had been deployed. 'In the architecture of the colonial pavilion, Eastern artisticism and Western technology literally stood side by side and opposite each other, as two poles, each with its own valuable strength.'[87] The pavilion, both the first and the second, received a lot of criticism after construction, and not just from a political perspective.[88] Architect J.Th. van Oyen (1893-1944) said from where he was in the Dutch East Indies that the result was an architectural scandal: 'instead of a good modern building in tropical architecture, here we come with a poor imitation of Balinese architecture'.[89] What Van Oyen apparently had failed to realise was that in the meantime modernism in Europe was declining.[90] In the same year, the 75-year-old Berlage was invited to sit in an editorial team that wanted to publish a series of books on Modern Architecture in the Netherlands.[91] The editors wanted to show which fine examples had been realised in the Netherlands, in the hope of inspiring others. W.M. Dudok (1884-1974) was one of the initiators. He arranged that several buildings of his were included in the first part of the series. One of these was the new Hilversum town hall, which was completed in 1931.[92] During the opening, reference was also made to the public bathhouse, which was built by Dudok in Hilversum ten years earlier. Dudok received a lot of praise. The father of Arnold Dikstaal was considered to be a driving force behind this project.[93] He had died unexpectedly a year after Arnold's arrival in the Dutch East Indies. Because of him, Arnold was able to work at Dudok for two years shortly before he left.[94] Dudok was Arnold's great inspiration.

Jakarta 1931 'Hotel des Galeries, expressionist modern'

At the end of 1930, there were plans to build a new hotel with the name Hotel des Galeries on the corner of the Molenvliet-Oost (now Jl. Hayam Wuruk No. 1) and the Harmonieplein (now Harmoni). An Arab developer had bought the land and wanted an expressive, eye-catching, modern building. Many 'Arabs', as referred to by the newspapers, invested in new real estate in the Dutch East Indies. Dikstaal wanted to make the design in the spirit of Dudok. He drew a plan, of which the presentation drawing appeared in various newspapers during the year. The design was expressive and sculptural and had something refreshing, something of confidence in the future, characteristic of the modernists. Even in the Netherlands the project was noticed. The *Algemeen Handelsblad* wrote: 'The Fermont-Cuypers firm has relinquished the traditional Cuypers style with this design, of which the front on Noordwijk (now: Jl. Ir. H. Juanda) has a particular appeal. It is in itself rewarding that it has saved us the famous arched galleries, which seemed to be inseparable from all products of their tropical architecture'.[95] Fermont, still in the Netherlands, read it with surprise. The journalist was apparently unaware that the firm had also completed totally different types of buildings with Eduard Cuypers for years than those with arcades. Hotel des Galeries was not the only building in

Paris, International Colonial Exhibition in 1931, with the Dutch East Indies Pavilion *PARIS GUIDE L'EXPOSITION COLONIALE INTERNATIONALE DE 1931* CEM

modern style that was being created at Fermont-Cuypers. In Semarang, for example, the finishing touches were put to the British American Tobacco factory. At the end of the year, the firm signed up for an extensive shopping and cinema complex in Jakarta.[96] The drawing was made by Thomas Nix, who was given plenty of leeway within the firm. He also made a plan for the expansion of the church in Bandung East and designed a Javanese church with presbytery.[97] His Catholic faith was certainly an advantage.[98] His drawing skills made a big impression. During a conversation with a client he would sketch the ideas in perspective on paper, sometimes even upside down for the convenience of his conversation partner, working with great flair from various vanishing points.[99] Through his studies in Delft and the discussions that took place there, he knew what was happening in Europe in the field of architecture. He must have shrugged his shoulders about Berlage's book *Mijn Indische Reis*, which appeared in 1931. Eight years after his trip, it was outdated and Berlage's opinion hardly mattered. A journalist from *De Indische Courant*, however, wholeheartedly recommended the book: 'Those who love the real Dutch East Indies will enjoy reading this book'.[100] Sales were disappointing, both in the Netherlands and in the Dutch East Indies. Was it the high price, was it the crisis, or was Berlage indeed a person of the past?

Laurent Logemann left the office after five years and joined the Municipality of Batavia (Jakarta) as a manager. That was special, because there were also many staff cuts in government departments through redundancy schemes.[101] Luckily the firm was popular among Catholic clients, who wanted to invest in new buildings thanks to fundraising. As a result they received projects from the Ursuline Sisters of the Little Monastery, next to the cathedral in Jakarta. The members of this group had bought land for a convent complex and a new student school, which had to be built partly behind and partly adjacent to their Julianaschool (now: SMA Santa Ursula) on the Waterlooplein (now: Lapangan Banteng). The brothers on the Koningsplein-Oost (now: Medan Merdeka Tim.) also wanted something new.[102] There were plans to build a brothers' house behind their school complex from 1906, designed by P.A.J. Moojen. Thomas Nix made the design. In March 1931 Han de Jongh sailed to Padang on Sumatra. In September of the same year he was in Banjarmasin on Kalimantan. In both cases to attend the openings of the Escomptobank. The building in Banjarmasin looked fresh and friendly. In fact, it displayed kinship with the larger offices in Jakarta and Medan in the proportions and in the façade layout. De Jongh was photographed at the opening, sitting on the ground, amid all the seemingly optimistic audience. Three years later, the building had to close

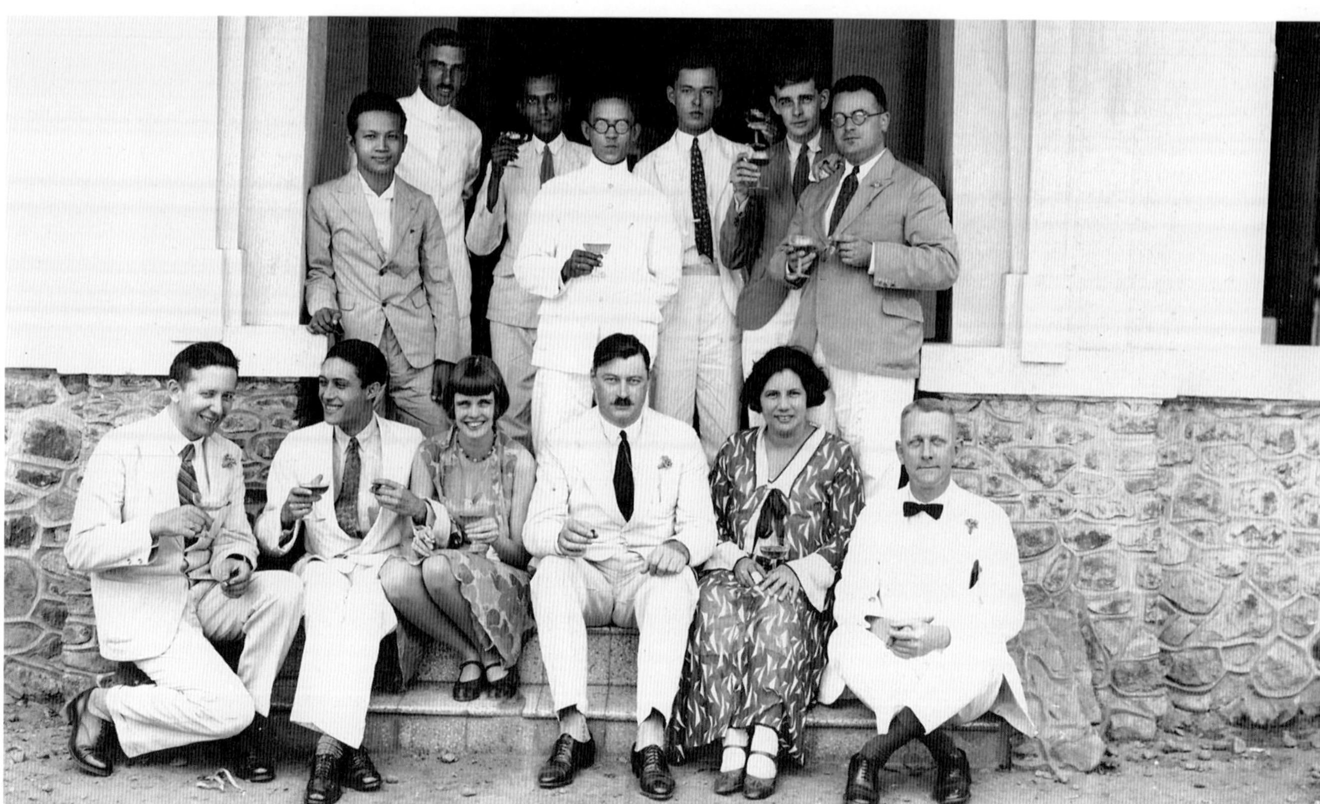

Jakarta, the Fermont-Cuypers team in 1933, sitting from left to right, include: Messrs Taen, Nix, Kaptijn and De Jongh. Secretary Mrs Ter Beeke-Heijnneman between them. Standing from right to left: Messrs Brouwer, Dikstaal, Schedler, Wijsman. They are celebrating the completion of a project CFN

Jakarta, sketch from October 1930 for Hotel des Galeries by Arnold Dikstaal CFC

its doors. The economic crisis hit the Escomptobank particularly hard, so therefore a large number of branches disappeared.[103] The banking institution continued to use the new building in Padang. It stood a stone's throw from the Javasche Bank on the Handelskade (now Jl. Batang Arau) This building still exists (now: Bank Mandiri).[104] More bad news followed. The *Algemeen Handelsblad* reported in May 1931: 'British American Tobacco Co.

Hilversum, the town hall from 1930, designed by W.M. Dudok CON

has decided to implement a drastic cut in business operations in Java. The factory in Surabaya will be closed, laying off 2000 workers, while the construction of the new factory in Semarang has been stopped'.[105] Photographs from the Fermont-Cuypers archive show that the large building with its modern appearance was completed in 1931 despite everything.[106] The government also continued to cut costs. For example, the head of the 'Landsgebouwendienst' (National Building Agency) received the instruction that 'numerous works, which had been put on the budget for the coming years, were postponed until later'.[107] The impact on Fermont-Cuypers was negligible as they barely worked for the government. Here and there, a school was created with money from Dutch Catholic circles, like Banka. Han de Jongh was there to attend the opening of the 'half building' in Pangkal Pinang, which was created with the limited budget. In the brochure for recruiting students, the complete plan of Fermont-Cuypers is shown, in the hope that this dream would become reality one day. The convent and the school complex in Belinyu were not built to the scale that the firm suggested.[108] The third project on Banka, in Muntok, was still under construction. Driving across the island, De Jongh must have reflected on his own childhood. His father was Chief Inspector of Opium Control at Banka until 1890.[109] Now he worked on the construc-

Jakarta , a bird's-eye view of the intended plan for the Sisters of the Good Shepherd named Mater Dolorosa with the Ciliwung river in the background. The riverside buildings are built at a more elevated level due to rising waters *HET NIEUWS VAN DEN DAG VOOR NEDERLANDSCH-INDIË* MARCH 29, 1930

Jakarta, Arthur Fermont and Theo Taen behind the drawing board CFF

Jakarta, Thomas Nix at his drawing board in 1932 CFN

tion of schools on the island of his youth. From Semarang, the office received an assignment for a large school and monastery complex for the Franciscans on Bodjong. Thomas Nix made the plan including an aerial view. After a long run, the girls' boarding house 'De Goede Herder' (The Good Shepherd) was finished in the municipality of Meester Cornelis (now: Jatinegara). There had been a lot of discussion about the land price of a part of the extensive site. Arthur Fermont, on behalf of the client, had wanted to buy part of the land for a symbolic sum from the municipality. The construction plan was, as he told the city council, 'for poor girls, so for a good cause'. A majority of the council did not share this opinion. They were Catholic girls and a Catholic interest was not a general interest. A fair price had to be paid for the land.[110] They did not agree, so only part of the large project could be built. Matthias Kaptijn, present at the inauguration, made some photos of the result.[111] Above the main entrance the Good Shepherd (*Goede Herder*) looks down on everyone who enters the building. Robert Deppe (1902-1943) made the relief. His studio in Jakarta later received more assignments from Fermont-Cuypers.

A changing of the guard had taken place at the palace in Bogor. Governor-General De Graeff, a man who to some extent sympathised with the Indonesians' move towards independence, made way for Jhr. B.C. de Jonge, a man who had no time for the nationalist movement. In the winter, Sukarno was allowed to leave prison. De Graeff had reduced his sentence, just before his departure, as a gesture of reconciliation, with the words: 'However reprehensible and unlawful his actions, however rash and impetuous his conduct may have been, Sukarno had been led by idealistic motives'.[112]

Amsterdam 1932. 'Everything that innovates calls itself motion'

In 1932, the first International Exhibition of Modern Architecture took place in New York. Initiators were Henry-Russell Hitchcock and Philip Johnson, who selected numerous examples of modern architecture that were successful in their opinion. This included the work of only one Dutchman, J.J.P. Oud (1890-1963).[113] At this exhibition, with many designs by German architects, the concept of modern architecture was further defined and given the international style tag.[114] This made little impression in Germany, where the economic crisis was hitting extra hard as a result of all the reparations the country had to pay as a punishment for the First World War. Almost every German threatened to lose confidence in the rest of the world and to follow Hitler as the last thing that remained. This generated a dynamic, a movement that could neither identify with modernism nor with its break with the past. That break had, as was experienced by many, 'only brought disaster'. Even the Soviet Union reconsidered modernism. The odd individual who still believed in modern architecture, sighed: 'The rough prevails and in parallel there are imitation classic styles.'[115] Berlage said that he did not see modernism 'as a beginning, but rather as the end': 'It symbolises the end of bourgeois society by the omission of the faculties and the acceptance of exclusively technical considerations. This new practicality fits perfectly with our era of rationalisation,' said Berlage.[116] The celebrated architect did not feel the spirit of the time. The opposition between the modernists and the group that had moved away from it, benefited the latter group. Civilian or not, most, given the result in the Soviet Union, had nothing to do with 'revolutions', not even in construction. Change arose through evolution, in which the movement, the eternal event and the dynamics were considered important.[117] The architect Sybold van Ravesteyn (1889-1983) stressed during a lecture, in the presence of Berlage, that 'architecture inevitably evokes feelings because it consists of form, colour and space'.[118] It was found that emotional aspects counted everywhere in Europe. Broder Christiansen signalled the arrival of a new style that he called 'Dynamics'. It saw this as a reaction to the 'New Objectivity'. 'When a new sense of life arises and is strong enough to express itself, a new style is created'.[119] The 'New Objectivity' has been dismissed, according to Christiansen, 'because it has reduced construction to radical simplification, overestimated the technology and eliminated the personal'. 'In the building style that emerged after modernism, the horizontal articulation is no longer defining,' according to Christiansen, 'but it is precisely vertical lines, processed in a tower or accent. Vertical lines contribute to a "dynamic", the eye is automatically drawn upwards when seeing a vertical line and that makes an impression.'[120] In Delft, Nicolaas Lansdorp (1885-1968) was awarded the chair in Architecture at the university in 1932.[121] He learned his trade from Eduard Cuypers and, like his former inspiration, he preferred actual building to theorising.[122] With Cuypers, Lansdorp shared a sense of tradition and the monumental, as well as the international orientation. Lansdorp, according to *Het Bouwbedrijf*, had much architectural conviction because of a 'suppleness of mind, which is of great value to someone who has to deal with a lot of work, because it keeps it fresh and always alive'.[123] Many of his public buildings in Amsterdam were given a striking tower, 'which draws the eye upwards'. Lansdorp showed his students that the designer should not only be guided by rational considerations, but also by expressiveness and dynamism, just as in the early days of the 'Amsterdam School'.[124] Among his students was Freek Dicke, who planned to graduate in 1933 and hoped to find work.[125] The crisis had caused a sharp downturn in housing production in Europe.[126] The Dutch government no longer started nor encouraged building initiatives. Architects who were dependent on 'social building' reproached the government about that. The time of construction subsidies had come to an end until 1945.

Jakarta, the expressive architecture of Hotel des Galeries, completed in 1932 and designed by Fermont-Cuypers CAA

Jakarta 1932, the view from the high tower of Hotel des Galeries on what is now called Harmoni CFC

Housing construction was left to the private initiative. With the exception of Italy, it was no different in the rest of Europe. Here and there, a government building was established. Most presented a classic look. Europe was in its 'monumental era'.[127] As the years went by, that style became even heavier in countries with a dictatorship. In the democracies the pillars and pilasters also returned, but with a more decorative undertone.

Jakarta 1932: 'May God protect Insulinde from greater disasters'

'Everywhere around us there is struggle and unrest. In Europe, the German-speaking peoples, who are now placed in a slave position, as it were, will cast off the confining economic restraints which may submerge old continental Europe again, and perhaps with far more fatal consequences, in a pool of shame and misery'. With these prophetic words, the official organ of the Association of Architects in the Dutch East Indies opened the New Year, and continued: 'With the chance that the Netherlands will not be able to escape punishment. Japan and China are also in heavy turmoil, and no one can foresee how the conflicts will go, nor how the tidal waves of hatred will be observed here in the Dutch East Indies. May God protect us in Insulinde from greater disasters than the unemployment that now exists'.[128] From 1932 the Dutch East Indies government took stock. What should it do now that private parties had less money available? Someone such as Thomas Karsten (1884-1945) continued to contribute a leading role to the municipal government. He was a recognised name there, also because he regularly spoke at conferences.[129] In addition, as a member of the editorial board, he frequently wrote in the only professional journal that the Dutch East Indies knew in the field of planning the *Indisch Bouwkundig Tijdschrift/Lokale Techniek*.[130] It made him very popular among a number of municipal authorities, because Karsten considered the municipalities to be important.[131] Possibly they found his approach at Fermont-Cuypers too planned, because Karsten was an urban planner, not a designer. At the firm they were barely occupied at the level of urban design and planning. They were builders. The opening of Hotel de Galeries produced a lot of advertising for their building skills. During the renovation, the *Bataviaasch Nieuwsblad* wrote: 'The entire project will be a splendid acquisition for Batavia's city appearance once the contours of the building in neon light in the evening stand out against the dark sky and once the terraces with brightly shining twilight lamps and beautifully set tables will be covered'.[132] Inside came visual art from Louis van der Noordaa (1894-1945), with whom the office regularly collaborated. 'With the appearance of an ocean liner, it's all in one of the most iconic locations in Batavia', according to a newspaper, 'The guests use superlatives to express their admiration, which increases when viewing the roof garden, from where there is a beautiful view of one of the busiest parts of the city'.[133] The new consul of Italy who had just arrived in Jakarta must certainly have seen the building, including the name Fermont-Cuypers, that could more or less be read behind the empty shop windows. Barely a year after the town hall of Hilversum, the firm enriched Jakarta with an Indonesian version of that building, striking, modern and expressionistic. Visible from the tram, the building was a landmark on the Harmonieplein (now: Harmoni). Arnold Dikstaal, the 29-year-old draftsman who provided the largest part of the design, must have felt 'Dudok' for a while. Due to the crisis, the retail spaces remained empty for a long time.[134] In order to guarantee income, after the hotel applied for suspension of payment in November of that year, the low tower functioned from 1932 as an advertising mast.[135] On August 24, the Van Heutsz monument, designed by Dudok, was unveiled in the new Gondangdia district.[136] 'Van Heutsz is far away from us, but he is also close', according to the Governor-General, 'because he has placed a milestone in the history of the Dutch East Indies, he laid a foundation to build upon, his politics have been continued; politics that, more than ever before, have furthered the prosperity, happiness and development of country and people'.[137] Arnold Dikstaal was also present at the unveiling of the monument. At about that time he worked on the design for a chapel at the Sint-Louis Institute in Ambarawa. After completing the design, he was told that he also had to lead the construction. He was forced to leave for Ambarawa, 500 kilometres away, with Mientje, his decisive wife.[138]

Amsterdam 1933: 'The tension increases enormously'

In the year in which Hitler took power in Germany, the Reichstag was burning, Japan advanced in China, occupied Shanghai and annexed Manchuria. In that year, mutiny broke out in the Indian waters on the Dutch warship 'De Zeven Provinciën' in protest against a wage reduction.[139] This could not have come at a worse time for the Dutch government.[140] The government knew the effects of the mutiny on the Potemkin barely 15 years earlier, which heralded the beginning of the Russian revolution. The Governor-General did not wish to negotiate with the mutineers.[141] The government in The Hague demanded an immediate surrender. When there was no response, a bomb was dropped.[142] That put an end to the mutiny and killed 23 people on board. As was to be expected, this led to fierce protests, especially among socialists and communists in the Netherlands. The Dutch government did not care much about what the left-wing had to say. And it was clear in its message to the extreme right: civil servants were not allowed to be members of the Dutch National Socialist Party (NSB).[143] Some newspapers brought the first reports of the persecution of Jews in Germany, along with dismissals, shop boycotts and their increasing isolation.[144] The tensions had gradually reached breaking point in the Netherlands. A country that did not unite, was further polarised in a battle between different camps. The fact that Catholics collected money for the construction of schools and hospitals in the Dutch East Indies matched that pattern of compartmentalisation.

Jakarta 1933: 'May the opening of this new building herald a better era'

In the colony, the tension among the Europeans increased as well. The Governor-General wished to be kept informed of the movements of the Japanese sea fleet and demanded loyalty from the Navy. The 'demagogic power' of Sukarno bothered him. He decided to banish this 'agitator'. This happened on August 1, 1933, as a result of which the calm apparently returned.[145] At Fermont-Cuypers a lack of work also gave the impression of calm. It is possible that Matthias Kaptijn arranged for two small assignments from Rangkasbitung, the capital city of Lebak, the city of Dutch writer Multatuli. On the Alun-Alun (large, open, lawned square) shortly afterwards, a Regency building was designed by them. The writer E. du Perron would write about this three years later: 'This alun-alun is spacious and beautiful, and next to the kaboepatèn a brand new building has been erected bearing the name 'Regentschapsraad'. 'Quiet Rangkasbitung is now a sweet, clean Dutch East Indies town, with that alun-alun at its centre, a small Chinese shopping area and two long streets, one of which is named Multatuli.'[146] Fermont-Cuypers completed a second project on this street, a small local hospital. *Het Nieuws van den Dag voor Nederlandsch-Indië*, announced the opening and made a modest report that the Reichstag building in Berlin had gone up in flames.[147] Germany was far away for the Europeans in the Dutch East Indies. 'According to the German rulers, the fire was caused by a Dutch communist'. Many Europeans must have thought how fortunate it was that there was a ban on the Communist party in the Indies. Shortly afterwards the new headquarters of the 'Nederlandsche Handel Maatschappij' (the Factorij) was completed in Jakarta, right next to the Javasche Bank.[148] Anyone who paid fifty cents could visit the modern building of the Dutch Trade Company. The proceeds went to charity, namely support for the unemployed.[149] The magazine *d'Oriënt* placed some photos but remained cautious in its comments. 'May the opening of this new building herald a better era, a period of ever-increasing prosperity', according to the editorial.[150] In another article, attention was paid to Hitler to end the reflection with: 'Whatever may the future bring?' The *Bataviaasch Nieuwsblad* reported that various speeches could be heard at the opening. A viewing took place under the direction of the architects. 'The building makes an excellent impression', according to the newspaper.[151] There was nothing else about the building itself.[152]

Shortly thereafter, Fermont-Cuypers received a request for the construction of a 'safe building' as an extension of the Javasche Bank, adjacent to the new building of the Factorij. Of course the question arose which style best suited this very enclosed building. The choice was made for a classic-looking design, adapted to the twenty-year-old bank of Eduard Cuypers

Rangkasbitung: 'In addition to the *kaboepatèn* (Regent's residence), a brand new building has been built bearing the word 'Regentschapsraad' (Regency Council). Rangkasbitung is now a sweet, neat Dutch East Indies town', according to E. du Perron. 'It appears that the times of Multatuli lie faraway' CFC

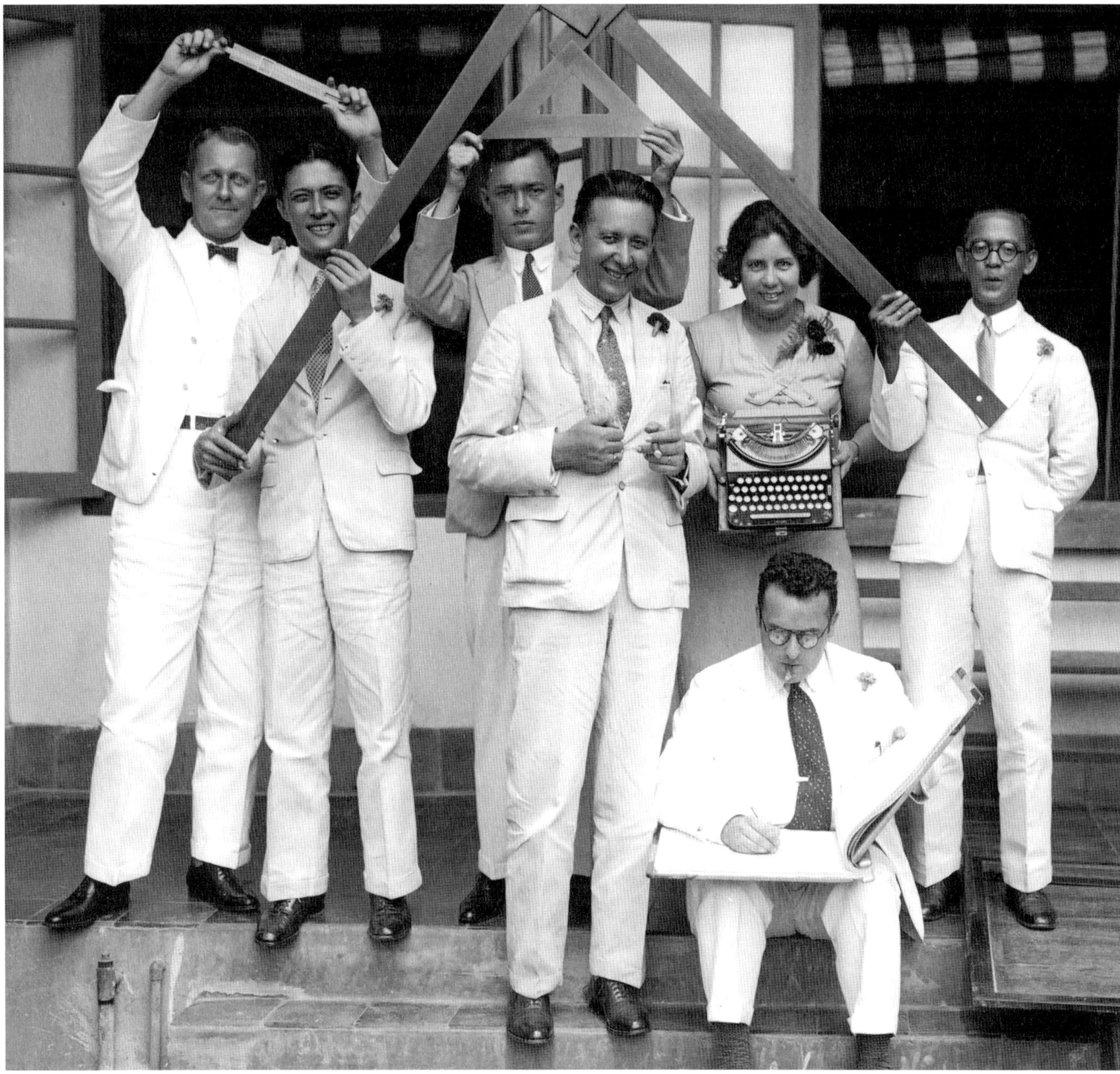

The core team of Fermont-Cuypers in 1936 on the steps of the office, from left to right: Han de Jongh, Thomas Nix, the draftsman Emiel Schedler, Theo Taen, Mrs. Ter Beeke-Heijnneman, the accountant Brouwer is seated with on the right the draftsman Philip Wijsman. Arthur Fermont was in Europe at the time CFC

to which the extension had to be connected. However, the firm advised the management to position the extension generously behind the building line, leaving enough space between the addition and the square to eventually build a new front building over the entire breadth of the plot. That plan, for the time being, went too far for the board of the bank, partly because of the crisis, but also because of internal resistance, because with the new building the now familiar façade had to disappear on Stationsplein (now: Jl. Stasiun Kota). The assignment was limited to the 'safe building'.[153] That was the end of Fermont-Cuypers's work for the time being. The bureau placed a request in the newspaper 'for approval of an amendment to the articles of association containing a reduction of the share capital by 50% by repayment of 50% of the nominal amount on each share'.[154] For the Reverend Clarissen Sisters, a building plan was designed for an abbey in Cicurug on West Java, but no assignment followed. J.Th. van Oyen (1893-1944), who had also sketched a proposal, was given the assignment. Van Oyen turned out to be a formidable competitor, also as a church builder. In Semarang he had already built a beautiful Reformed church building in 1928, now he also turned to the design for the Theresia Church in Jakarta, a project in which Fermont-Cuypers had already invested a lot of time. Thomas Nix had a view of the construction site from his house. He quickly made a new sketch plan, the umpteenth, but they did not get this assignment either. Van Oyen's plan was preferred. His design was based on a building without a tower and with a relatively simple and therefore not too expensive structure. At Fermont-Cuypers, the realisation must have dawned that no money was available for luxury building plans within the Catholic ranks. Later they were commissioned for a church building in Bandung, but now based on a design similar to that of Van Oyen's Theresia Church. Through the involvement of Theo Taen's sister-in-law, Laurentina de Sain, they were commissioned to build a school with a boarding school and a sister house in Bengkulu on Sumatra. She was the superior of the mission.[155] Theo Taen put a lot of time into it himself. Under the leadership of Mr. Beelen, a new foreman at Fermont-Cuypers, the beautiful ensemble of school buildings was completed a year later in a Dutch East Indies functional style.[156] After ten years of preparation, the construction of the Vincentius hospital started in Surabaya.[157] Matthias Kaptijn took on the job. His reputation developed as a 'hospital expert' and he regularly travelled to Rangkasbitung before the small hospital could be opened there. The delayed opening was due to the shortage of nursing staff.[158] But there followed, according to a newspaper, a 'wonder from God'. 'Six energetic Franciscan Sisters appeared directly from the Netherlands, with money that was collected there'.[159] There was even so much money, that a sister house and a small chapel could also be built. This resulted in a small Catholic enclave in Islamic East Java. It was not top architecture, but 'it contributes to well-being in the Dutch East Indies' was the general feeling.

On July 3, 1933, the *Het Nieuws van den Dag voor Nederlandsch-Indië* announced that the new chapel in Ambarawa had been consecrated a day earlier. Arthur Fermont and Arnold Dikstaal, who started to consider this building as 'his chapel', were present.[160] The same newspaper reported that the Javasche Bank in Semarang had bought a building plot for its new bank premises. Two years of internal decision making preceded this, but the bank was now in a hurry. Adjustments could no longer be made. It remained with Laurent Logemann's proposal, signed in 1930. Designers like Nix and Dikstaal had more affinity with the architecture of Hotel des Galeries. That certainly also applied to the businessman Tan Tjoan Keng. Fermont-Cuypers was allowed to design a villa for him on the Burgemeester Bisschopplein (now: Taman Suropati) in the new Menteng district. Because of the incline and the awkward size of the building plot, Fermont tried to haggle with the municipality on the land price on behalf of the client. The city council agreed to a reduced rate a few months later.[161] The design process could begin. Fermont was not directly involved with this. He decided to travel back to the Netherlands, where he wanted to stay with his family for a year and a half.[162] At the extraordinary shareholders' meeting of Fermont-Cuypers, Han de Jongh was appointed as second director and Matthias Kaptijn was appointed as a proxy holder.[163] At the end of 1933, Fermont first flew to Medan, he was the man of technical innovation, where he boarded the boat to the Netherlands. A newspaper reported that he was back in 1935.[164] Theo Taen decided to leave with his family for the Netherlands, also because the amount of work was disappointing. Thomas Nix and Arnold Dikstaal worked on the design for the villa of the Tan family and made a model of it. Even outside the regular work, Thomas Nix could channel his creativity, such as in the creation of sets for the theatre performances at the Canisius College. He oversaw the decoration and the actors' make-up. He also held regular lectures on architecture and urban design at this school.[165] In that year Freek Dicke arrived in the Dutch East Indies in search of work, at the instigation of his college friend Thomas Nix. Nix and Dicke knew each other from the Architectural Study Group in Delft, led by Granpré Molière since 1927.[166] Dicke also learned a lot from Professor Lansdorp, who, like Theo Taen, had worked for Eduard Cuypers for a long time. That created a bond, but unfortunately for Dicke, Fermont-Cuypers had nothing to offer him for the time being: there was no work. All firms were trying to win assignments in newspapers and magazines. Dicke then went to work as a drawing teacher at the Christian Lyceum in Bandung, where he also went to live.[167] He waited for the day when he could start working at Fermont-Cuypers.

On December 18 the KLM plane 'De Pelikaan' left for a speedy Christmas flight from Schiphol to the Dutch East Indies. Four days later the aircraft arrived in Jakarta, where the crew received an ovational welcome by a crowd that had gathered. Thomas Nix took pictures of this spectacle.[168] With more than three hundred Christmas cards the plane flew back to the Netherlands.

Amsterdam 1934: 'Fermont and Taen in the Netherlands'

Fermont visited his family in the Netherlands, but also negotiated the construction of a textile factory in Tegal. There was a lot of resistance against it. For the Dutch textile industry, the Dutch East Indies constituted a large market and that was in danger if there would be domestic production. Employees, trade unions and most political parties feared cheap labour from their own colony. After much deliberation the factory was allowed to come, but the agreements were such that the Netherlands benefited at the expense of the Dutch East Indies.[169] In order to keep Arthur Fermont informed about the progress of the Tan family villa, he received a few photographs of the model from Jakarta. It was a contemporary design. He received a second photo that year, shortly after the bamboo scaffolding had been removed from the building.[170] The architecture fitted in seamlessly with the latest developments in modern architecture through the

Jakarta, model of the villa designed by Nix and Dikstaal on Burgemeester Bisschopplein (now: Jl Taman Suropati) for Mr. Tan Tjoan Keng CFC

Jakarta, the building that Fermont-Cuypers originally designed as a villa and modified to become the Italian Consulate in 1934 CFC

introduction of smooth lines.[171] After the arrival of the ship 'Marnix van Sint Aldegonde' in Amsterdam, the whole family of Theo Taen was reunited in the Netherlands.[172] The older children had lived there since they went to secondary school. Theo visited Arthur Fermont a few times in his house in The Hague.[173] At the end of the year Taen left for the Dutch East Indies again intending to work for the firm for a maximum of six years. Then he wanted to return to the Netherlands with early retirement. That it would not last six, but twelve years, because of the war, was something he could not have imagined. He did notice in 1934 that it was threatening in Europe. In Germany, the Night of the Long Knives took place, and in the Soviet Union, persecutions and executions took place systematically under Stalin. It led to protests in the Netherlands, especially in Catholic and Protestant circles. Hardly anyone spoke negatively about Hitler in public. That was not opportune: the Netherlands wanted to remain neutral without risk.

Jakarta 1934: From villa to consulate

Developments in Europe were followed closely in the Dutch East Indies. Germany wanted to gain control of Austria. In a joint statement, France, England and Italy stood by Austrian independence.[174] The role of Italy during that consultation made an impression.[175] The villa of the Tan family in Jakarta was received favourably, when it emerged from the scaffolding. Especially by the Italian Consul, Mr. L. Cenzi, who was looking for a new home, and the villa strongly appealed to him. Architecturally, the building connected with modernism back in his own country. If it was adjusted in such a way that his consulate could occupy it, then he wanted to rent it. Mr. Tan Tjoan Keng agreed to this. Fermont-Cuypers made a renovation plan. They extended the ground floor and they added an extra entrance on the Van Heutsz Boulevard (now: Jl. Teuku Umar) The Italian coat of arms soon hung above that door and the Italian flag hung on the mast in the garden.[176] Photographs of the building have subsequently appeared in various books and magazines, but without mentioning the architectural firm.[177] That name is still clearly legible on the stone in the façade: 'Fermont-Cuypers'. The Pek family wanted a similar home in Menteng on the Oranjeboulevard (now: Jl. Diponegoro No. 51). Again the firm showed that it could be modern if requested by the client.

At the beginning of the year Matthias Kaptijn was still in Bengkulu for the opening of the new mission on the Alun-Alun. Six months later he visited Surabaya for the inauguration of the Vincentius hospital.[178] A distance of no less than 1,600 kilometres separates the two cities, with Jakarta in between. Such distances could occur for an architectural firm that built everywhere in the archipelago. On July, 2 1934, the *Soerabaijasch Handelsblad* reported that, 'despite the crisis, the new building of the Oranjehotel (now: Hotel Majapahit) in Surabaya has been completed and the first stone has been laid for the Javasche Bank in Semarang'.[179] For the latter event, Han de Jongh and Arnold Dikstaal were in Semarang in June.[180] Dikstaal ended up at the construction site of the Javasche Bank, where the construction process would take over one and a half years. Again he acted as an overseer, far away from Jakarta, where the design work took place. His wife and he moved to Semarang and both signed the certificate, which was bricked in when laying the foundation stone. Dikstaal realised that he had to study, to shed that eternal role of overseer.[181] He decided that this was his last project in that position. At the end of the year he led a journalist through the building under construction and shortly afterwards read a highly positive review in the newspaper.[182]

Amsterdam 1935: 'We live in a possessed world'

'A few unwelcome visitors broke into the offices of the Fermont-Cuypers firm on Molenvliet Oost, Batavia', according to a newspaper in the Netherlands. 'The gentlemen gained access by climbing into the building and left with a calculator worth FL. 350 and a typewriter of FL. 125. The police investigated the case'.[183] Was this sympathy from the Netherlands or did the newspaper have a vacant corner of the page left? The distance between the Netherlands and the Dutch East Indies was in fact greater than ever. Mr. H. Colijn, who was both prime minister and minister of colonies, told the Governor-General that more cuts had to be made.[184] Only the opposition and business world in the Netherlands were still involved with the colony. Social Democratic and Communist spokesmen repeatedly stated that the Netherlands had no business in the colony. They were applauded by the Indonesian nationalists.[185]

The government had a lot to do: the consequences of the crisis, the international balance of forces and the rise of the NSB.[186] Mussert, the leader of the Dutch National Socialist Party, felt triumphant. He decided to go to the colony and was the first leader of a political party that did so in the Netherlands. There, on one windy morning, Arthur Fermont rode on horseback over the North Sea beach of Scheveningen (The Netherlands), where he met the president of the Javasche Bank from Jakarta. He later said about this: 'Meeting between two gentlemen on the beach. A chat which led to the idea of demolishing the façade of the old building of the Javasche Bank in Jakarta and placing a new front building'. 'We were both there for our health', said Mr. G. G. Buttingha Wichers (1878-1945), that is, me on foot and him on horseback. And so we had a chat, from our individual standpoints, high and low, so the first plan matured'.[187] It remained an idea for the time being. Possibly they talked about the reuse of the pillars, the pilasters, the stained-glass windows and the other ornaments Eduard Cuypers had intro-

Surabaya, the Vincentius Hospital shortly before its opening in 1934 CFC

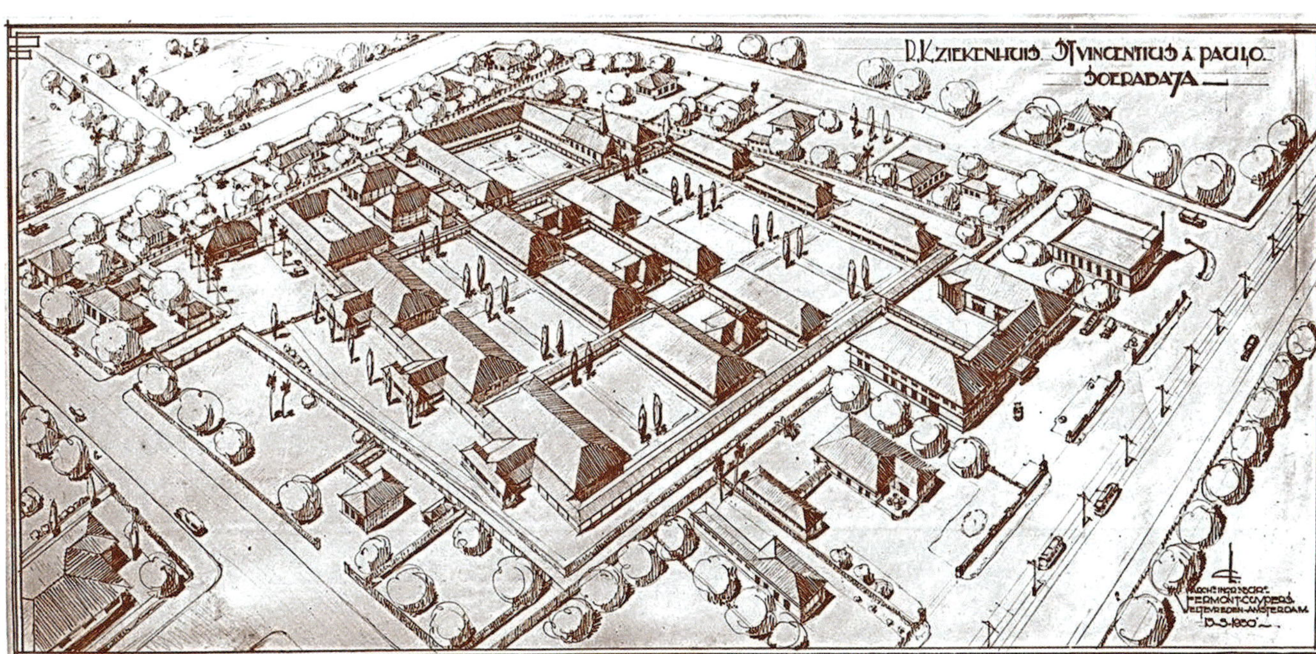

Surabaya, a bird's-eye drawing with the plan for the entire hospital grounds, signed by Laurent Logemann in 1930 CFC

duced in 1913. In spite of the criticism Berlage once had of the decorations, there was a different view at that time. Berlage had died and ornaments were back.[188] That was clearly visible at the world exhibition in Brussels where Arthur Fermont saw what the latest trends were in architecture and technology. The Netherlands was in a pavilion that attracted a lot of attention with a high tower crowned with three wrought-iron, stacked elements.[189] Thin steel columns and a realistic painted allegorical representation of people with provincial flags marked the entrance. Apart from the ornament, realism and wall decoration were also back. It all corresponded with recent Italian architecture.[190] The colonial section on the first floor was small compared to previous exhibitions. Within the pavilion, everything revolved around the technical achievements of the innovative Netherlands. The pavilions of other European countries were also inspired by Italian realism with marble plates, bronze fences, statues and plaques and vertical windows. Horizontality was out. Towers, columns and innumerable flag poles dominated the exhibition grounds. A month before the opening, Dutch historian Professor J. Huizinga (1872-1945) held a lecture in Brussels in which he said among other things: 'We live in a possessed world. And we know it. No-one would be surprised, if the madness suddenly erupted into craziness, leaving this poor European humanity behind in stupidity and foolishness, the engines still running and the flags still fluttering, but from which the spirit is gone'.[191]

Jakarta 1935: 'All things change, and we change with them'

'The new year has made its appearance and 1934, the year of increasing deterioration, has ended', according to the opening sentence in the official organ of the Association of Architects in the Dutch East Indies. 'If we are not mistaken then the lowest point of the crisis years has been reached and only a steadfast confidence in recovery will keep us upright'.[192] Indeed the construction got going again. Several buildings appeared from behind the scaffolding, often provided with a tower including one or more vertically placed flagpoles to which the red-white-blue was silhouetted against the tropical sky.[193] At Fermont-Cuypers it remained quiet. Work was carried out on a few schools and two churches that had to be ready for a tight budget in a short time.[194] In February, Theo Taen returned to Jakarta by ship.[195] Mussert took the plane to the Dutch East Indies where he visited the Governor-General twice, despite objections from Colijn.[196] He also visited the management of the Javasche Bank. Did they have something with each other or was it a formality? During lectures in the Dutch East Indies, Mussert stressed that he found the strong hand with which the Dutch East Indies was ruled a relief compared to parliamentary democracy in the Netherlands. Despite all rhetoric, the N.S.B. would recruit relatively few party members among Europeans.[197] The Europeans in the Dutch East Indies could not agree with the racial doctrine of the N.S.B. Many had distant relatives themselves who were considered non-European by Mussert and his followers. Moreover, unlike Mussert, they had more confidence in England than in Germany, which cooperated too closely with Japan. In a large Japanese newspaper, a redistribution of colonial property had recently been advocated. The Dutch East Indies was, according to the article, the first to qualify.[198] If they were already occupying themselves with politics at Fermont-Cuypers, it was within the Catholic church, especially because some work still came from there. On the back of the book *400 jaren Missie* there was a full-page advertisement, drawn by Thomas Nix. In the book itself, J. Th. Van Oyen, their formidable competitor, had placed an article that was richly illustrated with his own work.[199]

At Fermont-Cuypers, they attracted attention in a different way. A year earlier, they had designed a large statue of Christ, meant for the Jesuit jubilee, who had been working in the Indies for 400 years. After a sculptor had completed the large sculpture, it was delivered to the intended location next to the cathedral. There, a newspaper wrote, 'a tragic accident' followed. The statue fell from the transport truck onto a workman, who died. Without going into the death of the man, the newspaper said that an investigation would take place to the cause, with the following remark: 'during this investigation, the statue will not be unpacked, so that it remains unknown whether it is damaged'...[200]

In Jakarta, the 'safe building' under the direction of Han de Jongh began to take shape next to the Javasche Bank. The project had to be ready in September, but that happened in the absence of De Jongh. He had decided, as soon as Fermont was back, to take six months off for himself.[201] His wife was pregnant. They were both eager for their child to be born in the Netherlands. In August, Fermont was able to take over the baton from De Jongh again.[202] In Semarang, the finishing touches were put to the Javasche Bank under the guidance of Arnold Dikstaal. At the opening on December 14, 1935, Fermont referred to 'the new era' with the words: 'The new design for this building offered the opportunity to express the new zeitgeist'. Afterwards, lunch was served in Hotel du Pavillon. At the bottom of the menu, which the firm designed for this occasion, it said: 'All things change, and we change with them'. The building was floodlit in the evenings, because that was part of the new spirit. A newspaper said that this was 'the first lighting of this nature with gas in the Dutch East Indies'.[203] Dikstaal was not at the opening. He packed his suitcases for his period of leave in the Netherlands with the idea, after returning to the Dutch East Indies, of studying engineering at the Technical University in Bandung.[204]

Brussels, book cover of the world exhibition in 1935
CON

Brussels, the Dutch pavilion at the world exhibition in 1935 with a tower and wall paintings CON

Brussels, the entrance to the exhibition grounds in 1935. 'We live in a possessed world. And we know it. It would not be unexpected for anyone if the madness suddenly erupted into a frenzy, leaving behind this poor European humanity in stupidity and foolishness, the engines still running and the flags still fluttering, but the mind having disappeared', according to the Dutch historian J. Huizinga CON

Amsterdam 1936: '...for the time being, there is no reason to be worried'

After Germany entered the demilitarised Rhineland in March 1936, Dutch prime minister Colijn used the radio to utter the frequently quoted words: 'I ask the listeners that when they soon retire to their beds that they sleep as peacefully as they do on any other nights. There is as yet no reason to be worried.'[205] The Dutch athletes were able to prepare carefree for the Summer Olympics in Berlin, where nearly fifty countries would be represented in August. Trade between the Netherlands and Germany also continued. There was no reason to be worried. An American journalist thought differently about this and, in an editorial in the *Algemeen Handelsblad*, he said that Europe was on the verge of collapse. He feared that the summer of 1936 would be the same as that of 1914 and talked about the 'oppressive dreams of a sleepwalking continent'.[206]

The Dutch bishops did not sleep. In May, a letter was read in all Catholic churches where, in strong terms, a stand was taken against the N.S.B.[207] A group of writers founded a 'Committee of Vigilance', which fought the national socialist ideology. Dutch modernist author Menno ter Braak was one of them, another was poet and author Eddy du Perron (1899-1940) who, born in the Dutch East Indies, who planned to go back to his native country. He no longer felt comfortable in Europe. After the civil war broke out in Spain, Du Perron first left for Spain to join the 'Leftists'. 'If Spain is fascist in two months', according to the writer, 'France can be that in two years and the rest will follow in less than no time, including Holland'.[208] Arthur Fermont arrived in that Europe after leaving Jakarta on February 21, 1936. For the farewell dinner, Thomas Nix designed the menu. Nix drew a plane and a boat with which Fermont travelled and also the ship the 'Gneisenau', with people bringing the Nazi salute. It referred to a battleship recently launched in Germany. Back in Europe, Fermont saw his wife and children again, of whom Cyril, the youngest, was now fifteen. In answer to his question of how the children were doing, his wife replied as always: 'good'.[209]

The Netherlands still suffered from the crisis. The announcement in early September of the engagement of Princess Juliana with Bernhard von Lippe Biesterfeld provided some light. It was a happy event, even if it didn't actually solve much. The devaluation of the Dutch currency, the guilder on September 26 had a more positive effect. A day later, the Dutch East Indies guilder was also devalued. The Netherlands, with France and Switzerland, had for too long adhered to the gold standard with the president of the Dutch bank, Mr. L.J.A. Trip, as a big supporter.[210] After the French and Swiss currencies were devalued, the Netherlands, as the last country, could not do otherwise. The guilder lost 18 percent against the dollar and exports increased as a result. Fermont followed developments closely with his nose for money matters. In October he attended the funeral of a former director of the Javasche Bank. He walked behind the casket with Mr. Trip and countless other directors and former directors of banks and companies, many of whom were in the Dutch East Indies.[211] Fermont was there to be seen as a representative of his firm. In France, E. du Perron boarded in the direction of 'his country of origin'.[212] Disillusioned, he left Europe after discovering that more people in Spain feared communism than fascism.[213]

Jakarta 1936: A bank must exude solidity

On March 10, 1936, the *Bataviaasch Nieuwsblad* announced that the headquarters of the Javasche Bank in Batavia would be expanded, as a result of which the façade on the Binnen Nieuwpoortstraat, 'as it has been published on money notes for several decades, will get a completely new look'. 'Those who find it unfortunate that this typical and so familiar street view will disappear from Jakarta, will get the true impression that the character of the building shall be kept. The prestige of the entire bank with a grand design of the new façade will be retained'. 'Due to the time conditions, this plan was postponed,' according to the bank. The recently completed 'safe building' was part of the extensive design.[214] They worked on the plans at Fermont-Cuypers. In Eduard Cuypers' bank building there were two modest 'entrance gates', which indicated that this was not the main building. The new main entrance now came on the Stationsplein (now: Jl. Station Kota). The plan here showed a centrally located entrance in a symmetrical façade. The main structure corresponded with that of the adjacent Factorij ('Nederlandsche Handel Maatschappij', but the architecture was consciously different. The Factorij (now: Bank Mandiri Museum) was allowed to be innovative and modern, as a result of which the entire project came across as a building without a past. The Javasche Bank had history, that also had to be readable in the architecture of the new building.

The widely read magazine *d'Oriënt* showed in April 1936 some photos of 'the architectural style from the 'new Germany'. One of them was of the *Haus der Deutschen Kunst* in Munich, which had just been completed, with the caption that: 'now that the hoarding has disappeared, this monumental building can be seen in all its beauty'.[215] Although they had no affinity at Fermont-Cuypers with this strict classicist architecture, the revival of classicism in Europe offered them the chance to give the new front building for the Java Bank a classic look without being called 'conservative'. This allowed an architectural unity to arise between the buildings that were kept and the new building. The sketch made by Thomas Nix for the front building showed that the old columns of Eduard Cuypers had been given a new life. They were reused. That was on the one hand sustainable and they formed historical starting points on the other

Semarang, the Javasche Bank shortly after completion in 1935 CFC

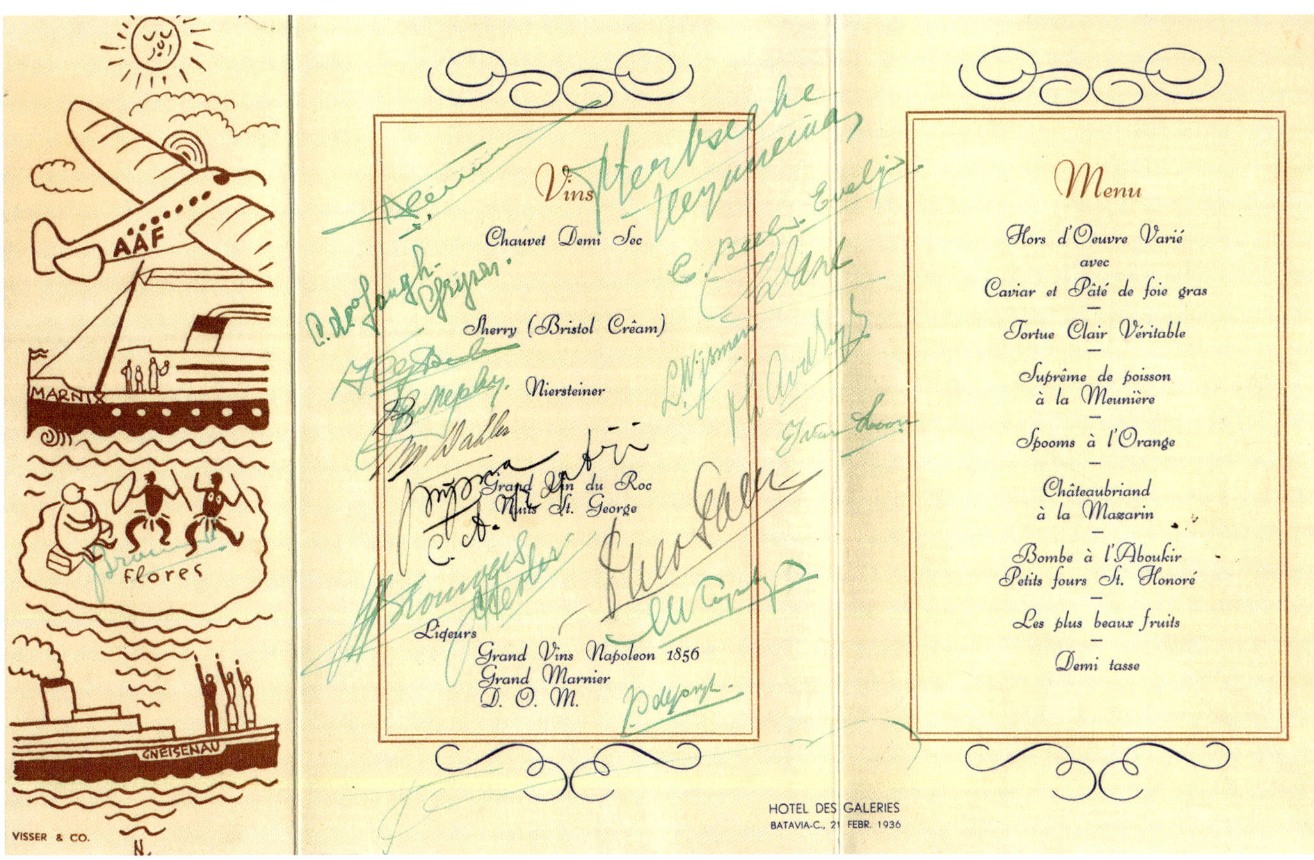

Vins
Chauvet Demi Sec
Sherry (Bristol Crêam)
Niersteiner
Grand Vin du Roc
Nuits St. George
Liqeurs
Grand Vins Napoleon 1856
Grand Marnier
D. O. M.

Menu
Hors d'Oeuvre Varié
avec
Caviar et Pâté de foie gras
Tortue Clair Véritable
Suprême de poisson
à la Meunière
Spooms à l'Orange
Châteaubriand
à la Mazarin
Bombe à l'Aboukir
Petits fours St. Honoré
Les plus beaux fruits
Demi tasse

HOTEL DES GALERIES
BATAVIA-C., 21 FEBR. 1936

Menu made in 1936 by Thomas Nix for Arthur Fermont's departure to Europe, signed by all employees and their partners CFC

Jakarta, sketch made by Thomas Nix for the new front building of the Javasche Bank in Batavia as it was published in the *Bataviaasch Nieuwsblad* on March 10, 1936 CFC

Jakarta, sketch of the old building made by Thomas Nix in 1936 CFC

Jakarta 1936, the major renovation, in which the columns are hoisted up from the original building and reused in the new façade CFC

hand.[216] Classicism stood for trust and solidity. Both belonged to a bank. Fermont-Cuypers did not have any fundamental choices between classical and modern. They sought the building style that best suited the project, the client and the situation. Traditionally, this was the firm's creed and they were not the only architects who worked in this way in the Dutch East Indies. Van Oyen switched from traditional to modern and vice versa, depending on the client. In Surabaya, he built modern shops for entrepreneurs with confidence in the future at Tunjungan, while elsewhere in Java he designed traditional-looking monastic complexes. J. Th. Van Oyen remained a formidable competitor in the Catholic circle for Fermont-Cuypers. The firm was pleased with the commission for a large monastery and school complex in Bandung. Thomas Nix created the design and Emiel Schedler, with whom he brilliantly collaborated, took care of the construction drawings. Meanwhile the major renovation of the Javasche Bank took place. While hundreds of construction workers in the blazing sun were creating reinforcing steels for the new building, others carefully removed Eduard Cuypers' columns from the old façade to store them for use in the new façade. The stained glass was also carefully removed for later reuse. The 'Hollandsche Beton Maatschappij' performed the work.

Due to the devaluation of the Dutch guilder, the economy, including the Dutch East Indies, began to emerge from the crisis. This also manifested itself in new assignments. The Bataafsche Petroleum Maatschappij (Shell) approached the firm with an assignment for no less than two office buildings, in Jakarta and Semarang. Trade was recovering, especially in the oil.[217] The architecture of both buildings resulted from years of experience with 'building in the tropics' and was also internationally oriented and 'business modern'. From the 'Nederlandsche Koloniale Petroleum Maatschappij', or 'De Koloniale' for short, also came an assignment. Nix and Schedler worked on this, under the watchful eye of Theo Taen in similar architectural style. The construction of an outbuilding could start at the end of the year. In 1937 the head office, with its frontage on the Koningsplein (now: Medan Medeka Tim.) had to be ready. That would be, according to a newspaper report, the first building in the Dutch East Indies where the installation of air conditioning had been taken into account from the very beginning.[218]

In Bogor, the changing of the guard took place in the government. Governor-General De Jonge made way for Tjarda van Starkenborgh Stachouwer. The successor was also not in favour of an independent Indonesia, even in the long term. These views were shared by most of the Europeans in the Indies and they identified with a conservative and autocratic Governor.[219] This did not stop the nationalists from submitting a petition in the Volksraad with the proposal to 'hold a conference on an equal footing between the Netherlands and the Dutch East Indies with the aim of Indonesia's independence through gradual reforms'. The petition was adopted with 26 to 20 votes, but this still had to pass the Governor-General for approval and then the Netherlands' government.[220]

Amsterdam 1937: 'The Netherlands belongs to the big colonial world powers'

In the Netherlands, only the communists and the socialists felt that the Dutch East Indies should eventually become independent. The message that the Netherlands had no place being there, was made clear with slogans such as: 'Indonesia separate from Holland' and 'No people are free to oppress another people'.[221] Other political parties pointed to the importance of the bond between the Netherlands and the Dutch East Indies. That idea was reinforced by the rise of fascism and national socialism in Europe, which made the position of the small countries uncertain. The Netherlands had a role among the great powers thanks to the ties with Dutch East Indies. As the threat intensified, the Netherlands stubbornly clung to the Dutch East Indies. For prime minister Colijn there was reason to not cooperate with a change in the status of Dutch East Indies within the kingdom of the Netherlands. He mentions as argument: 'The still insufficient state of social development of the vast majority of the Indonesian population'.[222] On January 7, 1937, there were celebrations in both the Netherlands and Dutch East Indies on the occasion of the marriage of Juliana and Bernhard. The Netherlands went wild, but the Dutch East Indies also, they read in the newspaper. Fermont received proof of this with a photograph of the decorated 'Harmonie' in Jakarta, made and sent by Kaptijn. On March 24, 1937, Fermont boarded a ship that brought him back to Jakarta. That's where the work called. He wanted to attend the opening of the new front building of the Javasche Bank. Although a notorious expo visitor, he found it more important than a trip to Paris, where two months later the Exposition Internationale des Arts et des Techniques opened.[223] Three countries were emphatically present: Germany, the Soviet Union and Spain. Spain was in the midst of a violent civil war. The Republican government was present with a pavilion in which Picasso's Guernica formed the centre. The pavilions of Germany and the Soviet Union faced each other and had to radiate power. On the high tower of the German pavilion was an eagle with swastika, representing the 'restored German national pride'. Germany First. A large picture of two young people, a man and a woman, 'storming forward together towards a bright future' dominated the Soviet pavilion.[224] The Dutch pavilion was a stone's throw away from both. On the glass façade stood in neon letters in French 'Néerlandais' and 'Indes Néerlandais' in between, also in neon, the flight path between colony and the Netherlands. Without the colony, the Netherlands did not count among flagpoles and parade architecture.

Paris, poster of the world exhibition in 1937 with on the left the German Pavilion and on the right the pavilion of the Soviet Union CON

Semarang, two decorated columns in front of the Javasche Bank because of the festivities surrounding the royal wedding of Dutch Princess Juliana with Prince Bernhard in January 1937 BROMMER (1995) P. 145

Jakarta 1937: Symbols of Western supremacy

The celebrations for the wedding of the Dutch Princess Juliana and Prince Bernhard were tightly orchestrated in the Dutch East Indies. Covered with lamps, countless buildings were illuminated in the evening against the backdrop of dark tropical skies. For the new Javasche Bank in Semarang there were two party pillars along the road. The floodlight lit up both the building and the pillars. Although it wasn't yet ready, in Jakarta the hoardings had been removed around the construction of the Javasche Bank. The building presented itself, from behind sixteen temporary masts, all bearing an orange pennant, with the family coat of arms of both spouses above the entrance. Thomas Nix made the sketch for that. A month later, the German community in the Dutch East Indies celebrated the 'Tag der Machtergreifung' with Hitler as a hero. All expressions of Western supremacy.[225] Newspapers and magazines published photos with Europeans in tropical uniforms with a swastika.[226]

Arthur Fermont immediately took up where he had left off after arrival in the Dutch East Indies. He visited the opening of the Textile factory in Tegal and shortly thereafter travelled to Palembang for the laying of the foundation stone of the Charitas Hospital and was then approximately five days later in Jakarta to guide numerous visitors through the new building of the Javasche Bank. It had a robust appearance. The 'unsatisfied attempt at Hindu-Javanese ornament motifs', as Berlage once called them disparagingly, had disappeared, but with that also the proof that Eduard Cuypers was the first to have an eye for the Indonesian ornament.[227] With the demolition of the old building, Jakarta lost a very special building.[228] Newspapers wrote full-page articles about the new building with headlines such as: 'A beautiful imposing front', 'Beauty inside and outside', 'De Javasche Bank after a beauty treatment'. One journalist was very impressed: 'After three cheers the management started the tour' 'In diesen heiligen Hallen kennt man die Rache nicht' (Revenge is unknown in these sacred halls), but the gold and the banknotes, and so I walk through a beautiful set of colours and ironwork, stucco and stained glass, impressive curves, practical turnstiles, in short, a new building with which both the interior and exterior of the Javasche Bank, is a building to be celebrated.'[229] Matthias Kaptijn made a small photo album from the bank as a reminder.[230]

In 1937 the economy continued to improve.[231] Dutch companies, which were affiliated with the Dutch East Indies, did well. De Rotterdamsche Lloyd paid dividends for the first time in years.[232] In the euphoria there were plans for a new terminal in the port of Jakarta. Optimism also prevailed at the Bataafsche Petroleum Maatschappij. The company agreed with the designs for the offices in Jakarta and Semarang. In Semarang the first stone was laid on July 10, in Jakarta on August 12, where, as usual, the son of the director in a sailor suit used the ceremonial trowel. The new building for 'De Koloniale' came out of the scaffoldings at the end of the year. It was part of the agency's design tradition, with the emphasis on symmetry in the façade, a large Dutch East Indies long-roof and a certain modesty. Just as with 'Duo', which had been built on the Koningsplein (now: Medan Merdeka Barat) almost ten years earlier, visual art was added to this building, which was in line with the client's taste. The Dutch sculptor Louis Van der Noordaa (1894-1945), who lived in Bali, made four statues: Labour, Engineering, Trade and Prosperity, heavy and robust, as symbols of Western supremacy. Fermont-Cuypers placed them in the façade as capitals in pseudo-pilasters above the main entrance. The stained-glass windows, from the studio of Robert Deppe (1902-1943), told the story of the company in full colour.

That the economy was recovering was also noticed by the municipality of Batavia (Jakarta). It decided to work on plans for the Koningsplein (now: Medan Merdeka). The municipality came, as in 1918 and 1934, with a plan, recreated by their advisor Thomas Karsten. Because the Dutch East Indies government, the owner of the country, saw no benefit in the earlier plans, they were not approved. The new vision was much like the first two. Again the city hall was centrally located in the open space. 'The central placement is the correct expression of Batavia's urban self-awareness', Karsten said.[233] Furthermore, other government buildings and sports fields with an all-sided sports stadium were visible on the grounds. During the presentation, the council asked questions about the construction costs and about the usefulness and necessity of the stadium. Possibly, referring to the Olympic Games in Berlin, the 'big impact of a stadium for the people' was especially true. The municipality discussed the matter with professionals, including Fermont-Cuypers, asking them what they thought about it. The Fermont-Cuypers firm responded with an alternative plan, in which the town hall, which really needed to be built, moved to the east and where the stadium, less visible, came to be behind. The firm had a model made of her plan by Robert Deppe. A pleasantly surprised headline appeared in the *Het Nieuws van den Dag voor Nederlandsch-Indië* upon seeing the Fermont-Cuypers plan: 'Beautiful City Park grows out of Ugly Grassy Plain'.[234] In response, a model of the municipal plan appeared, with many trees on Karsten's request. Both models were shown at the Pasar Gambir, the festive annual fair on the Koningsplein (now: Medan Merdeka). Visitors were able to respond: 'If you ignore the excessive "planting" of the municipality's model, the design of the Fermont-Cuypers plan seems more balanced, offers more possibilities for the future and is recommended in all respects from the viewpoint of urban beauty. and urban design', according to the *Bataviaasch Nieuwsblad* on September 4. Three weeks later, this newspaper once again paid attention to the plan of Fermont-Cuypers under the headline: 'The Koningsplein of the

Jakarta, in January 1937, the hoardings surrounding the new bank building were removed, to celebrate the marriage of Dutch Princess Juliana with Prince Bernhard the building was decorated with flags and pennants CFC

Jakarta, a photograph of the model made for the Koningsplein (now: Medan Merdeka). The plan was made by Fermont-Cuypers in 1937 CFC

Future'. The newspaper also indirectly covered Mussolini's visit to Berlin.[235] The fact that the government was making plans to move to Bandung in the event of a threat of war was not mentioned by any newspaper, nor was there any mention of an underground bombproof safe next to the Javasche Bank in Bandung. The gold supply had to go there, in the face of imminent war danger.[236] Fermont-Cuypers made the design, which, constructively, proved to be a complicated task. Han de Jongh, who was most adept at this, had left the office in June.[237] He had worked there for fifteen years; his time there was concluded with an enjoyable dinner with all employees, after which he left for the Netherlands to join his family. His vacant spot was filled by Freek Dicke, who quit his job as art teacher.[238] At the end of the year *De Sumatra Post* headlined, optimistically: 'Undefined feeling of threatening war has been chased away'. The newspaper said that America will not interfere in the events in Asia.[239] In another article, the 'German Colonial Aspirations' were dealt with in which a German newspaper was quoted as saying that the world could not ignore the aspirations of Germany.[240] At Fermont-Cuypers they concentrated on a message from Palembang, where, according to the same newspaper, 'a building was planned to house both the Escomptobank and the Algemeene Volkscredietbank'. 'Fermont-Cuypers is making the design', according to the newspaper,' the building will be ready in a year'.[241]

Amsterdam 1938: 'Architecture based on old styles is the ideal'

In 1938, the book *De Bouwkunst van ons Land* noted that "Het Nieuwe Bouwen' (New Objectivity), which had once exerted great influence through the work of gifted and assertive youngsters, has lost important points internationally'. 'Architecture, based on old styles, now seems to be the ideal, also of the modern proletariat', according to the writer.[242] In the Netherlands, only traditional architecture was built, even by Dutch architect J.J.P. Oud (1890-1963), a follower of The Style movement.[243] This early supporter of modernism designed the Shell building in The Hague, which was completed four years later, for a client, for whom Fermont-Cuypers also worked. It became a monumental edifice, full of ornaments. The buildings in Jakarta and Semarang looked fresh, modern and business-like in comparison. Meanwhile, Europe was anxiously watching as Germany expanded its power with the annexation of Austria in March and with Sudetenland in October 1938. In a radio speech, Dutch Prime Minister Colijn urged the population to await the future 'in calm confidence'. The government suspended the decision for the time being on the question whether the Netherlands would proceed with mobilisation or not. The outcome depended on the consultation in Munich between Hitler, Mussolini, Daladier and Chamberlain. In the meantime, after the so-called *Reichskristallnacht* on November 9 and 10, the flow

Koningsplein (now: Medan Merdeka), the plan of the municipality by Thomas Karsten I.B.T.

Two office buildings for the Bataafsche Petroleum Maatschappij (now Pertamina) in Semarang (top) and Jakarta (bottom). August 12, 1937; The foundation stone is laid by the son of the director in sailor suit PHOTO'S: CJW, CFC, CON

of refugees from Germany really began. Because most Jewish families were denied access to the Netherlands due to invalid documents, dramatic scenes arose at the border.[244] Under pressure from shocked public opinion, including the Vigilance Committee, the Netherlands allowed extra refugees. Housed in camps, they received the compelling request to emigrate as quickly as possible.[245] Under that constellation, the petition, aimed at full self-government for Indonesia, reached the Dutch 'Lager Huis' (Lower House) where, after extensive discussions, it was rejected by Royal Decree on November 16, 1938.

Jakarta 1938: 'Modernism for those who still believe in the future'

On January 17, 1938, *De Indische Courant* paid attention to the opening of two buildings by Fermont-Cuypers. In Jakarta the 'De Koloniale' where Matthias Kaptijn represented the firm and the Charitas Hospital in Palembang, which Theo Taen attended. Shortly thereafter, the firm received a new commission from the Netherlands Indies Tourist Office (NITOUR). This travel agency was on the corner of Rijswijkstraat (now: Jl. Majapahit) and Harmonieplein (now: Harmoni) and wanted a larger and more appealing building at that location. The neighbouring clothing store of Oger Frères also participated. Nitour was optimistic about the future and opted for a modern, future-oriented architecture. Despite the unfavourable political climate, the enthusiasm for travelling only increased. NITOUR organised three times as many trips as a few years earlier.[246] Stoomvaart Maatschappij Nederland and the Rotterdamsche Lloyd also benefited from this travel passion. The Rotterdamsche Lloyd continued the plan for a well-equipped passenger terminal in Tanjung Priok, for which Fermont-Cuypers was formally commissioned. It had to become a modern beacon in the port. In Bandung, the Savoy-Homann Hotel wanted to prepare for the arrival of tourists. The architect Albert Aalbers (1897-1961) designed a building in the modern style, which still stands out above the small-scale buildings in the immediate vicinity.[247] Fermont-Cuypers' design was more subtle for the new building for Nitour. They designed a smaller scale building that, in terms of architecture, responded to the three public spaces where it once bordered.[248]

With its vision of the Koningsplein (now: Medan Merdeka), the municipality of Batavia (Jakarta) did not make much headway. There were few responses to the previously presented plans. Most preferred the plan of Fermont-Cuypers according to the *Bataviaasch Nieuwsblad* on May 4. As usual, the experts did not agree: 'Only the architect J.F.L Blankenberg (1888-1958) was exclusively positive about the municipal plan'. In his explanation, he said: 'about the Fermont plan I only want to say that I miss the qualities that make the municipal plan so good'.[249]

The business community, which sat on the edges of the square, had difficulty accepting the central location that the municipality had assigned itself. They felt, as did Fermont-Cuypers, that the square space had to remain empty, and supported the idea that the stadium should be located behind the new town hall, where it was less visible. The municipality was far from happy with the alternative from Fermont-Cuypers. The mayor said that the town hall, as Fermont-Cuypers imagined it, was too large and therefore had to be made smaller, so that the stadium would also become clearly visible in their plan. The book that the municipality published about itself in 1937 contained a large folding map of the municipal plan, and only that plan.[250] In 1938, *De Ingenieur in Nederlandsch-Indië*

Three studies sketched by Thomas Nix CFN

offered plenty of room to the director of the City Development Service, who promoted the municipal plan on fourteen pages.[251] The designer, Thomas Karsten, previously did this as an editor in the *Indisch Bouwkundig Tijdschrift*.[252] Objections to the municipal plan persisted, to the displeasure of the man who commissioned Karsten at the time, the then director of the Department, H.A. Breuning (1901-1995). He detested Fermont-Cuypers.[253] The official organisation wanted to continue with its own plan. The *Bataviaasch Nieuwsblad* thought it unfortunate that the Fermont-Cuypers plan was overshadowed There were rumours that Fermont-Cuypers was aiming for the design and construction of the stadium. When the relevant journalist contacted the firm, they let him know that they would no longer take any initiatives. 'Fermont-Cuypers no longer wants to fight a losing battle', according to the newspaper.[254] The firm had another reason to step back from the 'Koningsplein' project – they were extremely busy. 'There is high demand for builders with experience in all disciplines', according to a newspaper, 'from engineers to good carpenters'. The cause was 'the authorisation of several large building projects, both for the government and for private individuals'.[255] The Fermont-Cuypers foremen were inundated in work, such as the two offices for the Bataafsche Petroleum Maatschappij, with a building opening first in Semarang and followed by the head office in Jakarta in October. At the latter site, there was an 'extra sense of elation because of the agreement reached the day before in Munich'. *De Indische Courant* devoted a lengthy article to 'De Bataafsche'. On the same page there were pictures of Hitler, Mussolini, Daladier and Chamberlain, the newspaper wrote: 'The Munich conference, which has been crowned a great success, has been the scene of some historical encounters'.[256] At the Bataafsche, a glass was raised to the new 'office palace'. The guests saw an interior in keeping with the latest trends in international architecture: white walls with reliefs, mosaic tiles on the columns, marble floors, robust bronze forgings, tiles in earthy colours, stained glass depicting ships, planes and technical installations and realistic visual art.[257] Architecturally, both in Semarang and in Jakarta, a representative building was created, which optimally responded to the tropics, with a modern business look. Shortly after these openings, Fermont left for Makassar, on Sulawesi, for the construction of a hospital. The municipality was not pleased with the first sketch proposals as they had specific ideas about the architecture of the buildings that were to be constructed along the new sea boulevard (now: Jl. Somba Opu). The municipality wanted a hospital as a 'multi-storey' house in modern architecture, identical to the neighbouring mayor's house. There was not enough money for that, Fermont told them. Moreover, a building in that building style at this location offered no guarantee of sufficient ventilation and cooling on the wards. In addition, the desired modern architecture was not low-maintenance, and that was a priority, given the prevailing western monsoon and the sea breeze. Fermont managed to convince the municipality. The hospital was created in the previously used pavilion building with the entrance building on the boulevard. At the same time, the firm worked on the design of the Brother school Sint-Raphael. That unfortunately for the municipality, was not on the sea boulevard.

In the night, which later became known as the *Reichskristallnacht* in Germany, a freshly printed newspaper in Jakarta stated that the new NITOUR building had been put into service.[258] 'With its modern look, the building is a fine counterpart to the Hotel des Galeries', the newspaper said, 'It has large, well-organised display windows for folders and pictures that will invite the passer-by to travel.' Matthias Kaptijn took photos of the building. A tram passed over the Harmonieplein (now: Harmoni). A week later, another newspaper reported NITOUR is curiously awaiting 'the attitude of the authorities towards the German Jews expected among the many tourists'. This 'in connection with the refusal of the Immigration Service to let six German Jews go ashore who wanted to visit the Dutch East Indies'. The newspaper states that 'Nitour has offered to send an employee with these people in such cases so that if one of them does not want to adhere to the programme, this can immediately be reported to the relevant authorities.'[259]

Shortly afterwards, a two-day congress of the 'Nederlandsch Indische Architecten Kring' (N.I.A.K.) took place in Bandung.[260] Theo Taen attended as a board member. On the agenda of the first day were many official documents, such as the remuneration and the pension of the attendees. On the second day, Thomas Karsten proposed that the members tour Bandung, led by Gerrit Hendriks (1890-1945), who worked for the municipality. The group paid a visit to the municipal cemeteries designed by Hendriks and to the Ciumbuleuit villa park. There, Taen was able to point out some villas under construction designed by Fermont-Cuypers. Everhard de Roo (1889-1942) then led the guests through the extension of the town hall and the group, led by the architect Aalbers, visited the Denisbank and the Savoy-Homann Hotel, both of which were his designs.[261] From the Denisbank, Theo Taen must have taken a look at the shop premises of the 'Samarangsche' on the other side of the street. They had carefully inserted this building into the row shortly beforehand. 'Today's Bandung wants to take new paths', wrote a newspaper, 'The outward streamlines of the great Denis building are already clearly visible. The shop 'Onderling Belang' is in the process of acquiring a new façade. [...] Imagine, dear reader, that the work on the modernisation of the Concordia cinema has begun [...] If a skyscraper is to be built in the Dutch East Indies, it will certainly be in Bandung', according to the newspaper.[262] Taen did not understand why such unrefined-

Jakarta, the NITOUR building on Harmonieplein (now: Harmoni) in 1938, designed by Fermont-Cuypers. This building was built for a Travel Agency (NITOUR) and a clothing store (Oger Frères) CFC

Two posters that encourage travel in the Dutch East Indies CFC

On September 6, 1938, a corso of floats paraded past the Fermont-Cuypers offices on Molenvliet Oost (now: Jl. Hayam Wuruk Tim) to celebrate Queen Wilhelmina's jubilee CFC

Bandung, the 1934 design made by Thomas Nix for the 'Samarangsche' on the Naripanweg (now: Jl. Naripan) CFC

Bandung, the Naripanweg (now: Jl. Naripan) in 1938, with the high roof of the 'Samarangsche' on the left and the Denis Bank on the right CTM

looking buildings, with towers and built in concrete with such closed façades had to predominantly determine the image in the old Indies city. He was not the only one at Fermont-Cuypers who thought this way.[263] Japan advanced further in China. The Indonesians reacted differently to this. Some chose the Chinese, whilst others opted for Japan. The nationalists felt that there would be a shift in power relations in Asia.[264] The exiled Sutan Sjahrir had an especially keen eye for this. He feared that the nationalist wishes would never be fulfilled if fascism won and was therefore committed to cooperation between the nationalists and the government.[265] European groups reacted differently to international developments. Most Dutch people who firmly believed in Dutch neutrality, did not think that this would happen so quickly. During Queen Wilhelmina's jubilee on September 6, everything was done again to underline their own identity with a 'reception in the palace', 'soldiers on the Waterlooplein' (now: Lapangan Banteng), a 'service of thanksgiving in the cathedral' and a long procession of floats. Kaptijn recorded this on photo. He recorded a miniature galleon that was from the Dutch 'Golden Age' and young people in Dutch costumes. On the photo you can see the office of Fermont-Cuypers in the background. Fermont travelled to Palembang for the opening of the Escomptobank and the Volkskredietbank and he visited the Children's Pavilion of the Carolus Hospital in Jakarta, where the official opening was conducted by the wife of the Governor-General. Taen sailed to Makassar to lay the foundation stone of the Stella Maris hospital and the Father school. Thomas Nix prepared for half a year's leave in Europe. He was in contact with Dutch poet and author Eddy du Perron for whom he made drawings to illustrate his books.[266] The writer asked him to become the editor of a journal to be set up in the Netherlands East Indies.[267] The idea appealed to Nix, but not now, as he was about to leave for Europe. That led Du Perron to write a letter to his friend, the Dutch painter Carel Willink (1900-1983) in the Netherlands: 'here in the Dutch East Indies everyone is afraid of Japan [...] The Indonesians are gaining self-confidence [...] We also want to leave, contemplating other countries. [...] A draftsman from here – son of my publisher Nix, Thomas Nix, engineer and Catholic, but a very nice man, is going to Holland today. I gave him your address. He loves to paint and admires you greatly.'[268]

Amsterdam 1939: 'Our country does not realise how big it is'

Whether Thomas Nix paid a visit to Willink is not known. Once, this painter actively participated in the international avant-garde until he had enough of all the experimentation and began painting in a realistic manner. Many painters in Europe of his generation did the same. In 1939, a painting on his easel depicted himself, sitting on a pillar with a burning city in the background under threatening cloudy skies. It symbolised the demise of European civilisation.[269] That's what it felt like in Europe. Nix and his wife decided to go to Paris, where he wanted to paint and be inspired by other artists. Whether that worked was the question. In March the German troops annexed Czechoslovakia, after which Hitler claimed Danzig. Soon after, Germany and the Soviet Union entered into a non-aggression pact. On June 5, 1939 Arthur Fermont arrived in the Netherlands again.[270] There, a month later, he visited the 'Rotterdam-Batavia' exhibition in Rotterdam. The speech of the Minister of Colonies may have been exactly what he was hoping to hear. 'Our country suffers from one problem: it does not realise how big it is', according to Minister Welter, 'The country suffers from an inferiority complex that stems from living in a small country, on a small scale and it has still not realised that overseas, it is a great power. But not only that, our people do not know what wonderful work it has done in the Dutch East Indies. It has created a rich country there of 2 million km^2, inhabited by 70 million people, managed and administered in a way that arouses the admiration of compatriots and strangers alike.' The mayors of Rotterdam and Batavia (Jakarta) attended the opening. The latter was on leave in the Netherlands and left shortly afterwards. Thomas Nix and his wife also left Europe halfway through the year.

Fermont stayed longer, also to consult with the 'Rotterdamsche Lloyd' and 'Stoomvaart Maatschappij Nederland' about their projects in Jakarta. He certainly visited Liège. There a world exhibition took place under unfavourable conditions. The 'Exposition Internationale de la technique de l'eau' should have lasted until November 1939, but closed its doors on September 2, due to a tragic accident and because Germany had invaded Poland, at which point Britain and France declared war on Germany.[271] The Netherlands had already called up its military forces a month earlier for a pre-mobilisation. It was quiet in the port of Rotterdam. Only the passenger transport to America and Asia increased. People with sufficient money left for safer places.[272] The 'Rotterdamsche Lloyd' ordered that the passenger terminal in Jakarta should be ready as quickly as possible. Fermont was in telephone contact with the firm in Jakarta to arrange various affairs and decided to stay with his family in The Hague. He waited for the events, even though waiting was not his style.

Jakarta 1939 A new building for an insurance company

For the nationalists in the Dutch East Indies, 1939 began disappointingly after the Dutch veto on their quest for independence. They united under the leadership of Thamrin in the Gabungan Politik Indonesia (Gabi).[273] Others, who once wanted to enforce independence, waited to see what was going to happen from where they had been interned. Theo Taen and Matthias Kaptijn kept the firm running in and from Jakarta, but there was virtually no work left. Taen designed a chapel at 'De Goede Herder', the institution that was completed eight years earlier. At the Canisius College, a chapel had to be built as an extension of the school complex that was built in 1930, even before Thomas Nix joined them. He was back in the Dutch East Indies and although he formally remained listed as a Fermont-Cuypers employee, he hardly worked for the office.[274] He channelled his energies into drawing, painting and organising exhibitions. At Fermont-Cuypers, they had lost the man of the smart, catchy sketches. The firm decided to make more scale models to make their design choices and the end result into something more visible. A simple model was thus produced for the passenger terminal in Priok, which Freek Dicke had designed. The Rotterdamsche Lloyd was in a hurry. The company wanted to use Jakarta as a home port for her passenger ships. The nationalists in the Volksraad were also in a hurry. They were afraid that they would lose their interlocutors if the Netherlands fell into the hands of Hitler, a man with grand colonial aspirations. Under the leadership of Thamrin, a motion was submitted in the Volksraad, now with the demand that a parliamentary form of government was set up in the Dutch East Indies, consistently called Indonesia. Theo Taen left for Makassar on November 1, 1939 to attend the opening ceremony of the Brothers school. In his opening speech, he recalled the origin of the plans and the completion. Almost perfunctorily, he expressed the hope that the building would meet all expectations.[275] Two weeks later he was present when the foundation stone was laid for the Mater Dolorosa chapel at the 'Goede Herder'. There were again many beautiful words, alternating with prayers. When the underground 'secret' bank vault in Bandung was put into service, the management of the Javasche Bank also wished for the best. Meanwhile, the firm put the finishing touches to a scale model, made for a new office building in Surabaya for Insurance Company 'De Nederlanden van 1845', a corner building at an iconic location in the old town.[276] The readers of *d'Oriënt* found a picture of the model in their magazine on Christmas Day.[277] An insurance company that believed in new building at this time was encouraging.

Amsterdam 1940: Law on Seat Transfers

The new Dutch government appeared to be unprepared for a possible occupation of the country. All instructions from the time of former Prime Minister Colijn, lay at the bottom of the desk drawers. Pressured by the business community, the Dutch Lower House passed a law in April that took into account that 'nightmare'. With the Law on Seat Transfers, the public limited companies established in the Netherlands were able to relocate their seat to other parts within the Kingdom and the managements were able to manage the company without an occupying force being able to influence it. The large shipping companies were the first to use the law. The Rotterdamsche Lloyd and Stoomvaart Maatschappij Nederland did relocate their seat to Jakarta. At the end of April 1940 the government was confronted in The Hague by a motion from the Dutch East Indies with the requirement to start discussions about future independence. The invasion of the Germans interrupted the handling of that request.[278]

Jakarta 1940: Unnamed ships sail back and forth

Early 1940 it was apparent that the municipality of Jakarta had not yet succeeded in making any headway with its plan for the Koningsplein (now: Medan Merdeka). The desired city hall was still absent.[279] The municipality wanted to organise a competition to invite four architectural firms to design the city hall, including Fermont-Cuypers.[280] Whether the invitation was ever issued is unknown. The building was never built.[281]

The new hospital opened in Makassar. There were many Dutch flags flying along the new sea boulevard. Taen attended the opening. He decided to write an article about this project in *Indisch Bouwkundig Tijdschrift*.[282] The construction of the port yard in Tanjung Priok progressed. A newspaper published a photograph of the scale model and wrote optimistically: 'Visitors coming to pick people up or drop them off will soon have an unhindered view of the sea from this building, while a comfortable waiting area is planned. The building will be flanked by a tower, which will be visible from a very long distance from the sea.'[283] A newspaper added hopefully in March: 'The busy season in the shipping connection between the Dutch East Indies and Holland will soon resume'.[284] Many American tourists were also expected. In January 1940, *Life* magazine published a positive article about the Dutch East Indies, 'This sprawling empire of 20,000 islands, covers a sea area wider than the U.S. It has 65,000,000 brown natives of 137 cultures (...) The Dutch have given every nation in the world a startling demonstration of how to get the best out of a colonial empire. They built a vast water system, multiplying the fertility of Java. They invited foreign capital under strict supervision (...) They stamped out disease, built railroads, overruled the local princes and set up a

Models made for the 'Rotterdamsche Lloyd' premises in Tanjung Priok and for 'De Nederlanden van 1845' in Surabaya and a stained glass windows designed by Robbert Deppe for the insurance company CFC

half-native parliament, the 'Volksraad'. In the article the natives are called 'the world's kindest people'.[285]

In April, two exhibitions took place featuring the visual artistic work of Thomas Nix, one of which was in the Kunstkring of Batavia (Jakarta). The shrinking team at the firm paid a visit. The press responded in a divided way: 'Thomas Nix has gained many impressions in the Dutch East Indies and in Europe, but they have not yet been processed. One sees influences of Carel Willink, De Chirico and Italian museums. The work shows a strong tendency towards baroque which makes it messy as a whole. In addition, his palette is dark and dingy. [...] One wonders whether Nix's work is not a bit too undeveloped to put it on display: there is still too little sense of a direction. [...] Nevertheless, for Nix, the satire still looks promising, perhaps in the form of the political print, which is now almost entirely absent in the Dutch East Indies.[286] Maybe this article helped Nix decide to once again pick up his architecture and urban planning. He started in 1941 at the Technical Department of the municipality of Bandung where, in addition to his profession, he could continue to paint.[287] Fermont-Cuypers had no more work. There was a bid for a church in Telukbetung (Bandar Lampung) on the southern tip of Sumatra, at the moment the Netherlands was invaded by Germany.[288] After the news of the capitulation arrived in the Dutch East Indies, there was a surge of patriotism among the Dutch.[289] Germans were arrested and interned in a chaotic manner, including Dutchmen with German names and even German Jews. *En masse*, support was given to the Governor-General, before his palace (now: Istana Merdeka). He responded with the following words: 'Continue to work and keep your faith'.[290] A month later he told the Volksraad 'that he was open to discussions about reforms', but only after the war.[291] The cruise terminal in Tanjung Priok was put into operation without any formalities or publicity. The latter was in any case the norm in the area surrounding the port. Around the new premises, mysterious loads were loaded or unloaded in large cases, shrouded in silence. Warring countries were not allowed to know what was going on there. Ships arrived and left again, unidentified. The place of departure and destination remained unknown. Painters changed the look of the port with their paint brushes. The brand new terminal was also painted The fresh white-washed building was now given a dingy colour in the hope that it was unrecognisable from the air.[292]

Jakarta, since the outbreak of the Second World War, unidentified ships arrived with mysterious loads in the ports, including Tanjung Priok
PHOTO C. BLAZER CMM

Jakarta, the premises of the 'Rotterdamsche Lloyd' in the harbour of Tanjung Priok, covered by the *Indische courant* on March 16, 1940, 'The busy season in the shipping links between the Dutch East Indies and Holland will resume very soon' PHOTO: C. BLAZER CMM

Amsterdam 1941: A Tri-partite pact: Germany, Italy and Japan

Some reports from the Dutch East Indies reached the Netherlands, where the press was under German control. One was that the Japanese delegation's leader said during a speech in Tokyo that the unequal distribution of wealth among population groups was the main cause of the unrest in the world. Japan, as a resourceless country, wanted to receive all the minerals from the possessing nations that geographically bordered Japan.[293] The leader of the Dutch National Socialist Party (NSB), Mussert announced after a visit to Hitler that he was convinced that the Dutch colonies would not be lost. 'The Netherlands will keep its place among the peoples'. Meanwhile, repression increased daily, mainly of Jewish citizens who were excluded from everywhere. Jewish emigrants from Germany were arrested. Associations had to exclude Jewish members. The Royal Institute for Engineers also did this, and, remarkably enough, it also declared it applicable for its departments in the colonies.[294] In the tri-partite pact between Germany, Italy and Japan, which was signed in Berlin, Japan was given the leading role in the so-called Great-Asian space, an area with undefined borders, but which was assumed to include the Dutch East Indies.[295]

Jakarta 1941: 'It is hard to find our Dutch friends'

In the upper room of the new building of the 'Nederlanden van 1845' in Surabaya, the opening was accompanied by some speeches. The Governor of East Java expressed his admiration for the architects, engineers and builders who 'assembled the building materials for such a large project during this difficult period of time. The construction of this office points to Dutch courage in hard times'.[296] The director of the insurance company wished that 'when the centenary will be celebrated in a few years' time, this may also be celebrated in the Netherlands under an 'orange sun' of the Kingdom of the Netherlands of 1945'. In the lower hall of the new building, three small stained-glass windows displayed the three events that could be insured against: Accidents, Fire, and Diseases, but not an approaching war.[297] A day later, the *Soerabaijasch Handelsblad* published a photograph of the new building. This was next to a long article about the bombed city of Rotterdam. Theo Taen did not express himself in superlatives in his speech. Shortly afterwards, he celebrated his 20-year jubilee at Fermont-Cuypers. There was little reason for a party because of what was happening in the world and due to the lack of work. Freek Dicke left for the municipal agency, the 'Landsgebouwendienst'. Everything was slipping through the fingers of Europeans. Thamrin, the moderate nationalist, was put under house arrest for suspicion of contacts with Japan. While he was sick in bed, his home was searched. He died a few days later.[298] The Indonesians blamed the government. His funeral culminated in a nationalist demonstration.[299] Thousands of people stood in white clothing along the route of the funeral procession, which passed the Harmonieplein (now: Harmoni), with the white Nitour building in the background. Sutardjo, the man of the petition, sighed: 'We now feel as if in our development we are encountering barriers everywhere. It is hard to find our Dutch friends'.[300] What Thamrin was not allowed to do was what a number of top officials had already been doing for four months. In Hotel des Indes consultations took place with a Japanese delegation, which eventually left because they considered the consultation to be a failure. They did not receive commitments for more intensive cooperation with Japan, nor did the Dutch guarantee that Japan would always receive the requested raw materials and goods. Meanwhile, at Fermont-Cuypers they were working on their, as yet, final assignment from the 'Scheepvaart Maatschappij Nederland'. The management in the Netherlands had authorised one of its members to act on its behalf in Jakarta.[301] An extensive head office had to be built between Stadhuisplein (now: Taman Fatahillah) and Kali Besar in the old town. From there, the company wanted to conduct global operations. A photograph of the scale model appeared in two newspapers. They reported that the Hollandsche Beton Maatschappij had begun construction, led by Fermont-Cuypers.[302] Old buildings were demolished, and the ground was prepared for construction. A little further a tram drove over a virtually deserted square in front of the railway station, between three new bank buildings, each of which radiated colonial power in a monumental way. It was a tranquil surreal image.

On Sunday December 7, 1941, Japan attacked Pearl Harbor. A day later, the Dutch government in exile declared war on Japan, followed by the mobilisation in the Dutch East Indies. All construction projects ground to a halt, including the 'Stoomvaart Maatschappij Nederland'.

A sketch. made by Fermont-Cuypers, showing the hall of the intended headquarters for the Stoomvaart Maatschappij Nederland CDJ

Jakarta, the funeral of M.H. Thamrin in 1941, with the NITOUR building in the background on the Harmonieplein (now: Harmoni) KITLV

Jakarta, a tram crosses the Station Square (now; Jl. St. Kota) in the kota tua neighbourhood at the end of 1941 with from left to right: 'Factorij', the Javasche Bank, the Escomptobank and in the middle of the photo the recently completed 'Nederlandsch Indische Handelsbank' by the architect Ch.P. Wolff Schoemaker CON

Jakarta 1942: The door remains closed for a long time

A quick victory followed the Japanese invasion. On March 4, 1942, the Japanese reached Jakarta. At 6.30 in the evening they stood in front of the Resident's office at the Molenvliet (now: Jl. Gajah Mada), opposite the Fermont-Cuypers premises. A large crowd of Indonesians had gathered and saw the Japanese as their liberators. Coming from the south of the city, the Resident and the mayor met the Japanese. Shots were fired at the Resident's office and shouts of 'boenoeh orang europa' ('death to the Europeans'). A Japanese colonel remained to take over authority in the capital with a proclamation. Four days later the overall capitulation took place. On March 10, 1942 trams were once again driving on the Molenvliet, where Fermont-Cuypers closed their doors, which remained closed for the next few years.

Architects who died during their internment or otherwise as a result of the war: **G.J. Bel** (1886-1945), **K.H.G. Bos** (1903-1943), **F.W. Brinkman** (1878-1944), **B.W.J. Deppe** (1902-1943), **F.C. Dhomen** (1901-1946), **J.J. van Dongen** (1881-1943), **J. van Gendt** 1885-1945), **G. Hendriks** (1890-1945), **G.C. Hildering** (1874-1945), **J.P. Hoogerbeets** (1892-1945), **H. Th. Karsten** (1884-1945), **Th. Koreman** (1881-1942), **H. Korver** (1881-1945), **W. Lemei** (1892-1945), **J.Th. van Oyen** (1893-1944), **E.H. de Roo** (1889-1942), **R. Rijksen** (1872-1944), **G.Th. Ubink** (1888-1945), **S. Snuyf** (1880-1944), **W. Westmaas** (1876-1945), **Prof. R.L.A. Schoemaker** (1886-1942).

1945-1949: From Dutch East Indies to Indonesia

After years of misery, a small group of emaciated employees from the pre-war office period came together to ask how they should proceed with Fermont-Cuypers. They had contacted Arthur Fermont in the Netherlands for whom there was only one answer: 'continue'! Most of them felt the same, as did Mr. Fischer and Mr. Beelen and, of course, Mrs. Ter Beeke-Heijnneman, who had been in charge of the secretariat since 1926. The 58-year-old Matthias Kaptijn pulled out and decided to go to the Netherlands. He followed Theo Taen and his wife Lies who repatriated immediately after their internment. Thomas Nix also left for the Netherlands with his wife and children. His youngest died shortly before arrival, because of all the previous hardships.[303] Taen, Nix and Han de Jongh formed an architectural combination that worked on the reconstruction of a coun-

Jakarta, the population greeting the Japanese as they march into the city in March 1942 NIOD

try that had to recover from the depths after five years of occupation. In addition, Thomas Nix wanted to complete a PhD in Delft focussed on the urban development in Indonesia.[304] They all left the Dutch East Indies and Fermont-Cuypers behind them. It was no longer spoken of in the Netherlands. The Dutch East Indies was now called Indonesia. It declared itself independent on August 17, 1945. However, this was not recognised by the Dutch government. Until 1949 colonial warfare took place in countless places in the archipelago, which lasted for a long time and cost many lives.[305] In Batavia, which was now called Jakarta, Fermont-Cuypers worked on the first post-war assignment. The K.L.M. commissioned a redesign of the Arnhem building on Jl. Ir. H. Juanda, once designed by Eduard Cuypers.[306] The official transfer of sovereignty to Indonesia took place at the end of 1949.[307] Both countries made concessions in the negotiations and differences of opinion remained. For example, the Netherlands excluded New Guinea from the transfer, much to the displeasure of Indonesia. A Dutch-Indonesian Union arose, which was little more than a joint venture.[308] Dutch business continued to find Indonesia an interesting country.[309] Fermont-Cuypers benefited from this in Jakarta. The firm advertised for architects, engineers and other experienced builders.[310] Arthur Fermont stayed in the Netherlands and asked his youngest son Cyril to go to Jakarta to strengthen the team.[311]

Jakarta 1950: A printing plant for the Republic

After the transfer of sovereignty there was a lot of work in the Indonesia, also for architects. 'The few architects are overwhelmed with work', sighed a Dutch architect at the time.[312] Many of his Dutch colleagues had left with the second wave of returnees.[313] As far as Jakarta was concerned, the large planned city expansion five kilometres south of Jakarta, in Kebayoran, had to be built.[314] At the beginning of 1950, Arthur Fermont heard in the Netherlands that Joh. Enschedé & Sons was approached by the Indonesian government with the request to set up a printing company in Jakarta for the production of banknotes and stamps. At Fermont-Cuypers in Jakarta, a study was begun led by of Fischer, who was appointed as director there, into potential locations for this printing company. The blast-proof vaults of the Javasche Bank in Bandung were an option, but one with many ifs and buts. This also applied to a number of other alternatives that were considered. The final recommendation was to build new commercial premises.

Indonesia Merdeka! Indonesia Independent! COF

Arthur Fermont was not sure that the team in Jakarta could handle such a large assignment as there were no architects left in the office. He polled in the Netherlands for people who were interested in Jakarta. He himself stayed at home in the Netherlands to procure more assignments for the office in Indonesia. He had stationery printed where, in addition to Fermont-Cuypers, 'Jakarta-The Hague' was written. The period 'Batavia-Amsterdam' was over.[315]

After Joh. Enschedé & Sons had finalised the commission, work began on the printing works. The commission was altered as a result of a new housing regulation issued by the republic, stipulating that a foreigner returning from leave would lose the right to his rental property. Many foreign companies decided to build their own homes for their employees, as did Joh. Enschedé & Sons. At Fermont-Cuypers, the plan was therefore expanded to include 40 homes on an area of almost 5 hectares. In terms of location, the choice was a large plot in the heart of the Kebayoran.[316] Business premises were built with a side room for a substantial extension, where different types of houses surrounded a quadrant. For Joh. Enschedé & Sons, this was something new. It had never developed printing works abroad, let alone a project with accommodation. A model of the proposed plan was made in the hope of convincing the Supervisory Board of Joh. Enschedé & Sons. But the business community in the Netherlands began to lose confidence in investments in a country where the economy was not doing well and where the president claimed that Indonesia would not have been 'the victim of crisis if the Dutch had recognised the independence of Indonesia in 1945'. 'They chose not to cooperate', Sukarno said, 'but they sent troops and have since then continued their unilateral behaviour'. 'I am against systems', according to the president,' and that is why I want to cancel the Union with the Netherlands as soon as possible', adding: 'After all I have said about our controversies with the Dutch, the impression may be that my words are inspired by feelings of resentment. I can assure you that I do not wish any ill-will towards the Dutch people'.[317]

Jakarta 1952: N.V. Percetakan Kebayoran

On January 1, 1952, the Percetakan Kebayoran started work on the printing plant, aiming to get it up and running within a year. The building elements in the façades are striking on the construction drawings of the main building. They were placed in a prefabricated framework, creating an Indonesian appearance. All homes resembled the pre-war types, which were also for Europeans. It became an extensive plan, with involvement from Karel Mekel. He was one of the architects who came over from the Netherlands that year.

The question at the firm was what should be done with the construction site in the city centre of Jakarta where the 'Stoomvaart Maatschappij Nederland' office was supposed to be built. Since the shipowner had rejected any building initiatives, people from Fermont-Cuypers were also eagerly searching for candidates for this location in the heart of the old city. In the meantime, the already strained relationship between

Jakarta, employees of Fermont-Cuypers in 1951, including on the left Mrs. P. ter Beeke-Heijnneman, celebrating her twenty-fifth anniversary with the firm, Mr. Beelen and Cyril Fermont and to her right Mr. Fischer and Karel Mekel CRF

Jakarta, the presentation sketch of Fermont-Cuypers from 1951 for the main building of the printing works in Kebayoran, in an architectural style that seeks connection with Indonesian architecture CJE

Indonesia and the Netherlands deteriorated further. The Dutch government was unwilling to change the status of West New Guinea. (Irian Jaya)

Jakarta 1953: Bank of China

In the course of 1953, the Bank of China presented itself as a potential customer for the construction site in the city centre. The first plan was similar in volume to the pre-war vision, only the architecture was different. Karel Mekel produced the design. He opted for post-war modern architecture that was a success all over the western world. He worked with simple main forms and standardisation in construction. During the design process, the number of floors increased from two to three, with modest provision for ventilation barely visible at the top. The municipality had concerns about the size. The firm used photomontages to convey the intended design, both on the Kali Besar and on the Stadhuisplein (now: Taman Fatahillah). They knew how to convince the officials. The tender could take place on the basis of the building plans; N.V. Nedam was the chosen building company.

The start of construction at the printing works was delayed. Discussions with Joh. Enschedé focused on the number of houses to be built. The management wanted to limit this number. On March 10, 1953, N.V. Nedam received the contract for the construction of the business premises, but doubts persisted regarding the number of dwellings. A month later the management travelled to Jakarta, where Fischer led them around the building site, where a few houses were finished. Arthur Fermont, as an intermediary, played a role in the background. After the death of his wife in December 1952, he had once come over from the Netherlands to visit his youngest son and his family. Naturally he also visited the firm's premises where a lot had changed. There were some small commissions, also for private homes, for which the team, gradually including more Indonesians, barely had any expertise.[318]

Jakarta 1954: Henk Roebbers comes over

Back in the Netherlands, Arthur Fermont came in contact with Henk Roebbers who had recently graduated. Fermont managed to recruit him for the team in Jakarta. Roebbers flew over in March. Dieuwertje, his wife preferred to sail over because it was much easier with a baby. Two months later, the ship 'Willem Ruys' docked at the passenger terminal in Tanjung Priok, which once again stood in its original splendour. Roebbers was full of energy and fresh ideas. He was a great supporter of architecture that brought innovation. The designer responded as much as possible to the very latest building techniques and made use of prefab building elements and a colour palette as Le Corbusier had recommended. That created an expressive, almost cheerful architecture that was a major departure from the heavy design of the 1930s.[319] Karel Mekel finalised the design for Bank Indonesia on Ambon.[320] The sketch shows a small building using an Indonesian architectural style. Where did the young republic want to go? Something local or international? They had no idea at Fermont-Cuypers. In February 1954, Joh. Enschedé made the decision not to build the houses to the west of the printing plant. Fischer said he found this very unfortunate.[321] The Indonesian economy deteriorated steadily and the Rupiah was constantly losing value. On May 7, 1954 Arthur Fermont wrote from the Netherlands that the houses had to be paid for in guilders. He was unable to distance himself from business operations in Jakarta. He also complained that everything took much longer than in his day. The expectations that he had once conveyed in his planning to the management of Joh. Enschedé proved to be unachievable. The completion date had been postponed for two years, as was incidentally the case with countless other projects in Kebayoran.[322] The time of colonial relations with top-down decisions was over. Consultation came in its place and that took time, especially in Indonesia.

Amsterdam Schiphol, Henk Roebbers leaves for Jakarta in 1954 and will contribute to a new start for the firm Fermont-Cuypers CRF

Jakarta, model made in 1953 for the printing works and staff residences in Kebayoran CJE

Jakarta, sketch made by Karel Mekel for the Bank of China CFC

Jakarta 1955: They still have each other

The Koningsplein was renamed Medan Merdeka after the revolution, which means Freedom Square. Sukarno wanted a glorious design and above all, a large green space with a monument to remember the struggle for freedom. In the old town, the first pile was driven into the ground on the construction site of the future Bank of China, while a tram, driving over the Stadhuisplein (now: Taman Fatahillah), passed the construction site. The tram passengers could just glimpse, because of the open space, the very first building that Eduard Cuypers had left behind in this city, the Hong Kong Shanghai Bank on the Kali-Besar. The new bank building, which would obstruct this view, bore no resemblance whatever to the old building that had been designed half a century earlier in the Dutch-Indies Building style that had been officially dictated. Now people worked with prefab building elements. This resulted in a robust, understated building. The municipality was pleased with such a building in the old city centre, because for most companies Kebayoran is the perfect location. There the final touches were put to the printing plant, where at the end of March 1955 the first 1 Rupiah banknotes rolled off the presses, five months before the official opening.

Vice President Hatta officiated at the opening on August 11, 1955. The board of Joh. Enschedé came over for the ceremony and sat on the front row. The Fermont-Cuypers team sat on the third row. The vice president addressed those present: 'We are all delighted to be in possession of a very modern printing plant. This plant is able to print paper money, bonds, stamps and other valuable papers. For the establishment and operation of a modern company such as this plant, it was still necessary to enlist the help of foreign technicians, as we do not yet have the required experience. This plant is a great asset to us and by having our paper printed here, we can reduce money forgeries to a minimum because the printing technology in this printing house is extremely up to date and modern. We hope that the workers in this printing house will find joy and peace in their work. I also hope that they will dedicate all their strength to the welfare of the homeland.' After these words a tour followed to inspect the printing works and view the staff houses with their classic appearance. In the new district of Kebayoran, houses were also created in a different architectural style, including some designed by Henk Roebbers. His wife sent a photograph of one of the houses to family in the Netherlands and wrote: 'This is one of Henk's houses, it's a beauty, especially now that it's almost finished and painted in all kinds of fantastic colours.' She regularly wrote to the Netherlands and experienced a more hostile atmosphere every day to everything Dutch.[323] On December 5, eight young Dutch families with twelve small children came together to celebrate the typical Dutch Sinterklaas party.

According to Henk Roebbers' design, buildings in Jakarta and Bandung were constructed in what would later be called Jenki Style CFR

Jakarta 1956: Unrest is everywhere

Craving western culture, the Roebbers couple sat in January 1956 in the Kunstkring of Jakarta. Listening to a recital of composer Benjamin Britten and tenor Peter Pears. Sukarno unilaterally cancelled the Dutch-Indonesian Union, as he did all the other agreements with the Netherlands, because he failed to get any further with the annexation of West Irian. 'The special position of the Netherlands, especially in the financial and economic field, has now come to an end', the Minister of Foreign Affairs added.[324] Roebbers did not want to accept this. At various construction sites in Jakarta and Bandung he saw a house or office building designed by him, using optimistic architecture, emerging from the scaffolding.[325] On March 25, 1956 the team from N.V. Nedam and the architects and foremen from Fermont-Cuypers came together for a simple dinner in the yacht club at Tanjung Priok. Although they were celebrating the official completion of the printing works, they spoke mainly about the situation in Indonesia. How long could they keep going with the growing smear campaign aimed at Dutch? Some compatriots were arrested, suspected of espionage and terrorism and also condemned. Dieuwertje Roebbers did not wait any longer. She booked the 'Willem Ruys' and left in August with her two small children from the terminal of the former 'Koninklijke Rotterdamsche Lloyd', now called the 'N.V. Nederlandsch-Indonesische Scheepvaart-Etablissementen'.[326] Henk stayed behind to finish his work. He visited the opening of the new bank building for Bank Indonesia on Ambon, designed by Karel Mekel, who had since left. Dieuwertje at that

Jakarta, the speech of Vice President Hatta at the opening of the printing works in Kebayoran in 1955. On the third row on the right are Henk Roebbers and Cyril Fermont. The production of banknotes and stamps could officially begin CJE

time sailed around the Cape of Good Hope, because the Suez Canal was closed because of the Suez crisis.[327] Shortly after her arrival in the Netherlands, the Soviet Union invaded Hungary. Unrest was everywhere.

Jakarta 1957: Fermont-Cuypers ceases to exist

In Indonesia, President Sukarno continued with rousing speeches and the threat of a boycott of Dutch companies. Strikes followed, restrictions on foreign money transactions were imposed. Some Indonesian politicians pointed out that measures were in the offing against Dutch companies as long as discussions about the West Irian were not finalised. At his six-monthly press conference, the mayor of Jakarta announced that some Dutch people had reported to him of feeling seriously threatened, and also by the slogans daubed on their homes and cars. 'Personally I am of the opinion,' said the mayor, 'that inscriptions such as *Bunuh Belanda* (murder the Dutch) cause unrest.'[328] Shortly thereafter, an anti-Dutch week followed, during which all Dutch people were denied access to restaurants, shops and other public buildings. Immediately after that, Indonesian workers were stimulated by the trade unions to occupy Dutch companies. On December 5, 1957, Sukarno declared that all Dutch people had to leave Indonesia immediately. There weren't many left. After Cyril Fermont tried unsuccessfully to sell Fermont-Cuypers, the transfer was made to some Indonesian employees. Fermont-Cuypers ceased informally to exist.[329] Fifty years earlier, Eduard Cuypers had been commissioned to build numerous bank buildings, the source of unity in the currency system within the archipelago. In the meantime, that currency was called rupiah. Every day, the banknotes rolled from the presses in printing works designed by Fermont-Cuypers. From now on, Indonesia could manage by itself.

In 1958, Cyril Fermont, Henk Roebbers and the others returned to the Netherlands with their families, where they had to make a new start, just as Theo Taen and Thomas Nix had done a few years earlier. In August 1958, they read in various Dutch newspapers that rumours were circulating in Jakarta

1954 Sukarno 1000 banknotes

A tram runs on Molenvliet West (now: Jl. Gajah Mada) with Hotel des Galeries on the right and behind it Molenvliet Oost (now: Jl. Hayam Wuruk) where Fermont-Cuypers ceased operating CON

about the imminent nationalisation of Dutch companies. There were only rumours, because a real decision was delayed. In early January 1960, the Indonesian government decreed that it had nationalised nine Dutch contractors, including Fermont-Cuypers.[330] Arthur Fermont also read this message in his newspaper in the Netherlands.[331] On the Molenvliet, now renamed as the Djalan Hajam Wuruk, the name Fermont-Cuypers disappeared from the façade on March 16, 1960. A tram followed the familiar route. The next day, the last tram lines were removed. Jakarta public transport only consisted of bus lines.[332]

Notes accompanying chapter 3

1 Joannes Benedictus van Heutsz died in Montreux (Switzerland) on July 11, 1924.
2 Witte (1976), pp. 129-130. The magazines in the Dutch East Indies in particular wax lyrical about the reburial of Van Heutsz.
3 Doel (1996), p. 222.
4 With a great sense of statement Sukarno chooses July 4, the day of the declaration of independence in the United States.
5 Sukarno was an engineer. Engineers strongly believe in manufacturability, that some even apply to a country.
6 Doel (1996), p. 215.
7 *De Telegraaf*, September 2, 1927.
8 *De Telegraaf*, September 2, 1927.
9 *Het Volk*, October 14, 1927. Stating that there is a 'most dubious phenomenon', the newspaper of the workers' party publishes the outcome of the investigation: Edison 70%, Mussolini 66%, Marconi 50%, Einstein 42%, Ford 25% and the pilot Lindbergh 25%. According to the newspaper, it casts a faint light on the feeling of the liberal 'Handelsblad bourgeoisie.'
10 *Nieuwsblad van het Noorden*, June 2, 1927.
11 *Het Vaderland*, August 29, 1928.
12 Dirk Burghard Logemann (1872-1964).
13 His diploma includes names such as: A. Boeken, B.T. Boeyinga, H. Evers, G. Friedhoff, J.P. Mieras, D. Roosenburg, J. Wils; quite famous architects in the Netherlands during those days.
14 *Bataviaasch Nieuwsblad*, July 2, 1927. First mention of 'Fermont-Cuypers'.
15 In 1923 in Pematang Siantar. In 1925 in Padang.
16 Emiel Schedler (1906-1986) and Philip Wijsman (1902-1970) worked at Fermont-Cuypers from 1926 to 1938. They entered service with the Architects and Engineering Company Taen Nix & Van Hasselt in Utrecht after the war.
17 *Algemeen Handelsblad*, August 15, 1904.
18 Helsdingen (1941), pp. 260-261. The train journey between Medan and Banda Aceh took even two days to complete in 1940.
19 Segaar-Höweler (1998), pp. 41-43. Groenewegen is commissioned to extend Jaski's church and to provide a tower, which must have been a bitter pill for Jaski.
20 *De Sumatra Post*, August 29, 1927.
21 *Bataviaasch Nieuwsblad*, November 3, 1926.
22 *De Indische Courant*, December 24, 1926. More than seven years later, Job & Sprey would complete the well-known front buildings of the Oranjehotel (Soerabaijasch handelsblad, July 2, 1934)
23 Laurent Logemann made a new drawing in October 1927, much like that of Kreisler.
24 *Algemeen Handelsblad*, February 3, 1928. Eduard Cuypers made the design together with H. Kannegieter. The beakers consist of yellow or lilac ornamental glass and are made of crystal from Leerdam.
25 Giedion (1954), p. 217. H.P. Berlage was one of those present at La Sarraz. He gave a lecture about 'The Relations between Government and Architecture'.
26 Woud (1983), p. 55. The direct reason is that modern architecture, Le Corbusier's plan, did not win, during a competition for the Peoples' Confederation building in Geneva, by 'conservative academism'.
27 Le Corbusier (1923), pp. 65-117.
28 Christiansen (1931), p. 55. Broder Christiansen (1869-1958) was a well-known philosopher in the 1930s who was loved by many who could no longer identify with modernism.
29 Bergson (1925), p. 9. Foreword: 'Bergson is the philosopher of evolution, change, movement, eternal event [...] Dynamic and not static [...] nothing is there, or it becomes a result of becoming'.
30 M.J. Granpré Molière, 'Modern art and its promises', from his speech when accepting his duties as professor at the Technical University in Delft on October 22, 1924.
31 Granpré Molière (1949), p. 47.
32 Granpré Molière (1949), pp. 33-36.
33 Molema (2010), p. 98. In the lecture 'Wat wij willen', from 1933 of the group of modernists at the Technical University in Delft, the name of Christiansen is mentioned in the same breath as that of J.J.P. Oud, Le Corbusier, Granpré Molière and others.
34 Christiansen (1931), p. 145.
35 Geest (1996), p. 12. To this group, of which Hans van der Laan (1904-1991) was the first chairman and professor M.J. Granpré Molière would succeed him, including: S.J. van Embden (1904-2000), C. Poyderoyen (1912-1993), J.J.M. Vegter (1906-1982), W.G.J. van Mourik (1914-2006), J.F. Berghoef (1903-1994), C.Th. Nix (1904-1998) and F. Dicke (1909-1985). Nix and Dicke were to work for Fermont-Cuypers for more than ten and four years respectively.
36 Vriend (1938), p. 176. J.J. Vriend made this statement in 1938.
37 Geest (1996), p. 12.
38 *De Sumatra Post*, September 13, 1928. Jaski had been in the city council for barely a year and a half.
39 *De Indische Courant*, December 3, 1929. Speech delivered by Mayor Schotman at the laying of the first foundation stone of the townhall.
40 Hulswit-Fermont and Ed. Cuypers completed in 1921 a bank building for the Java Bank in Cirebon.
41 *Het Nieuws van den dag voor Nederlandsch-Indië*, March 5, 1928, 'een schouwburg in Madioen'?
42 *Bataviaasch Nieuwsblad*, May 1, 1928.
43 Akihary (1998), pp. 89, 90.
44 *Het Nieuws van den dag voor Nederlandsch-Indië*, November 3, 1928.
45 *Het Vaderland*, November 3, 1928. Unfortunately, Grünberg does not participate in the initiation himself. He died a month earlier as a result of an explosion in the Malang ammunitions factory.
46 *Het Vaderland*, May 16, 1929.
47 The last building that Moojen designed was the building for the Kunstkring in Batavia (Jakarta) in 1913. Address: Jl. Teuku Umar No.1.
48 *De Indische Courant*, August 21, 1929. The following architects are approached by P.A.J. Moojen: Prof. dr. C.P. Wolff Schoemaker (1882-1949) in Bandung. H. Maclaine Pont (1884-1971) at Mojokerto. C. Citroen (1881-1935) in Surabaya. J.F.L. Blankenberg (1888-1958) in Jakarta. B.J.K. Cramer (1890-1978) in Rotterdam. F.J.L. Ghijsels (1882-1947) in Overveen (the Netherlands: NL). Th. Karsten (1884-1945) in Semarang. H. von Essen (1886-1947) in Rijswijk (NL). I.J. Gerber (1885-1949) in Bussum (NL).
49 *De Gooi- en Eemlander*, January 3, 1931 and November 8, 1931. After P.A.J. Moojen had opened the competition for all architects in the Dutch East Indies under some pressure, the winner W.J.G. Zweedijk from Surabaya, turned out to be his cousin. Moojen would later thoroughly adapt the design himself and then present himself as the architect.
50 Woud (1983), pp. 15-52. Due to lack of money, (social) housing construction stagnated everywhere in Europe, coupled with modernism.
51 A.F. Aalbers (30 years) and J.M. Groenewegen (41 years) were examples of this, as well as Arnold Dikstaal, who presented himself at Fermont-Cuypers. They had had a taste of modernism and wanted to put that into practice in a country where it was something new.
52 A.S. Dikstaal married in Hilversum in August 1929 and lived in Jakarta (Batavia) in November of that year.
53 The brother of Arnold Dikstaal was called Simon Arnoldus Dikstaal (1901-1942) and his nickname was Siem. He worked as a doctor in the Dutch East Indies. Without having done anything wrong, he was beheaded in 1942 by the Japanese on Kalimantan during the Japanese occupation.
54 Passchier (2008), p. 5. Passchier quotes what Thomas Nix told him in writing, namely that Dikstaal was called 'Siem' at Fermont-Cuypers. 'However, he was known as Arnold', according to his daughter-in-law during an interview on May 23, 2014.
55 The 'Rechtshoogeschool' is designed by M.B. Tideman (1888-1969) employed in 'Burgerlijke Openbare Werken' (Civil Public Works).
56 H.P. Berlage was a prominent Dutch architect (1856-1934).

57 *Het Nieuws van den Dag voor Nederlandsch-Indië*, May 10, 1929.
58 *Bataviaasch Nieuwsblad*, May 27, 1929.
59 *Bataviaasch Nieuwsblad*, May 11, 1929.
60 Kerchman (1930), p. 439.
61 The design is by H. Th. Wijdeveld. Berlage had selected him and P.A.J. Moojen took care of the contribution and furnishing of the collection from the Dutch East Indies.
62 In the Soviet Union, the 'New Objectivity', under the dictatorship of Stalin, made way for bombastic classicist buildings.
63 Mattie (1999), p. 158.
64 Woud (1983), p. 32. Van der Woud cites Giuseppe Pagano who wrote this in 1930 at the opening of the 'Novocomum' block of flats.
65 *Wonen-TA/BK* April 1977, p. 13. In the Netherlands, after the war, this architecture was regarded for years as 'an empty gesture' while Le Corbusier was emblazoned in those years. Le Corbusier's book Vers une Architecture contains the same elements, according to Auke van der Woud. Woud (1983), p. 32.
66 Bergeijk (2016), p. 111. Modernists like Le Corbusier, Elsässer and Jan Duiker thought they could go to Mussolini with their plans.
67 Woud (1983), p. 34.
68 Giebels (1999), p. 157. Sukarno was released early on December 31, 1931.
69 *Het Nieuws van den Dag voor Nederlandsch-Indië*, January 11, 1930.
70 *Bataviaasch Nieuwsblad*, February 6, 1930.
71 Borsi (1987), pp. 9-13.
72 Jong (1984), p. 350.
73 Delprat (1930) advertisement page (two pictures are switched in the advertisement).
74 *Bataviaasch Nieuwsblad*, August 15, 1930.
75 *Soerabaijaasch Handelsblad*, August 5, 1930.
76 De Indische Courant, May 16, 1930. Kaptijn was a municipal councillor of the Dutch East Indies Catholic Party. This party opted for a ballot box agreement with three parties that he could not accept, causing him to cancel his membership.
77 *Het Nieuws van den Dag voor Nederlandsch-Indië*, March 4, 1930.
78 *Het Vaderland*, March 2, 1930.
79 Jong (1998), p. 511.
80 Stroomberg (1930), pp. 130, 136, 266, 284, 420. With respectively: Javasche Bank (Jakarta), Handelsvereeniging Amsterdam (Surabaya), Chartered Bank (Jakarta), British American Tobacco (Cirebon), Hotel des Indes (Jakarta). With the Handbook of the Netherlands East Indies, the 'Division of Commerce' hoped to interest foreign companies in a branch in the Dutch East Indies.
81 Fasseur (1995), p. 43.
82 The Colonial World Exhibition in Paris takes place from May 6 to November 15, 1931.
83 *De Ingenieur*, July 3, 1931. The original design is from W.J.G. Zweedijk but was changed drastically by P.A.J. Moojen.
84 *De Indische Courant*, July 8, 1931.
85 *Algemeen Handelsblad*, June 29, 1931.
86 Bloembergen (2003), p. 306.
87 Bloembergen (2003), p. 316.
88 Bloembergen (2003), p. 307. The SDAP organ Het Volk and the communist magazine De Tribune had nothing to do with this 'imperialistic' display.
89 *De Indische Courant*, July 29, 1931.
90 J. Th. Van Oyen designed his beautiful modern 'Hellendoorn project' in Surabaya (Tunjungan) shortly afterwards.
91 The series 'Moderne Bouwkunst in Nederland' appeared between 1932 and 1936, edited by dr. H.P. Berlage, W. M. Dudok, J. Gratama, A.R. Hulshoff, H. van der Kloot Meijburg, J.F. Staal and J. Luthman.
92 *Het Vaderland*, July 14, 1931.
93 De Gooi- en Eemlander, April 17, 1931.
94 Bergeijk (1995), p. 165. Dikstaal's father was contractor and an influential dignitary in Hilversum and closely involved in the construction of the bathhouse in Hilversum, which was designed by Dudok around 1920. Thanks to his father's efforts, Dikstaal was allowed to work at Dudok in 1927 and 1928.
95 *Algemeen Handelsblad*, October 23, 1931.
96 Fermont-Cuypers Archive. It was impossible to discover where this project was planned. That this plan was not realised will be related to the crisis, which became very tangible at the end of 1931 in the Dutch East Indies.
97 Schlömer (1934), 'foto Djocja'. There may have been a competition that J. Th. Van Oyen won. His church building was consecrated on July 8, 1934. (Indische Courant July 8, 1934).
98 Perron (1984), p. 40.
99 Interview with Mrs. J. Nix-Hooij on April 6, 2016.
100 *De Indische Courant*, July 23, 1931.
101 *De Bouwkundige Ambtenaar.* The trade journal attached to the *Indische Bouwkundig Tijdschrift* complained between 1931 and 1936 about the impact of the economic crisis on the jobs and salaries of civil servants.
102 The Congregation of the Brothers of St. Aloysius (Brothers of Oudenbosch).
103 *Het Nieuwsblad voor Sumatra*, November 6, 1957; '1930 was the start of hard years for the bank. In 1932 the capital was reduced from Fl. 47 million to Fl. 40 million. A year later, a further write-off of purchased shares to Fl. 33.750000.- and amortisation of 60% of that amount to Fl. 13,500,000. The share capital was then set at Fl. 20,000,000.
104 *De Indische Courant*, March 30, 1931. Padang opening new Escompto building.
105 *Algemeen Handelsblad*, May 15, 1931.
106 Fermont-Cuypers Archive.
107 *Soerabaijasch Handelsblad*, December 16, 1931.
108 *Nieuws van den dag voor Nederlandsch-Indië*, June 30, 1931.
109 *De Tijd*, January 5, 1941. Mr. A.A. de Jongh, the father of Han de Jongh became mayor of Hoorn (the Netherlands) and died in 1941.
110 *Bataviaasch Nieuwsblad*, April 4, 1930.
111 *De Sumatra Post*, November 9, 1931.
112 Doel (1996), pp. 243-244.
113 From J.J.P. Oud was the housing project in Hoek van Holland from 1924 on this exhibition.
114 Until that moment the predicate 'International Style' was officially given to the 'École des Beaux-Arts'.
115 Loghem (1934), p. 192. J.B. van Loghem in a reaction to the new architecture in the Soviet Union.
116 *De 8 en Opbouw*, October 27, 1932, p. 223. Berlage during an interview on February 13, 1932 in Vooruit.
117 Bergson (1925), p. 9, 132. The philosopher H.L. Bergson calls it 'élan vital'.
118 *Het Vaderland*, October 25, 1933. Sybold van Ravesteyn (1889-1983) stated that the period in which Berlage created a furore 'did not produce any great ideas'. He calls this period 'the age of dissolution and decline of architecture that other countries have escaped'. The architects of the Amsterdam School were 'geniuses with their desire for plastic action'. Before any questions could be asked, Berlage had already left the hall.
119 Christiansen (1931), p. 9.
120 Christiansen (1931), p. 8.
121 N. Lansdorp (1885-1968) worked from 1902-1912, with some interruptions, with Ed. Cuypers.
122 Bergeijk (2014), p. 139. Lansdorp left an impressively large oeuvre.
123 *Het Bouwbedrijf*, 9 (1932), pp. 31-37. J.A.G. van der Steur: 'Feeling for local and national tradition, coupled with his sense of the monumental, did not prevent N. Lansdorp from moving in the direction of the strongly internationally oriented functionalism. He was open to new materials and new constructions [...].'
124 Nico Lansdorp worked at Ed. Cuypers office for many years together with the founding fathers of the Amsterdam School: Joan van der Mey, Michiel de Klerk, Guillaume la Croix and Piet Kramer.

125 F. Dicke became professor at the I.T.B. in Bandung, where he must have taught his architecture students skills that he had learned from professor N. Lansdorp.
126 Beusekom (1944), pp. 52-53.
127 Borsi (1987), pp. 94-173.
128 *De Bouwkundige Ambtenaar* 5, January 1, 1932.
129 Bandung (1931), Semarang (1933), Surabaya (1934), Jakarta (1937).
130 *Indisch Bouwkundig Tijdschrift/Lokale Techniek* with more than twenty articles by Thomas Karsten between 1932-1940.
131 Thomas Karsten would hardly build anything after 1932 by himself. He joined and worked for municipalities as an advisor in urban planning and planning.
132 *Bataviaasch Nieuwsblad*, May 4, 1932.
133 *Het Nieuws van den Dag voor Nederlandsch-Indië*, July 16, 1932.
134 *Het Nieuws van den Dag voor Nederlandsch-Indië*, September 16, 1931.
135 The building still exists but is unrecognisably maimed by façade architecture, fire damage and overdue maintenance.
136 *Het Nieuws van den Dag voor Nederlandsch-Indië*, August 23, 1932.
137 *Leeuwarder Courant*, August 24, 1932.
138 Interview with Mrs. M. Dikstaal-Van der Bijl on May 23, 2014.
139 Doel (1996), p. 245. While the commander and some of the officers were ashore, the crew took control of the ship on the night of February 4-5, 1933.
140 Langeveld (2004), pp. 31-35.
141 The mutineers wanted the salary reduction in the navy to be reversed.
142 Haasse (2010), pp. 367-368. Hella Haasse writes that the fear of communism in the Dutch East Indies was also behind this course of action.
143 Langeveld (2004), p. 360.
144 *Leeuwarder Courant*, April 19, 1933. With reference to the Handelsblad: 'De actie tegen de Joden in Duitschland'.
145 Doel (1998), p. 246. Sukarno was first interned on Flores on August 1, 1933 and later in Bengkulu. In February 1934 followed the arrest of, among others, Hatta and Sjahrir.
146 Perron (1956), p. 7.
147 *Het Nieuws van den Dag voor Nederlandsch-Indië*, February 28, 1933.
148 Beekum (2007). C. van de Linde (1886-1941) and A. P Smits (1881-1957) were two Dutch architects who were commissioned to work on this building by the Nederlandsche Handel-Maatschappij.
149 *Soerabaijasch Handelsblad*, January 12, 1933. '1239 persons viewed the building and, with their contribution of 0.50 cents, provided support for the unemployed'.
150 *d'Oriënt*, November 14, 1933. The article shows some shots of the building and a portrait photo of all three architects: C. van de Linde (1886-1941), A.P. Smits (1881-1957) and J.J.J. de Bruyn.
151 *Bataviaasch Nieuwsblad*, January 9, 1933. In this paper, the portrait photograph of both architects, C. van de Linde (1886-1941) and A.P. Smits (1881-1957) are briefly mentioned.
152 *Bouwkundige Weekblad Architectura*, October 10, 1931. In the Netherlands, the building would be praised architecturally and not just because the architects had the opportunity to present their work extensively in the *Bouwkundig Weekblad Architectura* well before they were handed over.
153 *De Indische Courant*, January 13, 1934.
154 *Het Nieuws van den Dag voor Nederlandsch-Indië*, October 18, 1933. Note: The bureau had a general meeting of shareholders of the N.V. Architecten- en Ingenieursbureau Fermont-Cuypers.
155 Sain (1968), p. 23.
156 *Bataviaasch Nieuwsblad*, June 22, 1934. On June 17, 1934 the consecration takes place.
157 *Bataviaasch Nieuwsblad*, August 7, 1920.
158 *Het Nieuws van den Dag voor Nederlandsch-Indië*, February 28, 1933.
159 *Het Nieuws van den Dag voor Nederlandsch-Indië*, March 22, 1933.
160 Interview with Mrs. M. Dikstaal on May 23, 2014.
161 *Bataviaasch Nieuwsblad*, February 17, 1934: 'Een aannemelijk bod'.
162 Arthur Fermont owned a house at Raamweg 13 in The Hague, where his wife and children lived from around 1930.
163 *Bataviaasch Nieuwsblad*, November 25, 1933.
164 *Het Nieuws van den Dag voor Nederlandsch-Indië*, November 17, 1933.
165 *Het Nieuws van den Dag voor Nederlandsch-Indië*, March 13, 1933.
166 Embden 1930, 'De geschiedenis van de Kring'. Yearbook BSK, 1930.
167 *Algemeen Handelsblad*, June 30, 1933.
168 Photo album of Nix family.
169 Jong (1998), p. 511.
170 The photo is located in the archives of the Fermont family as well as a photograph that was made shortly after completion of the building by M. Kaptijn and must also have been sent to the Netherlands.
171 Blijdenstijn (1994) p. 109. S. van Ravesteyn (1889-1983) and A. Staal (1907-1997) indicate this direction in the Netherlands. A. Staal; 'The new architecture is like a shiny, elegant automobile, clean and without the exhausting sight of visibly lasting structures'.
172 *De Indische Courant*, June 5, 1934.
173 The Hague, Raamweg 13.
174 Bullock (1983), p. 246
175 *De Indische Courant*, June 18, 1934. In Venice the first meeting took place between Hitler and Mussolini. 'Hitler and I did not meet to review the map of Europe or to increase the uncertainty,' Il Duce said.
176 *Soerabaijasch Handelsblad*, July 3, 1935. The offices of the Italian consulate moved from the Burgemeester Bischopplein 6 (now: Taman Untung Suropati), which was also the residence of Mr. Cenzi, to Tandjoenglaan 15 (now: Jl. Tanjung), which will be exclusively for the consulate.' Mr. Cenzi became a consul in the United States.
177 Voorneman (1937), p. 175; Voskuil (1989), p. 136; Temminck Groll (2002), p. 156; Leushuis (2011), p. 128; Passchier (2016) p. 84.
178 *Bataviaasch Nieuwsblad*, June 22, 1934. *De Indische Courant*, September 25, 1934.
179 *Soerabaijasch Handelsblad*, July 2, 1934. The front buildings of the Oranjehotel (now: Majapahit Hotel) were designed by the architectural firm Job & Sprey.
180 *Het Nieuws van den Dag voor Nederlandsch-Indië*, June 26, 1934.
181 *Bataviaasch Nieuwsblad*, October 6, 1939. As a result, Dikstaal must have decided to obtain a diploma. In 1939, Arnold Dikstaal will succeed as an architect at the Technische Hogeschool in Bandung in October 1939.
182 *De Indische Courant*, November 29, 1934. The article states: 'construction supervisor Dikstaal leads the journalist through the building in the making'.
183 *Bredasche Courant*, January 23, 1935.
184 Van der Wal (1968) Memories De Jonge, pp. 207, 281. 'We cut back on everything, took the most miserable measures, enraged the civil servants, (...) did too little education and public health, broke down what would have been much better'.
185 *De Tribune*, June 17, 1935. At their congresses, slogans resound such as 'Indonesia separate from Holland' and in the words of Karl Marx: 'No people are free to oppress another people'.
186 Meyers (1984), p. 86. The N.S.B. received almost 8% of the votes in the elections by the Provincial States, unique for a new party.
187 *Soerabaijasch Handelsblad*, November 5, 1929. Mr. Dr. G.G. Buttingha Wichers will be appointed president of the Javasche Bank on July 1, 1929.
188 In September, the publisher of the series 'Modernisme in Nederland' offers the books of and about Berlage, including Mijn Indische Reis for a greatly reduced price.
189 Van Thoor (1998), p. 99. The design is by D. P. Roosenburg (1887-1962).
190 Van Thoor (1998), p. 105. Van Thoor mentioned G. Cancellotti (1896-1986), E. Montuori (1907-1982), L. Piccinato (1899-1983), all founders of the Gruppo Urbanisti Romani.
191 Huizinga (1948), *Verzamelde Werken*, p. 315.
192 *De Bouwkundig Ambtenaar*, January 1, 1935.

193 New construction with dominant flagpoles: Surabaya; Hellendoorn buildings e.o (1933, J. Th. van Oyen). Surabaya; Oranjehotel front buildings (1934, Job & Sprey). Surabaya; Borsumij offices (1935, C. Citroen)
194 *Soerabaijasch Handelsblad*, January 29, 1935.
195 *Het Nieuws van den Dag voor Nederlandsch-Indië*, February 19, 1935. Taen goes to live in an apartment at Tanah Abang East 51/55.
196 Langeveld (2004), p. 360.
197 Jong (1984), pp. 370, 373. In 1935 there were about 4500 members. At the end of 1939 there were 1700 in a population of about 100,000 Europeans.
198 *Osaka Jiji*, September 30, 1935 and October 2, 1935. Keesings Historisch Archief 1935, p. 2037.
199 Schlömer (1934). Nix made the drawing for an advertisement in '400 years Mission in the Dutch East Indies' (400 years Mission in the Dutch East Indies).
200 *Het Nieuws van den Dag voor Nederlandsch Indië*, March 25, 1935.
201 *Algemeen Handelsblad*, March 28, 1935.
202 *Het Nieuws van den Dag voor Nederlandsch-Indië*, August 26, 1935.
203 *Het Nieuws van den Dag voor Nederlandsch-Indië*, December 14, 1935.
204 Bandung: Arthur Dikstaal passed the exam on October 6, 1939 as an architect.
205 Radio speech on March 11, 1936.
206 *Algemeen Handelsblad*, April 26, 1936. 'Europe for the Abyss', H.R. Knickerbocker.
207 *De Tijd*, May 22, 1936.
208 Meulen (1990), p. 76.
209 From information from the Fermont family.
210 Mr. L.J.A. Trip was president of the Javasche Bank from 1923-1928.
211 Haagsche Courant, October 17, 1936.
212 *Het Land van Herkomst* from 1935 is the title of a book written by E. du Perron about the Dutch East Indies.
213 Meulen (1990), p. 76.
214 *Het Nieuws van den dag voor Nederlandsch-Indië*, December 12, 1935.
215 d'Oriënt, April 4, 1936 p. 32.
216 Eduard Cuypers applied the columns as decorative elements from the past. At Fermont-Cuypers they actually did the same in the 1930s.
217 *Elsevier*, March 26, 2016, p. 80. Ben de Vries, 'In 1938, petroleum and related products covered 23.6 percent of the total export value of the Dutch East Indies, rubber accounted for 20 percent'.
218 *Het Nieuws van den dag voor Nederlandsch-Indië*, December 5, 1936.
219 Jonge (1998), p. 536.
220 Tichelman (1948), p. 25. On November 16, 1938, the motion would eventually be rejected by royal decree after extensive discussions in the Netherlands.
221 *De Tribune*, June 17, 1935.
222 Fasseur (1995), p. 211.
223 Fermont was a great lover of world exhibitions.
224 Van Loghem in *De 8 en Opbouw* 1939, 'Wat gebeurt er in de Sovjet-Rusland'
225 In February 1933, the National Socialists seized power in Germany.
226 *d'Oriënt*, February 6, 1937, p. 27.
227 Schoemaker (1923), p. 191.
228 Examples of the 'reorientation style' in the Netherlands include Rotterdam City Hall, the Bijenkorf in Amsterdam.
229 *Het Nieuws van den dag voor Nederlandsch-Indië*, June 12, 1937.
230 Kaptijn (1937). The photos in this book, which are almost all made by Matthias Kaptijn, also show all other bank buildings of the Javasche Bank, with dates, of which it must now be noted that this must not always have been the design date or the date of completion.
231 Doorn (2013), p. 248.
232 Scholten (1988), p. 22.
233 *I.B.T. Locale Techniek*, year 6, no. 6, November-December 1937, p. 169.
234 *Het Nieuws van den Dag voor Nederlandsch-Indië*, August 28, 1937.
235 *Bataviaasch Nieuwsblad*, September 25, 1937.
236 *Het Vaderland*, September 9, 1937.
237 *Het Nieuws van den Dag voor Nederlandsch-Indië*, June 30, 1937. In August, the shareholders of Fermont-Cuypers decide to grant Han de Jongh an honorable dismissal upon his request and appoint Theo Taen as his new second director. De Jongh leaves for the Netherlands. He worked for the firm for over fifteen years.
238 *Het Nieuws van den Dag voor Nederlandsch-Indië*, August 18, 1937.
239 *De Sumatra Post*, October 9, 1937.
240 *De Sumatra Post*, October 9, 1937.
241 *De Sumatra Post*, October 9, 1937.
242 Vriend (1938), p. 193.
243 Broekhuizen (1998), pp. 32-55.
244 In May 1938 the government introduced a stricter admissions policy.
245 But where to? The American president also said that he would 'stick to its strict immigration laws, whatever all other countries did'.
246 *Het Nieuws van den Dag voor Nederlandsch-Indië*, November 10, 1938.
247 In doing so, he follows in the footsteps of architects who use high-rise plans to oppose the existing city, such as: Le Corbusier, 'Ville Contemporaine' (1925); L. Hilberseimer: 'Großstadtarchitektur' (1927), 'Beton als Gestalter' (1928); J. Duiker: Hoogbouw (1930)
248 Fortunately, the building still exists, but all buildings in the immediate vicinity have been demolished.
249 Akihary (1990), p. 58. The architect J.F.L. Blankenberg (1888-1958) was commissioned shortly afterwards to design the official residence of the mayor of Batavia at the Burgemeester Bisschopsplein. (Jl.Taman Suropati)
250 Batavia als Handels-, Industrie- en Woonstad, G. Kolff & Co Batavia 1937.
251 *De Ingenieur in Nederlandsch-Indië*, year 5, no. 1, January 1938, pp. 1-14.
252 *I.B.T Locale Techniek* 1937, year 6, no. 6, pp. 159-172.
253 Breuning (1954), pp. 143, 145, 147. After the war, H.A. Breuning wrote a booklet entitled *Het voormalige Batavia*. In it he reports that there were counter-proposals to the municipal plan, which were 'clearly of lesser quality'. He casually condemns two buildings designed by Fermont-Cuypers on Koningsplein. 'The Koloniale is a gaudy building'. 'The B.P.M. building does not make a big impression'. Readers in the Netherlands who wanted to test this opinion had to do so without photographs of the buildings.
254 *Bataviaasch Nieuwsblad*, May 4, 1938.
255 *De Indische Courant*, October 22, 1938.
256 *De Indische Courant*, October 8, 1938.
257 Borsi (1987), pp. 175-184.
258 *Bataviaasch Nieuwsblad*, November 22, 1938.
259 *De Indische Courant*, November 15, 1938. The Immigration Service maintained its stance of refusing access, because it had the impression that they were 'not bona fide tourists' although travellers were in possession of tickets with which they could travel to America and England.
260 *Bataviaasch Nieuwsblad*, November 22, 1938.
261 *Bataviaasch Nieuwsblad*, November 22, 1938.
262 *Het Nieuws van den Dag voor Nederlandsch-Indië*, July 2, 1937.
263 Nix (1949), pp. 162-168. Thomas Nix argued that urban transformations should take place from the historic cityscape within predetermined building heights and on existing building lines. Large complexes of offices, flats are considered special buildings and must be assessed separately.
264 Jong (1998), p. 553.
265 Jong (1998), p. 553.
266 *De muze van Jan Companjie* (1939).
267 Perron (1990), *Brieven IX*, p. 248. Involving the magazine Noesantara.
268 Perron (1981), *Brieven VII*, p. 432.
269 Blom (1997), pp. 230-232.
270 *De Sumatra Post*, May 12, 1939.
271 The 'Exposition Internationale de la technique de l'eau' in Liège (Belgium) was opened on May 20, 1939 and should have lasted until November 1939. On August 31 however, explosives under two nearby bridges caused explosions leading to 20 deaths and 24 wounded as a result of thunderstorms. The explosives had been installed by the Belgian army to be able to blow up the bridges in case of war.

272 Klemann (2002), p. 346.
273 Doel (1996), p. 256.
274 *Naamlijst der Europeesche Inwoners 1941*, p. 687. According to this registry, Thomas Nix was still working at Fermont-Cuypers at the beginning of 1941.
275 During an interview with the author in 2015, the head of the school smiled as he agreed with this.
276 They follow in the footsteps of Berlage with his buildings 'De Nederlanden van 1845' in 1895 in The Hague. 1913 in Jakarta and in 1927 in The Hague.
277 *d'Oriënt*, December 25, 1939.
278 Jong (1998), p. 558.
279 Vletter (1997), p. 30. When the Koningsplein plan was adopted by the city council, the construction of the town hall in Wilhelminapark was mentioned as an alternative.
280 *De Indische Courant*, January 8, 1940. The other architects were J.F.L. Blankenberg, C.P. Wolff Schoemaker and Aalbers and De Waal.
281 The Mejid Istiqlal mosque has been standing on this location since the 1960s.
282 *I.B.T. Locale Techniek* 9 (1940), pp. 133-135.
283 *Het Nieuws van den Dag voor Nederlandsch-Indië*, February 16, 1940.
284 *De Indische Courant*, March 16, 1940.
285 *Life*, January 22, 1940
286 *Bataviaasch Nieuwsblad*, April 20, 1940.
287 *De Indische Courant*, September 16, 1941. Nix makes the design for an office building on the Houtmanplein (now: Lapangan Supratman) in Bandung for the Military Aviation and Topographic Service.
288 *Bataviaasch Nieuwsblad*, May 6, 1940.
289 Jong (1984) part 11a first half, p. 349.
290 Doel (1996), p. 255.
291 Jong (1998), p. 559. Speech by the Governor-General on June 15, 1940.
292 *De Indische Courant*, October 23, 1940. 'Unnamed ships arrive and depart'.
293 *Keesings Historisch Archief*, January 11-17, 1941, p. 4524.
294 *Bataviaasch Nieuwsblad*, February 28, 1941. As a result, Simon Snuyf (1880-1944) resigned in Surabaya as president of this organisation, despite his enormous service for the Dutch East Indies. He would die in an internment camp in 1944.
295 *De Telegraaf*, June 6, 1941.
296 *Soerabaijasch Handelsblad*, June 6, 1941.
297 Robert Deppe, the designer died in 1943 on the Burma railway among the Japanese.
298 Vletter (1997), p. 45. Thamrin was put under house arrest while he could invoke his parliamentary immunity. During a search on January 6, 1941, he was confined to his bed with kidney disease. Only after four days was a doctor allowed to visit him. He died on January 11, 1941 as a result of cardiac arrest.
299 Fasseur (1995), p. 209.
300 Doel (1996), p. 257.
301 Jong (1969), pp. 382-383.
302 *Bataviaasch Nieuwsblad*, October 31, 1941. *De Indische Courant*, November 3, 1941.
303 Doel (1996), p. 299. Between 1945 and 1949 there was the first wave of approximately 44,000 returnees.
304 *Stedebouw in Indonesië en de Stedebouwkundige Vormgeving* PhD dissertation under promotor Prof. M.J. Granpré Molière.
305 Kok (2010) The book Colonial War from Dutch East Indies to Indonesia shows in word and image what happened between 1945-1949.
306 *Het Dagblad*: Uitgave van de Nederlandsche Dagbladpers te Batavia, July 10, 1948.
307 Amsterdam, December 27, 1949.
308 The Dutch-Indonesian Union did not become a state body with its own powers.
309 Vletter (1997), p. 94.
310 *Het Dagblad*: Uitgave van de Nederlandsche Dagbladpers te Batavia, January 4, 1949.
311 Cyril Fermont married in 1946 in Jakarta with Riet Koene. They had a son in 1947.
312 *Bouwkundig Weekblad*, March 14, 1959, p. 130. Engineer M. Westerduin.
313 Doel (1996), p. 299. Between 1950 and 1956, approximately 140,000 people left for the Netherlands permanently.
314 Roosmalen (2008), p. 184. More than 4,700 houses were to be built in Kabayoran Baru, including shopping centres, schools.
315 Fermont worked more intensively than previously with the firm called 'Eduard Cuypers' in Amsterdam.
316 Djalan Palatehan no. 4 block K5, Kebayoran Baru.
317 *Keesings Historisch Archief*, no. 1062 from October 21-27.
318 Vletter (1997), p. 94. Dutch companies had to make agreements about the number of Indonesian employees in their company.
319 In Indonesia this building style is called 'Jengki'.
320 The Javasche Bank became the central bank of Indonesia in 1953 under the name Bank Nasional Indonesia (BNI) which later changed to Bank Indonesia (BI).
321 Archive of Joh. Enschedé Haarlem.
322 Roosmalen (2008), p. 184. The first stone for this district was laid on March 18, 1949. Instead of the planned 2,700 homes that should have been completed in 1949, no more than 1,800 were built for two years, with the result that it took until 1954 before the neighborhood was more or less ready.
323 The Netherlands reluctantly attended a conference in The Hague with Indonesia about changes in the previously concluded agreements, among others regarding New Guinea and made no concessions.
324 *Friese Koerier*, February 24, 1956. Statement by the Indonesian Minister of Foreign Affairs.
325 Passchier (2016) p. 231. The Indonesians would later speak about Jengki style, where Freek Dicke, as a professor at the Technical University in Bandung, had a leading role.
326 In her suitcase was the *Javabode* of April 20, 1956 containing a leading article about the death of Leon Jungschläger. That was probably the deciding factor for the departure.
327 On July 26, 1956, President Nasser of Egypt announced the nationalization of the Suez Canal.
328 *Javabode*, November 5, 1957.
329 Vletter 1997, p. 95. On May 20, 1958, the Indonesian government announced that Dutch companies were nationalized with retroactive effect from January 1, 1958.
330 *De Tijd*, August 12, 1958.
331 Contrary to what was previously recorded, Arthur Fermont lived until November 17, 1967.
332 Duparc (1972), p. 28. March 16, 1960 was the day of the disappearance of last tram from Jakarta's streets.

Jakarta, the construction of the Bataafsche Petroleum Maatschappij (Pertamina building) sketched by Thomas Nix CFT

4 LIST OF WORKS

1 1927 Bandung: Borromeus Hospital
2 1927 Banda Aceh: Catholic Church
3 1927 Semarang: St. Xaverius School
4 1928 Belawan: Harbour buildings of 'Ned.-Indische Scheepvaart Mij.'
5 1928 Yogyakarta: Seminary
6 1928 Pontianak: Javasche Bank
7 1928 Medan: Escomptobank (now Bank Mandiri)
8 1928 Surabaya: Staff residence at Petodjo Ice factory
9 1928 Cilacap: Nederlandsche Handel-Maatschappij'
10 1928 Tanjung Karang: Catholic Church
11 1928 Malang: Towers of the Sacred Heart Church
12 1929 Kediri: Javasche Bank (now: bank Indonesia) and staff residence
13 1929 Subang: The Clubhouse, (now: Wisma Karya Museum)
14 1929 Bandung-East: Catholic Church
15 1929 Surabaya: Catholic Church Ketabang (design)
16 1930 Jakarta: Presbytery for planned Theresia Church
17 1930 Jakarta: Theresia church (design)
18 1930 Jakarta: Shop buildings with upstairs dwellings
19 1930 Jakarta: Canisius College
20 1930 Jakarta: Duo Passenger Terminal (now: Ministry)
21 1930 Jakarta: Hotel des Indes, main building designed by A.I.A.
22 1930 Madiun: Town Hall
23 1930 Madiun: Theatre and/or cinema
24 1930 Purwokerto: School complex
25 1930 Purwokerto: Catholic Church
26 1930 Ambarawa: St. Louis Institute
27 1931 Padang: Escomptobank (now: Bank Mandiri)
28 1931 Belinyu: Convent and school
29 1931 Pangkal Pinang: Catholic Boarding school
30 1931 Semarang: British American Tobacco factory
31 1931 Jakarta: Carolus Hospital, main building, convent, chapel
32 1931 Banjarmasin: Escomptobank
33 1931 Jakarta: 'The Good Shepherd' Girls' school
34 1931 Solo: Catholic Church and presbytery (design)
35 1932 Jakarta: Hotel des Galeries
36 1932 Muntok: Catholic church, convent, boarding school
37 1932 Semarang: Franciscan Sisters' school
38 1932 Jakarta: Van Lith school with chapel
39 1932 Pekalongan: Primary school and Fröbel school
40 1932 Jakarta: Sancta Ursula convent
41 1932 Rangkasbitung: Regency Council of Lebak
42 1933 Rangkasbitung: Hospital
43 1933 Jakarta: Dutch-Chinese Primary School
44 1933 Jakarta: Sancta Maria Teacher Training School
45 1933 Ambarawa: Chapel at St. Louis Institute
46 1933 Purworejo: Catholic Church
47 1933 Palembang: Boarding school and Fröbel school
48 1934 Jakarta: Mater Dei vocational School
49 1934 Bengkulu: Schools, convent, chapel
50 1934 Surabaya: Vincentius hospital
51 1934 Yogyakarta: Seminary expansion
52 1934 Jakarta: Tan Villa/Italian Consulate
53 1934 Jakarta: Brother house
54 1935 Cirebon: Dutch-Chinese Primary School
55 1935 Jakarta: Pek Villa
56 1935 Jakarta: Bank vault building Javasche Bank (now: Bank Indonesia)
57 1935 Jakarta: Tarcisius Primary School
58 1935 Bandung: Pandu Church, presbytery, club building
59 1935 Semarang: Javasche Bank (now: Bank Jateng) and staff residence
60 1935 Pekalongan: St. Peter's Catholic church and presbytery
61 1936 Bandung: 'Maria Sterre der Zee' schools and convent
62 1937 Tegal: Textile factory
63 1937 Tegal: Ursuline schools
64 1937 Jakarta: Front building of Javasche Bank (Museum Bank Indonesia)

65 1937 Jakarta: Urban plan for Koningsplein/MONAS
66 1937 Bandung: Bank vault at Javasche Bank (now: Bank Indonesia)
67 1938 Jakarta: Kolff printing works
68 1938 Palembang: Charitas Hospital
69 1938 Semarang: 'Bataafsche Petroleum Mij.', (now: Pertamina)
70 1938 Jakarta: N.K.P.M. building 'Koloniale' (now: Departemen Energi)
71 1938 Jakarta: 'Bataafsche Petroleum Mij.' (now: Pertamina)
72 1938 Palembang: Escomptobank en Volkscredietbank
73 1938 Jakarta: Dutch East Indies Tourist office (NITOUR)
74 1938 Jakarta: St. Carolus Hospital, children's pavilion
75 1939 Wonosobo: Institute for the Deaf and Mute
76 1938 Sungailiat: Primary school and Brother house
77 1939 Lahat: Schools and convent
78 1939 Bandung: Ciumbuleuit villas
79 1939 Makassar: Brother school
80 1939 Makassar: Stella Maris Hospital
81 1940 Jakarta: Canisius College (extension)
82 1940 Jakarta: Mater Dolorosa Chapel
83 1940 Semarang: Business School (extension),
84 1940 Jakarta: Harbour establishment
85 1941 Surabaya: Offices of 'De Nederlanden van 1845'
86 1954 Jakarta: Bank of China
87 1954 Jakarta: Housing at Pertjetakan Kebayoran printing works
88 1955 Jakarta: Ruznar and Go residences
89 1955 Jakarta: Pertjetakan Kebayoran printing works
90 1956 Ambon: Bank Indonesia,
91 1956 Jakarta: Essence Indonesia

5 CATALOGUE OF WORKS

Jakarta 1936, construction workers on the roof of the new extension of the Javasche Bank (now: Museum Bank Indonesia) CFC

1 | 1927 Bandung: Borromeus Hospital, Joseph pavilion

CITY: Bandung
ADDRESS: Dagoweg 80/Jl. Ir. H. Juanda No. 100/-
ARCHITECT: Th. Taen, L. Logemann
YEAR: 1927
CLIENT: Sisters of Mercy of St. Carolus Borromeo from Maastricht (the Netherlands)
CURRENT SITUATION: new building of Rumah Sakit Santo Borromeus
SOURCES: *Indische Kroniek*, October 27, 1921; *Bataviaasch Nieuwsblad*, July 2, 1927; HET NIEUWS VAN DEN DAG VOOR NEDERLANDSCH-INDIË, July 2, 1927; DE INDISCHE COURANT, October 10, 1930; *Kruistriomf*, year 7, 1924-1925, p. 269; Gorris (1937), pp. 361-364

The St. Carolus Borromeus Hospital in Bandung opened in September 1921 under this name. The house that the Sisters used was called the clinic of Dr. Merz. In 1923, a thorough renovation began. Because of a generous donation a large chapel could even be erected. The first stone was laid on February 18, 1925. The inauguration of the building was held on August 3, 1925. The architect of the chapel is unknown. In the meantime, alterations were carried out within the existing hospital complex, such as the elevation of the galleries, the construction of a mortuary, the expansion of the laundry, the arrival of an X-ray department and a telephone booth.
In 1926, Fermont-Cuypers worked on a design for a hospital pavilion. The tender is dated December 11, 1926. The next day the work began, the result of which was visible on July 3, 1927. The building was later demolished. It was built in Indies objective style throughout, with the sleek, whitewashed walls, a high roof with generous overhangs, open galleries and river pebbles applied to the walls. The main entrance had a generous awning. A ventilation tower was visible on the roof of the main building. The damp-proof course consisted of river stone, which was also incorporated in the walls at height differences corresponding to the ground level and the surrounding terrain. The layout of the building illustrates the simplicity which was typical of Fermont-Cuypers. Through the main entrance on the Dagoweg, the visitor entered a small hall with a nurse's room and a consultation room on either side. The hall continued through a corridor where patient rooms were located. These met the latest requirements in hospital construction at that time. Each room had its own front gallery, where the beds could be moved easily if desired. In the corridor of the pavilion, Fermont-Cuypers tested out new noiseless Emboolit floors. The service rooms were located in a separate part of the pavilion, so that patients were not inconvenienced by other hospital activities.
In the early thirties, *De Indische Courant* wrote the following about this hospital: 'It is not only important from a social point of view, but also architecturally, it is a jewel for the city. Often "fully booked" not only in the first class, but also in the other treatment classes. Many residents of Bandung and planters from the Preanger, and even far beyond, have been nursed successfully, after a short or longer period of time in the hospital. Not only by the meticulous nursing and food, the extremely fresh and cool location, but also by the wonderfully spacious and cool rooms'. The newspaper also made mention of 'a radio in every room' which was a novelty.

Bandung, the completely renovated hospital with the chapel in 2011 CON

Bandung, the St. Joseph pavilion of the Borromeus Hospital shortly after the opening in 1927, with adjacent chapel, which also belongs to the hospital CFC

Bandung, corner of Dagoweg (now: Jl. H. Juanda) in 1928 with the St. Joseph Pavilion and the patient accommodation on the Potterweg (now: Jl. Singa Perbangsa) CFC

Bandung, the entrance to the St. Joseph Pavilion on the Dagoweg (Jl. H. Juanda) around 1930 CFC

Bandung, the wards of the St. Joseph Pavilion on the Potterweg (now: Jl. Singa Perbangsa) in 1928 CFC

Bandung, the gallery of the St. Joseph Pavilion on the north side of the building with beds in the open air in 1928 CFC

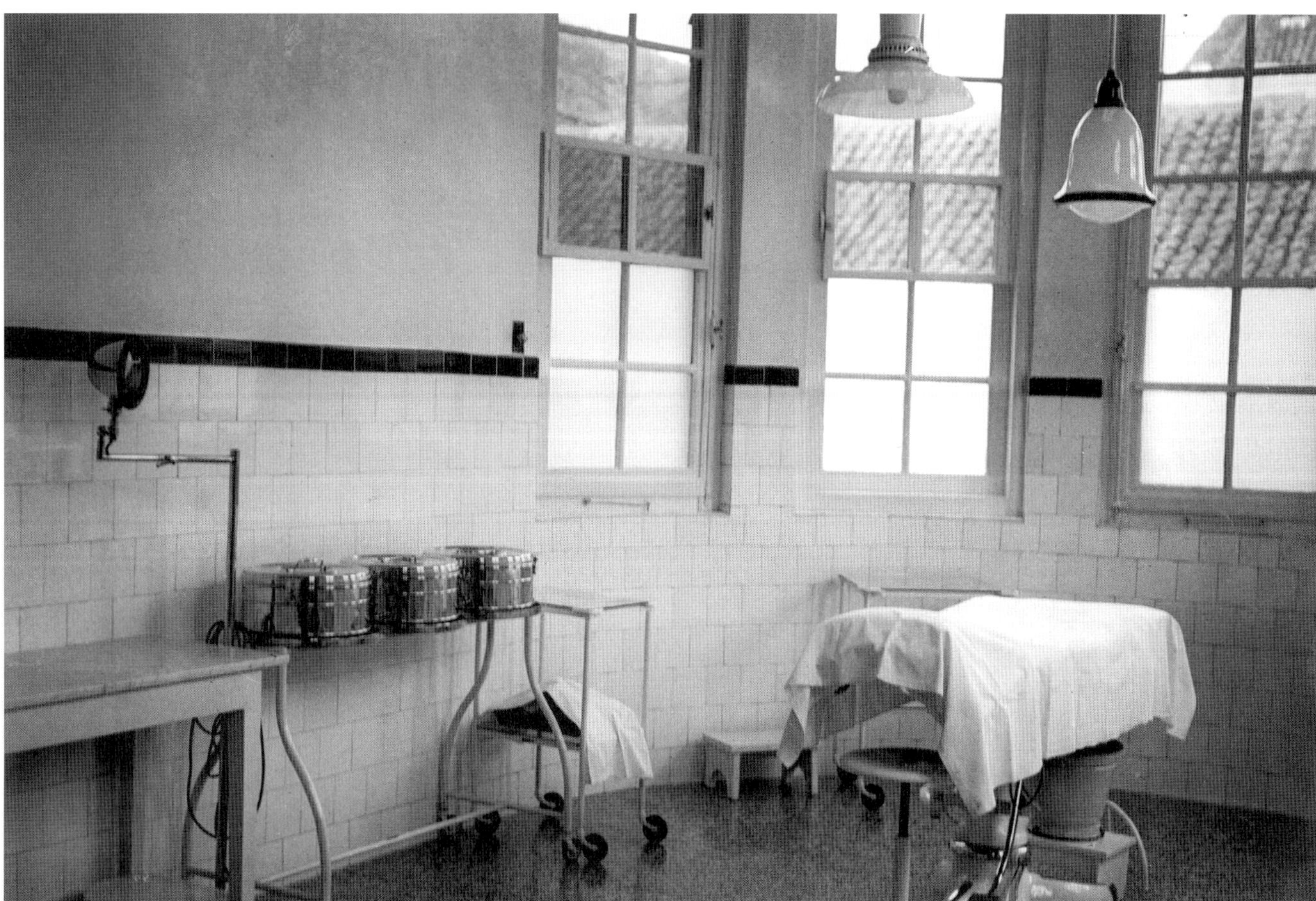

Bandung 1928, Borromeus Hospital, a treatment room in St. Joseph Pavilion CFC

2 | 1927 **Banda Aceh: Catholic Church**

CITY: Banda Aceh
ADDRESS: Pastoor Verbaaksingel 2/Jl. Jenderal Ahmad Yani
ARCHITECT: Th. Taen, A. Kreisler
YEAR: 1927
COMMISSIONER: Roman Catholic Church council
CURRENT SITUATION: Gereja Katolik Hati Kudus Yesus
SOURCES: *Bataviaasch Nieuwsblad*, March 17, 1925; *Het Nieuws van den Dag voor Nederlandsch-Indië*, March 17, 1925; *De Indische Courant*, March 17, 1925; *Algemeen Handelsblad*, April 7, 1925; Catholic Documentation Centre Nijmegen: photos of the construction of the church

On March 17, 1925, a few newspapers announced that a new presbytery was being added to the old church, as restoration proved to be more expensive than a new construction. 'With some luck, a new stone church will be erected next to the presbytery', *Het Bataviaasch Nieuwsblad* reported, 'for which the Architect and Engineering Office Hulswit-Fermont has already submitted an attractive design and sketch'. Alfred Kreisler (1888-1980), who worked for the firm at the time, produced that drawing. The new church replaced the forty-year-old barn church, where pastor Verbraak (1835-1918) once lived. 'The current pastor would like to see a monument to his predecessor placed in front of the new church building', the newspaper said.

Willem Jaski acted as building supervisor. Jaski took photos of the construction, starting from when the foundation stone was laid. He recorded the moment the bells were hoisted up into the tower, and, of course, the consecration on December 19, 1927. Since then, the church building with its tower marks the area near the bridge over the Aceh River. In terms of construction, the building consists of a prefabricated concrete frame filled with masonry, with a white plaster finish, as was usual in the tropics. The circumference of the church is approximately 36 metres by 16 metres. It is a church of the Christocentric type with narrow, low side aisles, which did not offer seats. There are deep buttresses on the outside of the clearstory, where the roof still protrudes. As a result, the windows of the clerestory with their atmospheric stained glass are deeply recessed, where direct sunlight never comes through. The small window openings in the aisle are hidden under the protruding lean-to roof. The main entrance is centrally located in the narrow southeast side, the choir is oriented towards the northwest. The main entrance has a large awning. Three framed, narrow and high window openings emphasise the verticality of the tower, which is next to the nave of the church. The square crown with a plate protruding from four sides and above that, several openings and a square plate with a smaller circumference, pointing to the simple spire above.

More than 77 years after the consecration, an all-devouring tsunami overwhelmed the city of Banda Aceh on December 26, 2004. Thousands of people died. Almost all buildings were lost, but the mosque and the church remained standing. The church building was refurbished after this disaster.

Banda Aceh, the Roman Catholic Church in 2015 CON

Banda Aceh, sketch made in 1926 by Alfred Kreisler (1888-1980) of Fermont-Cuypers CFT

Banda Aceh, the Roman Catholic Church shortly after completion in 1927 CON

3 | 1927 **Semarang: St. Xaverius School**

CITY: Semarang
ADDRESS: Karreweg 91/Jl. Dr. Cipto No. 91/-
ARCHITECT: Th. Taen
YEAR: 1927
CLIENT: Jesuit Fathers
CURRENT SITUATION: new building for Kb-TK-SD Pl Xaverius
SOURCES: *De Locomotief*, May 14, 1927; *De Locomotief*, May 17, 1927; *De Limburger*, August 9, 1927; Hoof (1934); Christinus (1940), pp. 253, 302, 305; Archive of Brothers from Maastricht

On May 17, 1927, the inauguration of the St. Xaverius School took place on the Karreweg (now: Jl. Dr. Cipto) in Semarang. There is still a school on the location, but the buildings from 1927 no longer exist. The Jesuits took this initiative to build a 'school for poor children', but they did not have much money available. They were therefore drawn to a relatively cheap piece of land outside the urban area. Fermont-Cuypers made the design for a competitive price. It left the construction to a local contractor. The open main buiding with entrance was on the Karreweg (now: Jl. Cipto). The entrance led to the large open playground of about 50 by 70 metres, surrounded by the classrooms in quadrant formation, consisting of a single-storey building and a high roof with an overhang. The open side of the classrooms bordered the square. It was known as a 'subsidised European School for the poor', which did not attract many scholars, as few parents wanted to admit that they had no money. The initiators managed the institution until 1937 from their Canisius Foundation. Then the brothers from Maastricht, who set up a number of educational institutions in Semarang, took over the school. In 1937 the school had seven classes. In that year there were four brothers and two lay people working there, ensuring that the negative 'poor image' the school still had gradually disappeared.

Semarang, the school in the early 1990s CBM

Semarang 1927. the simple buildings on the Karreweg (now: Jl. Dr. Cipto 91) CBM

Semarang, pupils from the Xaverius school in the 1930s CBM

4 | 1928 Belawan: Harbour buildings of 'Nederlandsch-Indische Scheepvaart Maatschappij'

CITY: Medan Belawan
ADDRESS: Oceaankade-Sumatraweg/Jl. Sumatra
ARCHITECT: A.A. Fermont, H. de Jongh
YEAR: 1927
CLIENT: 'Rotterdamsche Lloyd' and 'Stoomvaart Maatschappij Nederland'
CURRENT SITUATION: the terminal no longer exists
SOURCES: *Het Nieuws van den Dag voor Nederlandsch-Indië*, May 5, 1927; *Het Nieuws van den Dag voor Nederlandsch-Indië*, May 9, 1927; *De Sumatra Post*, May 11, 1927; *De Sumatra Post*, October 17, 1927, Delprat (1930), p. 101

At the beginning of May 1927, *Het Nieuws van den Dag voor Nederlandsch-Indië* published a call for tender. It involved new premises for the N.I.S.E. ('Rotterdamsche Lloyd') in Belawan (Deli), including the sheds and the iron roofing. The specifications and the conditions were, with accompanying drawings, available for payment of fifty guilders per set to the architecture firm of Hulswit-Fermont-Cuypers in Jakarta. That was where the interested parties met Han de Jongh, someone with expertise, who seven years earlier, as an engineer was closely involved in the port works of Belawan. A scale model had been made of the intended buildings along the quay. A journalist from *De Sumatra Post* reported on May 11, 1927: 'We hear that at the new berths for mail ships in Belawan, on behalf of the N.I.S.E. and 'Stoomvaart Maatschappij Nederland', large sheds will soon be built, including the necessary offices, customs departments and the like. The design work has been assigned to the engineering firm of Fermont-Cuypers, who has made it into a scale model'.

The new quay was about one kilometre long and was positioned further seaward than the old part. The business premises of the aforementioned shipping companies as well as those of the 'Koninklijke Pakketvaart Maatschappij' (now: PELNI) would also be built. It became an extensive project with sheds with a depth of 36 metres and storage areas equipped with cranes for loading and unloading freight of three and five tons. The quay width was approximately 14 metres.

After completion of the project, in which Jaski played a major part, the renovated Belawan cruise terminal received thousands of passengers for years. They then travelled by car or by train to Medan, 25 kilometres away, the springboard of Sumatra. To demonstrate that they were also skilled at utilitarian projects, Fermont-Cuypers posted an advertisement with a photo of this complex in the book *De Koloniale Roeping van Nederland*, which was published in 1930. Nowadays, Belawan no longer has a passenger terminal. The building has disappeared. Only cargo ships now moor at the former Ocean Quay.

Belawan 1930, a departing ship in front of the premises CTM

Belawan 1930, desk for processing administration within the building CTM

Belawan, the terminal shortly after completion in 1928 CMM

5 | 1928 **Yogyakarta: Seminary**

CITY: Yogyakarta
ADDRESS: Telamajalaan/Jl. Ahmad Jazuli No. 2
ARCHITECT: Th. Taen
YEAR: 1927
CLIENT: Jesuit Fathers
CURRENT SITUATION: Universitas Sanata Dharma
SOURCES: *De Indische Courant,* October 1, 1926; *Katholieke Illustratie*, February 15, 1928; *Limburger Koerier,* January 25, 1928; *Soerabaijasch Handelsblad*, July 12, 1934; Hoof (1934), p. 336; Archive of Jesuits European Low Countries, Kadoc Leuven (B)

Yogyakarta, the building from the inner garden in 2015 CON

On October 1, 1926, *De Indische Courant* reported that the plans for the construction of a major seminary in Yogyakarta had reached a definitive stage. Fermont-Cuypers delivered the design. The construction costs were estimated at approximately 80,000 guilders. This plan responded to an earlier vision of Eduard Cuypers in Amsterdam, made in 1922 on the terrain in the residential area Kota Baru that was more than 2 hectares. Cuypers started out with an ensemble of three parallel U-shaped buildings, situated in the westernmost part of the site. All buildings, including the church, were grouped around a cloister garden. The new plan was based on a strongly simplified building cluster without a large garden. A large volume had to be created for the limited budget, which simplified the design. The main building with a length of 93 metres contained two storeys with an Indies roof. On December 18, 1927 the complex was blessed. There were quite a few dignitaries in attendance, because the project in Yogyakarta was considered an important event for the whole of Java. The bishop came over from Jakarta. The day started with a high mass in the crowded Saint Anthony Church. Afterwards, the company went to the new Seminary where almost all Catholics from Yogyakarta attended the service. After a speech from the bishop in Bahasa, a few more speakers followed. Two days later, the Sultan and the Resident both graced the profane opening with their presence. The school complex was available now to 45 pupils who wanted to become priests. There would be many more. In the Netherlands, the *Katholieke Illustratie* of February 15, 1928 published the result with some pride. This building did not stay this way for long. In 1934 Fermont-Cuypers was given a follow-up assignment for an extension to both the rear and the front of the main building.

Yogyakarta, front façade of the new seminary in 1928 CNJ

Yogyakarta, the Seminary building overlooking the railway and the river, early 1930s CNJ

6 | 1928 **Pontianak: Javasche Bank**

CITY: Pontianak
ADDRESS: Residentsweg/-
ARCHITECT: Th. Taen
YEAR: 1928
CLIENT: The Javasche Bank
CURRENT SITUATION: no longer exists
SOURCES: *De Indische Courant*, October 4, 1926; *De Indische Courant*, May 18, 1928

Eduard Cuypers, who died in 1927, must have been very satisfied - Hulswit-Fermont-Cuypers were commissioned in September 1926 to build a new Javasche Bank in Pontianak on the Residentsweg (now: Jl. Pak Kasih). The management of the bank decided to replace the old building where the agent also lived, with a new building. The property no longer exists. The design, made in Jakarta, seemed very similar to previous designs. The foundation consisted of reinforced concrete bins or caisson. Part of it also served as a water reservoir. The safe was not placed in the basement because of its considerable weight, but in an outbuilding to spread the weight. Because of the soft soil, the firm kept the construction light. The superstructure consisted of a framework of reinforced concrete with double walls of plastered thin metal. The roof construction consisted of steel, covered with wooden roof tiles (*sirap*).
The main shape of the building connected with the bank buildings in Pematang Siantar (1923) and Padang (1925), but also near the town hall of Valkenswaard (the Netherlands) , which Taen designed shortly before his departure for the Indies. The façade consisted of two equally tall floors with three wide axes. In front of the entrance in the middle axis, because of the elevation on which the building stood, a wide staircase led up to a protruding awning with a balustrade for the deep balcony, which extended in front of the loggia above, supported on both sides by two linked, square columns. In the side axes there were narrow, sleek double-paned windows. A protruding roof overhang provided shade. On the ground floor there was a large, flexible room with dividing walls. The upstairs apartment had its own entrance and consisted of a hall, a front and a rear gallery and four rooms. The toilets were located on the first floor of the building. All floors were covered with tiles with black edges and a plinth. *Jati* (teak) wood panelling was used on the walls and incorporated in the ceilings.
The opening took place on May 7, 1928. In a short speech, Arthur Fermont handed the property over to the agent of the Javasche Bank, who gave the wife of the Resident a silver key with the request to open the building. The Resident emphasised in his speech the importance of the Javasche Bank for Pontianak. Arthur Fermont elaborated on the various technical details of the building, after which the group went outside for a group portrait. 'The building, which overlooks the river, can be called a jewel for Pontianak', according to *De Indische Courant*. In the 1930s, after the departure of the Resident, the address would change to Larivepark 3.
The bank building disappeared simultaneously with several other small-scale properties. The road is now called Jalan Pak Kasih and serves as a wide urban road around Pontianak, a city with more than half a million inhabitants today.

Pontianak, with the white building of the Javasche Bank in 1941 in the front PHOTO ZWAAN (1980) P. 158

Pontianak 1928, the newly opened Javasche Bank facing the Residentsweg (Jl. Pak Kasih) and the bay CAA

Pontianak 1928, the back of the Javasche Bank with the outbuilding where the safe is housed CAA

7 | 1928 **Medan: Escomptobank**

CITY: Medan
ADDRESS: Kesawan 109/Jl. Jend. Ahmad Yani No. 109
ARCHITECT: Th. Taen
YEAR: 1928
CLIENT: 'Nederlandsch-Indische Escompto Maatschappij'
CURRENT SITUATION: Bank Mandiri Kesawan Medan
SOURCES: *De Sumatra post,* November 12, 1926; *De Sumatra Post*, July 12, 1927; *De Sumatra Post,* August 29, 1927; *Het Nieuws van den Dag voor Nederlandsch-Indië*, September 3, 1928; *De Indische Courant*, August 18, 1928

In November 1926, *De Sumatra Post* discovered that Mr. Jaski, acting for Hulswit-Fermont-Cuypers, had bought the lot on the corner of Kesawan and the Kerkstraat (now: Jl. Palang Merah), Fermont-Cuypers let the newspaper know it had bought the piece of land for its own account. No particular destination had been given yet. In early 1927 it became known that the Escomptobank would be built at that location. On Saturday, August 27, 1927, the foundation stone was laid according to the well-known ritual. The agent of the bank, the staff, Fermont, Jaski and the overseer of Fermont-Cuypers, Mr. Van Driel all attended the ceremony. The son of the president-director from Jakarta laid the first stone, after which the agent of the bank in Medan gave a speech about the strong growth of the company, which made the new building inevitable. Then the attendees raised their glasses in a toast and the official building charter was placed in a cylinder with all coins, from half a cent to Fl. 10 and bricked into the construction, as dictated by the 'adat', the unwritten rule in Indies construction.
The building opened its doors on September 1, 1928. President-director Sandrock and Arthur Fermont were photographed afterwards. The building covers a floor area of approximately 36 by 28 metres and faces Kesawan on the narrowest side. This prominent building in Medan consists of a relatively low basement and a tall entrance floor. The middle part has three axes, the side wings each have two axes. Behind, the side façade again protrudes. At the front, behind the basement on the ground floor, there is a covered corridor with a tight rectangular opening in each axis. The municipality of Medan must have demanded for urban planning reasons that the building must have this covered gallery on the Kesawan. Unlike the neighbouring building of the Varekamp bookshop, which presented itself with large display windows onto the arcade, this bank building did not seek to attract the passing pedestrians. On the entrance floor there is a clean design of a cross frame in each window axis, which lies entirely flush in the plane of the façade. The building seems quite closed as a result of its relatively small window surface. The roof overhangs with the façade. The basement houses the big cash safes with safe deposit, the archives, a dining room and toilets. The entrance floor contains the large hall for the public, surrounded by the agent's room, the securities department, the cashier's desk and the bookkeeping. In the roof there is a simple light-cum-ventilation dome. Architecturally, the building bears a resemblance to the branch at Noordwijk (now: Bank Mandiri, Jl. Juanda in Jakarta), both in terms of proportion and in the façade section and with the striking roof, which also provided the distinctive Escompto ornament, consisting of three horizontal lines with the vertically placed flagpole.

Medan, the building in 2019 CSL

Medan, the Escomptobank shortly after opening on September 1, 1928 CON

Medan 1928, central hall of the Escomptobank (now: Bank Mandiri) with counter functions CFC

8 | 1928 Surabaya: Staff residence at Petodjo Ice factory

CITY: Surabaya
ADDRESS: Radersmastraat/Jl. Kidal
ARCHITECT: Th. Taen
YEAR: 1928
CLIENT: Petodjo Ice factory
CURRENT SITUATION: the houses are still there, the factory has disappeared
SOURCES: *Bataviaasch Nieuwsblad*, February 24, 1928; Groeneveld de Kater (1934), p. 101

This accommodation no longer exists as it was in 1928, it has been thoroughly renovated, but it can be seen in a photo book with works built by the N.V. Nedam construction company. On February 21, 1928, the tender for these three houses at the Petodjo Ice Company took place at Fermont-Cuypers. With Fl. 45,275, the Nedam construction company had the lowest bid and it also had an impressive track record. Each of the single-floored square houses had a pavilion roof and a particularly simple floor plan. A small central hall with the living quarters on one side and the sleeping quarters on the other. The rooms were higher than in Europe, so natural ventilation could take place through small openings. The houses stood out because of their large roof overhangs and wide windows. They were on the Radersmastraat and a side street that was later named Petodjoweg. On the map of Surabaya, the complex lay between the Gubeng station and the former NIAS (medical school: 'Nederlandsch Indische Artsen School'). It was the Petodjo company's fifteenth ice cream factory in the Dutch East Indies. During the opening speech, mention was made of two other factories that were still under construction, one in Sumatra and one in West Java. 'With this, the Union of Ice Factories', says one of the speakers, 'forms a belt of ice on the belt of emerald.' The brief presentation of the company's business during the opening described how the company worked with two freezers, each with capacity for more than 2,500 kg of ice per hour or 60,000 kg per day. In total, the company produced a maximum of 120 tons of ice per day. During the construction of the factory, an expansion of two more tanks had been allowed for. Ice clients included hotels, guesthouses and larger establishments. It was also worth noting that the new ice factory had a new system of hardening the ice water for absolutely crystal-clear ice.

Surabaya, three houses at Petodjo Ice Factory, a few years after completion CBN

9 | 1928 Cilacap: Harbour Office of 'Nederlandsche Handel-Maatschappij'

CITY: Cilacap
ADDRESS: Factorij-weg Donan/-
ARCHITECT: Th. Taen
YEAR: 1928
CLIENT: 'Nederlandsche Handel-Maatschappij'
CURRENT SITUATION: Destroyed in WW II
SOURCES: *Het Nieuws van den Dag voor Nederlandsch-Indië*, January 27, 1928; Gongrijp (1948), p. 455; Jong (1984), pp. 925-926. Dutch National Archives: 'Nederlandsche Handel Maatschappij' 2,20.01/13143

The 'Nederlandsche Handel-Maatschappij' owned one of the first companies to have warehouses in Cilacap, the only port on the south coast of Java. These were used for the storage of sugar and were located with a small office, directly on the loading and unloading quay at the harbour. In 1927, it was decided to build a new building and Fermont-Cuypers was commissioned to design a warehouse with office space and several large halls for the storage of goods. A warehouse was planned on the ground floor with an office floor above it, with windows opposite each other that could be opened, allowing the sea breeze to cool the interior.
Het Nieuws van den Dag voor Nederlandsch-Indië of January 27, 1928 contains the call for tenders: 'On the 20th of this month, the construction of the *gudang* of the Nederlandsche Handel-Maatschappij was opened for a bid and commissioned by the Architects and Engineers Bureau Fermont-Cuypers. Registered candidates were: Braat - Soerabaia for Fl. 61,800; De Unie - Bandung for Fl. 64,100; De Vries Robbe & Co - Semarang Fl. 69,400; Sunda - Bandung Fl. 74,100; Lindeteves-Stokvis - Batavia Fl. 77,579'. As the lowest bidder could not meet completion dates as prescribed in the specifications, the work was awarded to 'NV Constructie Werkplaats and Technisch Bureau De Unie' in Bandung. The substructure of the *gudangs* (warehouses) was subcontracted and awarded to the 'Hollandsche Beton Maatschappij Batavia' for Fl. 71,520.
The economic crisis broke out shortly after completion of the project, hitting the sugar industry in particular. Unsold sugar accumulated in 1935 to a stockpile of 2.5 million tons, the same size as the total production of the harvest year 1931-1932. 140 of the 178 sugar factories had to be closed. After the sugar business gradually recovered during the 1930s, the Second World War broke out.
On March 6, 1942, the Japanese bombed all the harbour works, warehouses and the railway station. These building disappeared as well. The National Archives in The Hague has the construction drawings of the halls.

Cilacap, harbour office of the 'Nederlandsche Handelsmaatschappij' and company halls in 1929 CFC

Office space on the first floor CFC

10 | 1928 **Tanjung Karang: Catholic Church**

CITY: Tanjung Karang
ADDRESS: Stationsavenue/Jl. Dipo/-
ARCHITECT: Th. Taen, L. Logemann
YEAR: 1928
CLIENT: Priests of the Sacred Heart (S.C.J.)
CURRENT SITUATION: no longer exists
SOURCES: *De Tijd*, January 2, 1929; *De Tijd*, January 18, 1929; *De Telegraaf*, September 11, 1933; *Het Nieuws van de Dag voor Nederlandsch-Indië*, December 18, 1933

On December 5, 1928, the Roman Catholic Christ the King Church in Tanjung Karang was consecrated. Pastor Van Oordt also took up residence in the new presbytery. 'The church and the presbytery are simple, make a friendly impression and are an asset to Tanjung Karang', according to the journalist of *Het Bataviaasch Nieuwsblad*, who then continued: 'The well-known architects and engineering firm Fermont-Cuypers, responsible for the design and construction, completed the entire project in the short period of three and a half months. The result was a simple church hall with half-timbered walls, an overhanging gable roof with a high peak on the roof turret with bell. The result was entirely in accordance with the design sketch that Laurent Logemann made on October 12, 1927. The church no longer exists, it was on the Stationsavenue (now: Jl. Dipo). The construction consisted mainly of wood as the safest solution in an area with earthquakes, such as the Lampong district in the southern tip of Sumatra. The press in the Netherlands also paid attention to the consecration and did not fail to mention that after the ceremony, the attendees toured 'through the neat building and the presbytery'. In 1933, *De Telegraaf* said of a volcanic eruption: 'Monday, half past six, loud bangs were heard at several places in the Lampong districts. Several people saw fan-shaped white smoke develop in a westerly direction, emitting lightning flashes and electrical discharges. Reports from the population reported that the Gunung Beliran is active on the border between Kroë and Kota Agung. Later in the day there was an ash rain in the earthquake-struck area, where the church building stood proudly'. At the end of 1933, Aneta wrote: 'Yesterday, Sunday, it was 5 years ago that the Catholic Church in Tanjung Karang (the first in the Lampungs area) was opened'.

The parish has occupied a different building for years.

Tanjung Karang, the church and presbytery, sketched by Laurent Logemann CFC

Tanjung Karang 1929, the church and presbytery, architect Fermont-Cuypers CFC

11 | 1928 **Malang: Towers of the Sacred Heart Church**

CITY: Malang
ADDRESS: Kajutangan/Jl. Mgr. Sugiyopraneto No. 2
ARCHITECT: M. Hulswit (design from 1904), built by A. Grünberg
YEAR: 1928
CLIENT: Church council of Sacred Heart Church in Malang
CURRENT SITUATION: Gereja Hati Kudus Yesus
SOURCES: *De Indische Courant*, July 24, 1928; *Het Vaderland*, November 3, 1928; *De Indische Courant*, November 5, 1928; *De Indische Courant*, December 14, 1928

In Europe, many a church tower was built later than the church itself. That also happened in Malang. From the outset, Marius Hulswit's 1904 design took into account the construction of two towers. Because of the costs, however, the church arose without the towers. In 1927, more money was available. Hulswit himself, who died in 1921, could no longer build the towers. On July 24, 1928 the newspaper reported the start of the construction: 'Today the construction of the two towers of the Catholic church on Kajutangan has begun'. This beautiful place of worship, which is located at one of the busiest points in the city centre, was built in 1905 and consecrated the following year. In the absence of the necessary funds, the two towers, which were designed at the front of the building, were omitted, so that the church has the front view we know today. For many years funds were collected and saved by the successive clergymen in Malang. They were finally ready to complete the façade by erecting the two towers. A. Grünberg, the director of the municipal works, was instructed to carry it out. He coordinated with the Hulswit-Fermont-Cuypers firm in Jakarta. Unfortunately, Grünberg did not live to see the completion of the project. On November 3, 1928 he died in the explosion of the fireworks factory in Malang, whereby many people died. During the consecration of the renovated church on Sunday, December 16, 1928, the priest stood still in remembrance of the deaths of Grunberg, and undoubtedly, of Hulswit. A newspaper wrote: 'The church bells have been hoisted up and can now resound all over the city'. Another newspaper informed its readers: 'The interior of the church has also undergone a metamorphosis through various improvements. In the past, the dome was only painted in two colours. Nowadays, the use of five harmonious shades presents a wonderful combination. The main colour of the church dome is cream, while the frames and capitals are painted in gold, blue, green and brown. The arches of the 15-metre-high dome are therefore all the more attractive.' The newspaper concluded: 'Several other parts of the interior of the church also underwent a renewal or improvement so that this church can now be regarded, without any doubt, as one of the finest places of worship in the Dutch East Indies'.

Malang around 1930, the church shortly after two towers were built CON

12 | 1929 Kediri: Javasche Bank with staff residence

CITY: Kediri
ADDRESS: Groote Postweg-Insulindestraat/Jl. Brawijaya No.2
ARCHITECT: Th. Taen, L. Logemann
YEAR: 1929
CLIENT: The Javasche Bank
CURRENT SITUATION: Bank Indonesia (front building). The residence no longer exists
SOURCES: *De Indische Courant*, May 8, 1929; *Het Nieuws van den Dag voor Nederlandsch-Indië*, May 11, 1929; *Bataviaasch Nieuwsblad*, May 15, 1929; *Bataviaasch Nieuwsblad*, May 31, 1929; *Bataviaasch Nieuwsblad*, October 9, 1929; *Het Nederlandsche en Ned.-Indische Huis Oud & Nieuw* (1930), pp. 14-17

On July 2, 1923 a new branch of the Javasche Bank in Kediri started doing business in an old house. On May 8, 1929 the official opening of the new bank premises took place. The building now functions as a front building for a large bank building, the house has disappeared. Both structures were erected on the location of the first house and the adjacent plot purchased for this purpose, at the intersection of two main through roads and near the station. The bank and the house formed an attractive ensemble.

The old bank building functions as a historic building now. It has a length of 28 metres with a width of 18 metres. The main body behind the front building has a square design of 18 by 18 metres. The building is simple and built in a modern objective style. It has a basement that protrudes about two metres above ground level, a bell-floor and a roof. In the smaller front building, the entrance is accessible via a wide staircase. An iron gate was used to close off the entrance. In front of the entrance and above the stairs there is a large awning with a flat roof, supported at the front by four linked columns on both sides. The slightly lateral side axes of the front building display the same stone cross-bar frame on the first floor as in the side walls. The front building has a roof that connects to the pavilion roof of the main body. There is a defined roof overhang for shade and a strong ventilation dome protrudes from the tent roof. Double exterior walls also provide coolness. In the agent's house, which no longer stands, it was also very cool because of the large roof, ventilation openings on all sides and the windows that could be closed with shutters. In some places the walls are so deep that cupboards have been incorporated into them, so they weren't freestanding in the room. The partition walls and cabinet panelling are made of teak (*jati*). At the top of the walls there are horizontal strips of stained glass. Two flights of stairs lead down to the basement with the vault. This consists of concrete walls, floor and a ceiling of half a metre thickness.'Machinefabriek De Nijverheid' in Kediri manufactured the burglary-free frameworks in the basement. There was steel purlin in the roof. The steel window frames came from Semarang. The Hollandsche Beton Maatschappij executed the concrete construction.

Kediri, the bank building from 1929 now fulfils a representative function COF

Kediri 1929, the eighteenth bank building for the Java Bank, designed by Fermont-Cuypers, the bank agent's residence to the right CFC

Kediri, the home of the agent of the Javasche Bank shortly after completion in 1929 CFC

Kediri, Javasche Bank on the corner of the Groote Postweg and Insulindestraat CFC

13 | 1929 **Subang: The Clubhouse**

CITY: Subang
ADDRESS: intersection Jl. Ade Irma Suryani Nasution No. 2
ARCHITECT: Th. Taen, L. Logemann
YEAR: 1929
CLIENT: 'Maatschappij ter Exploitatie der Pamanoekan & Tjiasemlanden'
CURRENT SITUATION: Wisma Karya Museum
SOURCES: *Het Nieuws van den Dag voor Nederlandsch-Indië*, August 27, 1929; *Soerabaijasch Handelsblad,* October 8, 1929; *Haagsche Post*, March 16, 1940

The first foundation stone was laid on Monday, January 15, 1929. It was for the new clubhouse for the 'Pamanukan & Tjiasemlanden' in Subang. The opening, planned on August 31, 1929, on Dutch Queen Wilhelmina's birthday, did not take place until October 8, because the wooden floor of the large auditorium had not been delivered on time due to a misunderstanding. The entire project replaced the old premises, in which 'one had to make do with what there was', according to the members present at the opening. The old clubhouse had only one room where everything had to take place, from film screenings to bar and from theatre to a bowling alley. Every activity has its own space in the new building.
The beautiful building has marked an important crossroads in Subang since then. The broad single-storey building with an Indian roof has a spacious open veranda on the front supported by square columns. This connected directly to the side gallery. The high roof with overhang provides shade and ventilation. The damp course, made up of river pebbles, appears as a special plinth. The same pebbles were used in the low walls on the grounds. Above that, the wall has been plastered. There were informal rattan seats in the open porch. To the left of the main entrance was the billiard room with two tables and a large pool table with accessories, still leaving enough room 'to add some tables for bridge enthusiasts'. In the middle of the front gallery was the bar, with a black marble topped counter and high bar stools. 'Ever since the official opening', according to a newspaper, 'the bar is enjoying great popularity'. To the right of the bar was the large auditorium, a large cool room, 'simply but tastefully decorated', with in the corner near the stage 'the new concert Pathéphone', the mechanical predecessor of the gramophone player. The theatre facilities offered sufficient opportunity to optimally receive artists on tour. Behind the bar and to the side of the room there was an open space enabling the circulation of outside air. This bordered the warehouse and office of the secretary and the kitchen. The back of the building offered space for the bowling alley, with the clubroom at one end and a garage at the other. The kitchen had a complete kitchen installation. A visitor called the new building 'damned good'. Someone else who travelled a lot around Java said: 'If you ignore the four main places of Java for a moment, then I would not be able to name one place for you in Java, where there is a club building that can match your new interior.'

Subang, the building now houses an attractive museum CON

Subang, recently completed club building for the 'Pamanoekan en Tjiassem-landen' company in 1929 CFC

Subang, river pebbles define the look of the building and the walls around the new club building in 1929 CFC

14 | 1929 Bandung: Catholic Church

CITY: Bandung
ADDRESS: Groote Postweg-Emmalaan/Jl. Kamuning No. 25
ARCHITECT: Th. Taen.
YEAR: 1929
CLIENT: Convent of St. Agatha, Cuijk (the Netherlands)
CURRENT SITUATION: Gereja Katolik Salib Suci
SOURCES: *Bataviaasch Nieuwsblad*, May 15, 1929; *Bataviaasch Nieuwsblad*, May 31, 1929; *Bataviaasch Nieuwsblad*, October 9, 1929; *Het Nederlandsche en Ned.-Indische Huis Oud en Nieuw* (1930), p. 122; *Kruistriomf* 10 (1930-1931), pp. 373-374; HNI CUY 0353382

On October 9, 1929, this church was consecrated by the Bishop of Jakarta. The construction had only taken four months. One longitudinal side of the church is parallel to what was then the Emmalaan (now: Jl. Kamuning) . Photos from 1930 still show the church without presbytery and other buildings. They were part of the extension in 1931, designed by Thomas Nix. The completion of the presbytery, which connected to the choir of the church via a meeting room, took place on April 23, 1931. The school complex from 1931 is also adjacent to this.

The church occupies a floor area of approximately 18 by 26 metres and provides 400 seats. The main entrance, with a 24-metre-high tower next to it, is located on the then Groote Postweg (now: Jl. Jenral Ahmad Yani). Due to the limited budget, the tower does not contain any timepiece. The side walls of the church could remain low by using a high and steep gable roof. The church's nave consists of five areas: the one behind the tower is blind, the three areas that then follow are articulated with slender piers, each with windows on either side consisting of three linked windows in the shape of a standing rectangle. The area adjacent to the choir contains an extension for the confessionals on both sides. The almost square choir connects to the high façade in the axis of the building.

Inside, the open roof does not contain visible structural parts. The roof's triangular shape returns as a theme in the contours of the choir. Even the panels on either side of the choir, which serve as background for the images, acknowledge the roof's angular main shape. There is a sense of unity in the entire church, despite the simple design. The church and the presbytery are still in full use and the parish treats the church's interior with great care, conserving the church's authenticity.

Bandung, the interior of the church in 2013 CON

Bandung, the church on the day of its consecration in 1929 CFC

Bandung, front of the church on the Groote Postweg (now: Jl. Jeneral Ahmad Yani) in 1929 CFC

Bandung, the back wall of the church was visible for only a short time, before the presbytery and outbuildings were added in 1931 CFC

15 | 1929 Surabaya: Catholic Church Ketabang (design)

CITY: Surabaya
ADDRESS: Van Sandickstraat/-
ARCHITECT: L. Logemann (design: October 20, 1929).
YEAR: 1929
CLIENT: unknown
CURRENT SITUATION: never built
SOURCES: *De Tijd,* December 11, 1930; *De Tijd,* January 13, 1931; *De Indische Courant*, October 7, 1932; HNI CUYZ 0353366

At the beginning of 1931, *De Tijd* announced that about a year and a half previously the Catholic Church of Surabaya had taken an option on a piece of land between Tambaksari and Patjarkling, near Karang Kajam. A third Catholic church was to be built here for Surabaya, but funds had to be collected for it first. 'It will,' says a newspaper, 'still take some time before construction can take place'. Fermont-Cuypers made a design for this church that was never built. Laurent Logemann made the drawing which shows a high front building between two towers with the equally high church hall at right angles to it, all in uncluttered, Art-Deco style, with some gothic elements. Fermont-Cuypers may have thought of putting the drawing of the church on a postcard. The sale of this increased the chance of completion. In 1932 *De Indische Courant* announced that the site was in use for the Theresia school, a Melania school and a Fröbel school (now: Jl. Kalijudan No. 25–33). At the end of 1932, construction began on a new presbytery, by two of the firm's former employees, Henri Estourgie (1885-1964) and Rijk Rijksen (1872-1944). Presumably that was a clear signal that Fermont-Cuypers stood no chance of obtaining the commission. The services took place in the 'auxiliary church' in the Theresia school. A new church building was never built.

Surabaya, postcard with the planned church on Ketabang CFC

16 | 1930 **Jakarta: Presbytery for planned Theresia Church**

CITY: Jakarta
ADDRESS: Soendaweg 3/Jl. Gereja Theresia No. 2
ARCHITECT: Th. Taen
YEAR: 1930
Assignment: Jesuit Fathers
CURRENT SITUATION: rectory/rumah pendeta Theresia
SOURCES: *Het Nederlandsche en Ned.-Indische Huis Oud & Nieuw* 1930 p. 121; *Het Nieuws van den Dag voor Nederlandsch-Indië,* February 17, 1930; Hoof (1934), p. 359

After the completion of the Theresia school in 1927 (Santa Theresia Highschool, Jl. H. Agus Salim No. 75 Jakarta), Fermont-Cuypers hoped to soon get the assignment for the already planned presbytery and church. The firm had already made a draft sketch for this in 1926, presumably by Alfred Kreisler. This shows the presbytery on the left and a cross church with a tower on the right, pointing to the nearby intersection. This sketch was published in *Het Nederlandsche en Ned.-Indische Huis Oud & Nieuw* in 1930. Several meeting and prayer rooms formed a connection between the presbytery and the church hall. The steeple is more or less as in Ed. Cuypers' sketched proposal made in 1923 for the Saint Joseph church in Meester Cornelis (now: Jatinegara), where the firm failed to obtain the commission. When there was enough money, the construction of the presbytery began. The house consists of one storey with a very high roof with considerable overhang. Its narrow side, including an entrance, faced the road and shows an Dutch East Indies objective style. The house has wide, rectangular windows with ventilation openings above them. Fermont-Cuypers used stained-glass windows here for a luxurious look. The inauguration of the presbytery took place on October 31, 1930. Mass was held in the Theresia school. This school served on Sundays as a temporary church until the new church was completed, designed by J. Th. van Oyen.

Jakarta 1930, a photograph of the presbytery that was completed shortly before, taken from the as yet uncultivated terrain for the Theresia church CFC

17 | 1930 **Jakarta: Theresia Church (design)**

CITY: Jakarta
ADDRESS: Theresiakerkweg-Soendaweg/-
ARCHITECT: Th. Taen, A. Dikstaal, C.Th. Nix
CLIENT: Jesuit Fathers
YEAR: 1930 (Dikstaal) and 1933 (Nix)
CURRENT SITUATION: not built
SOURCES: *Het Nederlandsche en Ned.-Indische Huis Oud & Nieuw* (1930), p. 121; Driel (1931); *Bataviaasch Nieuwsblad*, May 29,1933; *De Ingenieur in Nederlandsch-Indië* (1934), no. 8; Buys (1934); HNI CUY 0353374

On May 29, 1933 Fermont-Cuypers was told that the architect J.Th. Van Oyen (1893-1944) had been commissioned for the Theresia Church in Menteng, and not their firm. Ed. Cuypers had already sketched a design for this church in 1926. Three years earlier, they had submitted a new design proposal, which was printed on a postcard. This drawing was signed by Arnold Dikstaal in August 1930, but in the drawing style and design it closely resembled Laurent Logemann's design of the church at Ketabang in Surabaya in October 1929. The proposal testified to high ambitions. This church presented the same style as the Protestant Nassau-church (now: GBIP Paulus) of the A.I.A. architects which would be built three years later in Menteng. In order to prevent the project going to Van Oyen, Thomas Nix made one last attempt with an amended design in 1933. That proposal was not received positively either. Building on this location required 17-metre-long piles. The fewer piles, the better, Van Oyen must have thought. He designed a church with a hood of reinforced concrete in a cross shape. His proposal was calculated by the Hollandsche Beton Maatschappij N.V. that would also go on to build Van Oyen's church. At Fermont-Cuypers it was a bitter disappointment, especially for Thomas Nix, because he lived with his family on the Theresiakerkweg (now: Jl. H. Agus Salim), with a view of the building site. One experience wiser, he later took revenge with the design for the Pandu-church in Bandung.

Jakarta, A third design proposal from 1933 for the Theresia church by Thomas Nix at Fermont-Cuypers. This church building also failed to materialise CFC

Jakarta, design for the Theresia church by Arnold Dikstaal from October 1930 CFC

18 | 1930 Jakarta: Shop buildings with upstairs dwellings

CITY: Jakarta
ADDRESS: Citadelweg/Jl. Veteran I
ARCHITECT: Th. Taen
YEAR: 1930
CLIENT: Project developer
CURRENT SITUATION: various entrepreneurs and the PBBI (Badan Pelestarian Pusaka Indonesia)
SOURCES: *Het Nieuws van den Dag voor Nederlandsch-Indië*, March 4, 1930; *Het Nieuws van den Dag voor Nederlandsch-Indië*, June 16, 1931

The project on the Citadelweg (now: Jl. Veteran I) was one of the first forms of project development in Jakarta for shops with upstairs apartments. The economic crisis meant that banks did not easily lend money to starting entrepreneurs who wanted their own premises. In addition, suitable rental properties were in short supply. 'Rich Arabs', as they were called in the newspapers, seized their opportunities. One of them, from Singapore, decided to invest in a project on the Citadelweg, where the existing old buildings were bought up and demolished. Fermont-Cuypers made a plan with four connected retail properties including upstairs apartments. They were situated along the building line on the Citadelweg, as indicated by the municipality. The number of shops and apartments could be expanded with a further minimum of five shops and upstairs apartments, if the rental of the first phase was a success. In 1931, they were indeed built. Building plans were not found nor were photographs taken shortly after completion. The connected block displays a lower ground floor of shop windows, interrupted every two shops by a portico with four doors to the shops on both sides and to the entrances to the double upper accommodation. Above the portico, a small crescent-shaped dormer window is located on the gable roof for ventilation. The residents on the first floor looked out on the old citadel.

PBBI (Badan Pelestarian Pusaka Indonesia) is now on Jl. Veteran No. 1A No. 27.

Jakarta, the shops on the Citadelweg (now: Jl.Veteran I) around 1940 CFC

19 | 1930 **Jakarta: Canisius College**

CITY: Jakarta
ADDRESS: Menteng 40 and Gang Menteng/Jl. Menteng Raya No. 64
ARCHITECT: Th. Taen, A.A. Fermont
YEAR: 1930
CLIENT: 'Strada Vereeniging' to establish a General Secondary School
CURRENT SITUATION: Sekolah Kanisius
SOURCES: *Bataviaasch Nieuwsblad*, October 4, 1926; *Bataviaasch Nieuwsblad*, October 26, 1926; *De Tijd*, November 13, 1926; *Het Nieuws van den Dag voor Nederlandsch-Indië*, January 11, 1930; *Bataviaasch Nieuwsblad*, February 6, 1930; *Het Nieuws van den Dag voor Nederlandsch-Indië*, February 6, 1930; Archive of Jesuits European Low Countries Kadoc Leuven (Belgium)

In 1926, J. Kurris S.J., who had until then been a teacher at the Roman Catholic Higher civic school in Amsterdam, was appointed as the first principal of the Peter Canisius College in Jakarta. That school still had to be built. After the purchase of the building on Menteng 40 with surrounding grounds, the board, with the cooperation of the municipality, also received access to the large plot of land to the rear, which continued on to Menteng Ketjil (now: Jl. Menteng Kecil). Fermont-Cuypers was then allowed to set up a building scheme, which determined the correct location of the new buildings. The programme included a series of linked buildings around a courtyard, with nine regular classrooms, an assembly hall and five special classrooms for biology, physics, chemistry, signature- and line drawing. The gymnasium was planned centrally in the courtyard. The planned and later built chapel linked the old main building at Menteng with the new building behind. Between the main building and the future chapel was a courtyard with sleeping quarters for the boys' boarding house on both sides. In making the building plan, Fermont-Cuypers allowed for future expansions on the west side of the courtyard. They hoped for the purchase of Menteng 44 and 46. In January 1930, the school announced the grand opening with a collage of four photographs of the new building, the old main building and the new principal in the middle. The opening took place on February 6, 1930 by the Apostolic Vicar of Jakarta. The director welcomed everyone in the assembly hall bedecked with flower arrangements, after which Arthur Fermont, who had supervised the construction, formally handed over the school to the principal. Then everyone went to the temporary chapel for the mass, after which, upon returning to the assembly hall, the inauguration of the building was completed.

Among the many speakers was the mayor of Jakarta, Mr. Meyroos, who said he was surprised at the 'neat, simple and highly efficient complex'. He also mentioned that nothing of it was visible from the public road because the new building was hidden behind the old Indies houses along the road. As the land on that side could not yet be purchased, it was literally impossible to build on the road. Fermont-Cuypers made several albums with photos of all new buildings. One of these was sent to the school board, the other to the Netherlands, where it ended up in the archives of the Jesuit Fathers, the initiators of the project. The photographs show buildings in an Indies functional architecture, all equipped with a large roof, galleries on the open inner sides, river pebbles processed in the damp-proof course of the outer boundary walls. The assembly hall had a roof construction, with partial hipped ends for ventilation. The interiors show ceilings with ceiling panels and teak furniture, designed by the office.

Almost all buildings have subsequently been replaced by new buildings.

Jakarta, an aerial photograph of Canisius College (Kanisius) in 1940. The buildings built in 1930 are central. The buildings with the light roofs date from 1940 CNJ

Jakarta, Canisius College in 2017 with new buildings. On the left the chapel from 1940, designed by Fermont Cuypers INTERNET COF

Jakarta 1930, students of the Canisus College in front of the school CNJ

Jakarta, the northern boundary of the Canisius College with the informal access on Gang Menteng, that was in use until 1940 CNJ

Jakarta, room for drawing lessons in the Canisius College in 1930 CNJ

Jakarta, the school buildings including the gymnasium in 1930 CNJ

20 | 1930 **Jakarta: Duo Passenger terminal**

CITY: Jakarta
ADDRESS: Koningsplein-West 3/Medan Merdeka Barat No. 3
ARCHITECT: Th. Taen, L. Logemann
YEAR: 1930
CLIENT: 'Stoomvaart Maatschappij Nederland' and the 'Rotterdamsche Lloyd'
CURRENT SITUATION: Ministry Kementerian Koordinator Bidang Pembangunan Manusia dan Kebudayaan
SOURCES: *Bataviaasch Nieuwsblad*, May 27, 1929; *Het Nieuws van den Dag voor Nederlandsch-Indië*, March 4, 1930; *Het Nieuws van den Dag voor Nederlandsch-Indië*, March 26, 1930; Archive of Fermont-Cuypers: *Ontwerp voor een passagegebouw voor de N.V. Duo te Weltevreden*, September 30, 1928; HNI CUYZ 0353362

After the 'Stoomvaart Maatschappij Nederland' and the 'Rotterdamsche Lloyd' had merged under the name of N.V. 'Duo', a competition was organised for the design of joint offices on Koningsplein (now: Medan Merdeka Barat) in Jakarta. At Fermont-Cuypers, Laurent Logemann spent a lot of time on this project. The result was presented in a bid book on September 30, 1928. Seven months later, a newspaper in Jakarta reported that the firm had been given the commission. The promise was that the project would be completed within six months. The sketches show the intended building from different angles. The completed building actually contained very few of the many architectural references to shipping. The opening took place on April 1, 1930.
The entire project was beautiful because of its objective simplicity and practical adaptation to the tropical conditions. The still existing building complex consisted of a single storey with a generous roof. The roof was covered with Roman tiles, specially imported from Europe. The requirement of two separate offices, each with its own entrance united under one roof, led to a concept of two broad wings behind a connecting main building with the entrance at the front in between. The building has a width of 55 metres and a depth of 52 metres and stood on its own in a spacious garden. To the left and to the right behind the main entrance were the wings of the separate offices. The colourful coats of arms of the shipping companies were to be seen between the three large windows above the main entrance. Whitewashed as they are now, they are barely visible. The windows contain stained glass with scenes from the shipping industry, which become visible again when the plate is removed from the inside.
The temporary building housed the agent's office of both the 'Nederland' and the 'Lloyd'. The left wing of the building was occupied by the passage office of the 'Nederland' and in the right wing that of the 'Rotterdamsche Lloyd'. Their layout was, with some difference in space ratios, almost identical. An elongated public hall stretched out behind the entrance to both offices. Behind a counter was a large, open office space. This space was more extensive for the 'Rotterdamsche Lloyd' than for the 'Nederland'. Behind it were closed office spaces. Lavish tiling everywhere determined the image. The large garden to the rear provided space for outbuildings, including some garages. The grouping of the offices behind the main building on both sides of a courtyard guaranteed a quiet workspace, of which, according to a newspaper, 'the lighting and the ventilation meet the highest requirements'.

The sleek building is now the gatehouse of the Ministry of Culture. The two wings, stripped of the original interior, serve as a reception room and mosque. Behind the old building, there is now the office tower of the Ministry.

Jakarta, the Duo passenger terminal on Koningsplein (Jl. Medan Merdeka Barat) shortly after completion in 1930 CAA

Jakarta, the building in 2013 PHOTO: DENNY RACHMAT GHAFFARI

Jakarta 1930, Duo passenger terminal, courtyard CFC

Jakarta 1930, Duo passenger terminal with the entrance to 'Stoomvaart Maatschappij Nederland' = 'Rotterdamsche Lloyd' CMM

Jakarta, counters of 'Rotterdamsche Lloyd' in Duo passenger terminal in 1930 CMM

Jakarta, counters of 'Stoomvaart Maatschappij Nederland' in Duo passenger terminal in 1930 CFC

21 | 1930 Jakarta, Hotel des Indes, main building designed by A.I.A.

CITY: Jakarta
ADDRESS: Molenvliet West/Jl. Gajah Mada/-
ARCHITECT: A.I.A. architects (F.L. Ghijsels, N.E. Burhoven Jaspers); building management: Fermont-Cuypers
YEAR: 1930
CLIENT: Hotel des Indes Batavia
CURRENT SITUATION: demolished in 1971
SOURCES: *Bataviaasch Nieuwsblad*, December 10, 1925; *Bataviaasch Nieuwsblad*, July 11, 1927; *Het Nieuws van den Dag voor Nederlandsch-Indië*, May 17, 1930; Gelink (1948)

On July 11, 1927, *Het Bataviaasch Nieuwsblad* announced that the Hotel des Indes had plans to demolish the older rooms, which stood in a row in line with the new kitchen, in order to create a modern large dining hall with a lobby, a ladies' salon and a reading room over a width of 200 metres between the neighbours 'Eigen Hulp' and 'Pension Oriënt'. This plan was, as the newspaper reported, 'worked out according to very modern ideas from the Architects and Engineering Office Hulswit-Fermont and Ed. Cuypers'. 'Before the implementation of this plan can be started,' continued the newspaper, 'the above outdated rooms will first be replaced by new apartments in connection with an increase in hotel guests. That is why the architects have worked out the plans for various expansions'. Alfred Kreisler drew this 'big plan' in November 1925. Laurent Logemann altered elements of this design two years later However, in 1929 the hotel management opted for a plan from A.I.A. architects, which was significantly more modern. Fermont-Cuypers was commissioned to oversee and manage the work. On May 17, 1930, the new building of A.I.A. was completed.
Hotel des Indes formed the setting for the Van Roijen-Roem negotiations on May 7, 1949. These led to the release of Sukarno and Hatta and ultimately to the formal transfer of sovereignty to the Indonesian Republic. In 1960, Indonesia confiscated the hotel and from that moment on it was called Hotel Duta Indonesia. In 1971, the famous hotel made way for a regular shopping complex.

Jakarta, Hotel des Indes on Molenvliet West (now: Jl. Gajah Mada), viewed from the viewing tower of Hotel de Galeries across the road in 1932 CFC

Jakarta, sketch made by Alfred Kreisler of Hulswit-Fermont-Cuypers, for a new main building of Hotel des Indes, dated November 12, 1925 CFC

Jakarta, revised sketch for a new main building of Hotel des Indes made by Laurent Logemann working for Fermont-Cuypers, dated October 25, 1927 CFC

Jakarta, sketch of the proposed main building of Hotel des Indes, which the client ultimately chose. Designed by F.J.L. Ghijsels of A.I.A. architects in 1928 CWH

22 | 1930 **Madiun: Town Hall**

CITY: Madiun
ADDRESS: Residentslaan/Jl. Pahlawan No. 37
ARCHITECT: Th. Taen, L. Logemann
YEAR: 1930
CLIENT: Municipality of Madiun
CURRENT SITUATION: Balai Kota Madiun
SOURCES: *Soerabaijasch Handelsblad*, August 5, 1930; *Soerabaijasch Handelsblad*, April 27, 1931; *Locale Techniek* (1933), no. 1; Gonggrijp (1934); HNI CUYZ 0353364

The municipality of Madiun, established by ordinance on June 20, 1918, was granted legal status in 1928, with the right to its own mayor. Schotman, who previously held that position in the much larger Cirebon was appointed to put things in order in Madiun during the last five years until his retirement. He became decisive. He wanted at least a new town hall. In June 1929, the council agreed to the final design, made by Fermont-Cuypers for a sum of Fl. 117,000. It was to be located on the Residentslaan (now: Jl. Pahlawan), a long road with avenue planting. Laurent Logemann first sketch encompasses a romantic scene, with friendly little windows, two small entrance doors and a balcony over much of the length of the council chamber on the first floor. The final plan looks cleaner. The town hall consists of four buildings around a green courtyard. The main building together with both wings has a front width of 48 metres. In the left wing (north side) is the secretariat, at the rear are the civil works and in the right wing the other services. The actual town hall of 18 by 12 metres on the Jl. Pahlawan consists of two high floors, a tiled roof and a tower with a clock. In the 33-metre-deep front gardens, with lawns and cypresses, a semi-circular driveway made its way to the 4-meter-long protruding *porte-cochère*. On the awning, there was also the municipal coat of arms as well as a flagpole. Under the awning is the main entrance that leads into a vestibule, with walls covered with carrara marble. The mayor's chamber and the committee room can be accessed from the vestibule. Both are clad in *jati* (teak) panelling and in the upper windows there is stained glass. The vestibule gives access to the covered gallery at the back, as well as the stairs to the first floor in the tower. The council chamber covers almost the entire first floor of the main building. The lamps and decorative panels were designed and made in Madiun. The division in the council hall for the press and public could be removed, creating one spacious room.
The one and only town hall complex that Fermont-Cuypers designed is essentially a purely Indian design; a main building located on the road, with the administration, the other buildings located behind, all with workrooms under a well-ventilated roof and accessed via a covered gallery. Only the main building distinguishes itself architecturally. This represented the Dutch authority, visible in architecture, which apart from plastering, displayed a relationship with the architecture of what is later called 'De Delftse School' in the Netherlands.

Madiun, design for the town hall sketched by Laurent Logemann. The drawing shows two entrances, which were replaced in the modified design by a central access CFC

Madiun, the new town hall in 1930, with the coat of arms of the municipality executed in coloured faience above the front gallery. To the left and right of the main building are the entrances to the service wings CFC

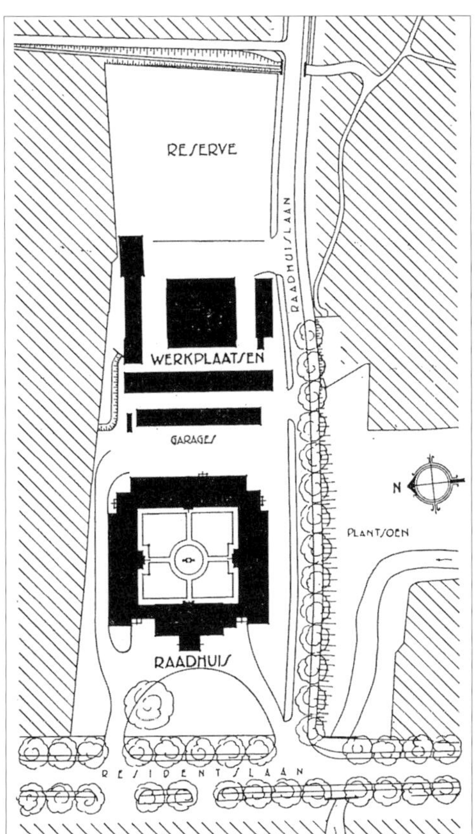

Madiun, the Residentslaan (Jl. Pahlawan) is the main road of the city. The tower strongly defines the cityscape from the southwest *LOCALE TECHNIEK* JANUARY 1933

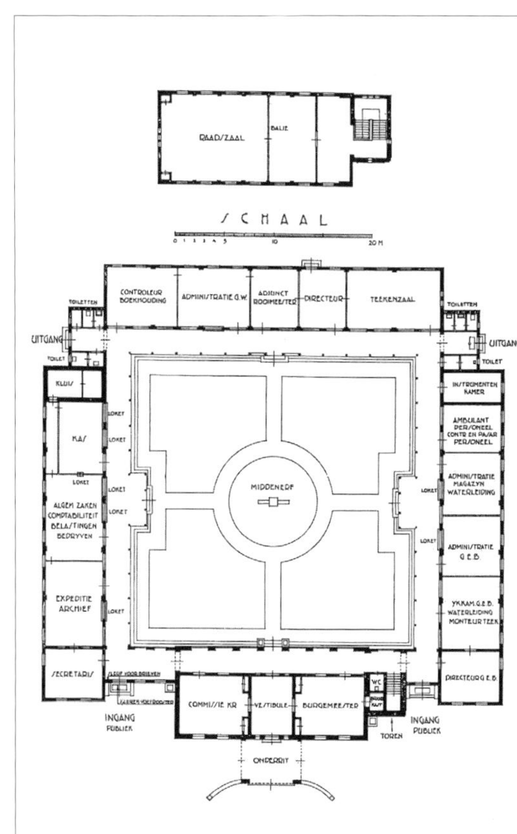

Madiun: In the main building are the rooms of the mayor and the committee. The staircase in the tower leads to the council chamber above *LOCALE TECHNIEK* JANUARY 1933

Madiun 1930, the corner tower from the courtyard *LOCALE TECHNIEK* JANUARY 1933

Madiun 1930, the gallery behind the main building with the rooms for the committee and mayor on the left *LOCALE TECHNIEK* JANUARY 1933

Madiun, front view of town hall and porte cochère in 1930 CFC

OORKONDE

IN DEN JARE NEGENTIENHONDERD NEGEN EN TWINTIG
OP DEN 30STEN VAN SLACHTMAAND
ONDER HET BURGEMEESTERSCHAP VAN
ROELOF . ADRIAAN . SCHOTMAN
WERD VAN DIT
RAADHUIS DER GEMEENTE MADIOEN
ONTWORPEN EN GEBOUWD DOOR
HET ARCHITECTEN EN INGENIEURS BUREAU
FERMONT - CUYPERS
WELTEVREDEN - A'DAM
DE EERSTE STEEN
GELEGD DOOR
ELLEN . LUCIE . EMELIE
VAN DEN BOS - ZEYDEL
MOGE DIT BOUWWERK EEN ZINNEBEELD ZIJN
VAN VOORUITGANG EN GEMEENSCHAPSZIN

wd RESIDENT | BURGEMEESTER | RAADSLEDEN
SECRETARIS
REGENT | DIRECTEUR VAN G.W. | ARCHITECT.

Madiun, the charter, as was bricked in with the first stone CFC

Madioen, het raadhuis in de jaren dertig CFC

Madiun, the town hall in 2017 PHOTO: ANDRIK AKITA INTERNET

23 | 1930 **Madiun: Theatre and/or cinema**

CITY: Madiun
ADDRESS: Residentslaan 45/Jl. Pahlawan-Jl. Kalimantan/-
ARCHITECT: Th. Taen, L. Logemann
YEAR: 1930
CLIENT: Municipality of Madiun
CURRENT SITUATION: demolished, now: Sekarang Sri Ratu shopping centre
SOURCES: *Het Nieuws van den Dag voor Nederlandsch-Indië*, March 5, 1928; *De Indische Courant*, August 16, 1928; *Soerabaijasch Handelsblad*, March 30, 1929; *Soerabaijasch Handelsblad*, July 12, 1929; *Soerabaijasch Handelsblad*, December 31, 1929; *Soerabaijasch Handelsblad*, August 5, 1930; *De Indische Courant*, August 5, 1930; *Haagsche Post*, March 16, 1940; HNI CUYZ 0353368

On August 1, 1930 the flags were flying, not only because of the town hall, but also because of the opening of the theatre. This had been made possible thanks to a legacy of Miss M.E.J. Manuel. She donated her estate to the municipality, on condition that it would be in exchange for a theatre built on the leafy Residentslaan (now: Jl. Pahlawan) in the grounds of her home, where she lived until her death. Based on discussions with the Madiun society for amateur dramatics, Fermont-Cuypers made a design for a long hall of approximately 26 metres, with 400 seats and a large stage. During the planning process, the drama society backtracked. It wanted to continue using its own club building, after which the plans underwent an adjustment to enable profitable exploitation. The adapted, more elongated room could also serve as a cinema. Together with the seating on the balcony, it offered 380 seats in the hall and 120 on the balcony. The construction costs amounted to Fl. 120,000. The building was set back about 30 metres from the building line. A wide and impressive awning hung above the entrance. On either side there were low towers with a very protruding awning along the roof edge. Somewhat behind it was a middle section with an extremely protruding roof. In spite of the sleek design and the plastered façades, the entire project appeared somewhat expressionist. There was a front wing on both sides of the main entrance. In the right wing there was a bar with restaurant, in the other wing, the municipal library with reading room.
The building was replaced by a shopping centre in the 1970s.

Madiun, the theatre/cinema in the 1950s, a building that the city acquired thanks to an endowment CON

24 | 1930 Purwokerto: School complex

CITY: Purwokerto
ADDRESS: Schoolweg/Jl. Jend. Gatot Subroto No. 44
ARCHITECT: Th. Taen
YEAR: 1930
CLIENT: Ursuline Sisters from Weltevreden
CURRENT SITUATION: SD Santa Maria Purwokerto
SOURCES: *Bataviaasch Nieuwsblad*, August 15, 1930; *De Indische Courant*, August 16, 1930; *De Tijd*, May 18, 1935; *Algemeen Handelsblad*, May 18, 1935; Archive of CEK; Photo album of Ursuline Sisters from Weltevreden

A day after the consecration of the church in Purwokerto, on Sunday, August 10, the apostolic vicar blessed the new school complex on the same street. The mother superior of the Ursuline Sisters of the convent on the Postweg (now: Jl. Pos in Jakarta) attended both ceremonies. The school system in the colony differentiated according to culture and race, as a result of which different schools existed for Europeans, Indonesians and Chinese. All schools taught in a western manner and in Dutch. This government-imposed system was kept up to standard by the Department of Education and Religion by regularly inspecting each school. Besides government schools, religious communities were also allowed to start schools, for which they were granted subsidy after approval. The Ursuline Sisters started their school in Purwokerto. Fermont-Cuypers created the design for the school complex. The buildings for the European Primary School, the Dutch-Indonesian Primary School and the Domestic School barely differed. There were classrooms grouped together with a covered play area around an open school garden. In the middle of the garden was the statue of Saint Angela, the 'common denominator' of scholars and sisters. In 1935, another expansion followed with a Dutch Indonesian School for girls in the same simple building style. None of the original school buildings are still in existence.

Purwokerto 1930, the classrooms of the European school on the left. In the background the covered accommodation for all children CFC

25 | 1930 **Purwokerto: Catholic Church**

CITY: Purwokerto
ADDRESS: Schoolweg/Jl. Jend Gatot Subroto/-
ARCHITECT: Th. Taen
YEAR: 1930
CLIENT: Missionaries from Tilburg (MSC, the Netherlands)
CURRENT SITUATION: disappeared
SOURCES: *Bataviaasch Nieuwsblad*, August 15, 1930; *De Indische Courant*, August 16, 1930; Archive of CEK: AR-Z117, inventary 'Ursulinen van de Romeinse Unie'

Purwokerto, the entrance to the church on the day of the consecration in 1930 CEK

Purwokerto had 25,200 inhabitants in 1930, including about 700 with a European background. On Sunday August 10, 1930, the new Catholic Church, named 'Christus Koning' was consecrated. It was a relatively compact building, on the spot where the Schoolweg (now: Jl. Jend Gatot Subroto) crossed the river Kranji. The priest must have thought that this was just the beginning. The building, designed on a structural grid, could be extended in its length as soon as more money was available. This type of church was developed by Fermont-Cuypers in response to the economic crisis. The building cost Fl. 35,930. The construction of the building was kept simple. The central nave consisted of a box with a width of about 16 metres. On the two long sides there was a low extension under a tiled, lean-to roof, which formed an awning above the front main entrance. A roof turret was placed in the middle of the roof. On the long sides, there were wide windows under the overhang of the roof. At the top of the church hall there were windows under the overhang of the hipped roof. This not only allowed indirect daylight, but also provided ventilation. Inside, the church was an example of cubist modernity, reflected in the furniture, pillars, capitals and in the ceiling with rectangular and square boarding. The church had a lower course of river pebbles. The flags had been hoisted on the day the church was consecrated by Monsignor Van Velsen, the apostolic vicar of Jakarta. A well-attended reception in the presbytery followed the ceremony. The Resident of North Banjumas and the assistant Resident of Purwokerto as well as the Regents of Banjumas and Purwokerto all attended this opening. Allthough the church withstood the years 1942-1949 relatively well, it disappeared afterwards.

The building was far too small for the Catholic community in the fast-growing city with already more than 250,000 inhabitants. A new church building is now in use.

Purwokerto, the church on the day of its consecration, Sunday August 10, 1930 CFC

Purwokerto, interior of the church shortly after completion in 1930 CEK

26 | 1930 **Ambarawa: St. Louis Institute**

CITY: Ambarawa
ADDRESS: road Semarang-Djokja/Jl. Mgr. Sugiyopranoto No. 191
ARCHITECT: Th. Taen, L. Logemann
CLIENT: Brothers from Maastricht (the Netherlands)
YEAR: 1930 and 1931
CURRENT SITUATION: SMP Pangudiluhur
SOURCES: *Het Centrum*, September 13, 1928; Archive of KITLV M1997A2595 'Instituut St. Louis Muloschool met Europeesch Internaat'; CEK: Documentation 4822, drawing January 31, 1930, no. 21-1-35N, May 12, 1930, September 16, 1931, September 18, 1931; Hoof (1934), pp. 359, 367; Christinus (1940), pp. 150, 183-185; Linden (1981), p. 37

Before Fermont-Cuypers' involvement as architects with this Institute, a start was made on August 8, 1928 with the construction of a few classrooms near an existing house. In 1929, Fermont-Cuypers made the first drawings for a large school complex with a boarding school and a monastery. The firm designed a large front building with classrooms and the brother house. Phased extensions could take place behind this. A school complex with a school garden was created behind the western part of the new front building, while space remained behind the eastern part for a future monastery complex. The chapel was to be built between the school and the monastery. Behind the school and the planned monastery, there was a spacious playground created. The boarding school with two large dormitories, including associated laundry and bathrooms were built behind the playground. East of this main set-up, the firm planned an infirmary, kitchen, dining room, laundry facilities and storage rooms around the old house, aiming to demolish the old building as soon as all new buildings were ready. The priest Joachim van der Linden wrote about this in 1981: 'Despite the fact that the institute started the school in 1928 with seventeen interns and a year later thirty-three, there was a lack of confidence in the future. In spite of this, the Superior General agreed to an extension, because the old Boarding school did not offer sufficient classroom space'. 'The architecture firm Fermont-Cuypers created beautiful plans, but they were immediately rejected as being too expensive'. Simplified plans followed in February 1930. Consecration of the new building followed on November 2, 1930. The final plan, designed by Fermont-Cuypers, was never fully implemented, only the most essential was achieved and that is what has remained to this day. 'Now we know that the malaise - the notorious 1930s - slowed down the influx to St. Louis', Van der Linden believed. The old house survived, wedged in between other structures, as can be clearly seen on the aerial photo from 1936.
Included in the commission for the Institute, Fermont-Cuypers were also asked to design a 'cemetery chapel' for the small Catholic cemetery in Ambarawa, which had been put into use shortly before. This first Catholic cemetery chapel in the Dutch East Indies was consecrated on July 19, 1931. In it, Mass for the deceased was held at least once a month for years. Nowadays the little chapel has fallen into disrepair.

Ambarawa, some students in 1933 CNJ

Ambarawa, aerial photograph of the St. Louis Institute from 1936, when the chapel was built that towered above everything. The original house stands to the right of the chapel, it is almost entirely surrounded by other buildings KNILM/CFC

Drawing of the front building made by Fermont-Cuypers CEK

Ambarawa, the original school furniture still in use in 2015 CON

27 | 1931 **Padang: Escomptobank**

CITY: Padang
ADDRESS: Handelskade/Jl. Batang Arau No. 42
ARCHITECT: Th. Taen
YEAR: 1931
CLIENT: Nederlandsch-Indische Escompto Maatschappij
CURRENT SITUATION: Bank Mandiri Muaro
SOURCES: *De Indische Courant*, March 30, 1931; *Het Nieuws van den Dag voor Nederlandsch-Indië,* March 30, 1931

In 1930 in Padang, the Escomptobank moved to a building designed by Fermont-Cuypers on the Handelskade. The building, of which no old photographs were found, was built on a small plot. The festive opening took place on March 29, 1931. All trade offices on the quay hung out the flag that day. 'Not only the so popular tricolour', *De Indische Courant* reported, 'but also a variety of flags, whose countries were represented by the consulates of the foreign powers'. At about 11 o'clock, a large crowd gathered in the new building. They came through the front door, up a staircase, into an area that gave access to the surrounding rooms of the agent, the bookkeeping, securities and to the public hall. In the vestibule and the hall, the ceramic tiling extends up as high as the doors. The agent's room was given an extra rich decoration with a wooden floor and furniture with ebony frames. Stained glass was used in the windows of the façade and the vestibule, creating beautiful colour effects with the tiling. The securities room was kept completely separate and provided direct access to the safe in the basement. After the tour, the agent of the bank, Mr. Koetsier, welcomed the guests and thanked them for their interest. He told the story of the construction of the building and thanked the municipality for its cooperation. As the second speaker, Han de Jongh took the floor, 'under whose direct supervision the building, according to the newspaper, had come about. A number of speakers followed, including the Mayor of Padang. The newspaper continued: 'A treasure of floral arrangements, offered by friends and relations, adorn the new bank building. Drinks and various delicacies were shared generously.'

Although the building is remodelled from the inside, this characteristic bank building is still there, with the typical Escompto-crest on the roof above the entrance consisting of three horizontally staggered beams and the vertically placed flagstaff. The building is still surrounded by a few other buildings from the colonial times such as, the former Javasche Bank (Jl. Batang Arau No. 66) and Güntzel & Schumacher (Jl. Batang Arau No. 70).

Padang, Bank Mandiri in the building of the former Escomptobank in 2015 CON

28 | 1931 **Belinyu: Convent and school**

CITY: Belinyu
ADDRESS: Pandjiweg/Jl. Mayor Syafrie Rachman No. 103
ARCHITECT: Th. Taen
YEAR: 1931
CLIENT: Sisters of the Divine Providence from Amsterdam
CURRENT SITUATION: SD Santa Agnes 2
SOURCES: *Bataviaasch Nieuwsblad*, June 30, 1931; *Het Nieuws van den Dag voor Nederlandsch-Indië*, June 30, 1931; *De Indische Courant*, July 2, 1931; CEK AR-2167. CEK AR/P036/1891; Drawing of September 6, 1929

On November 1, 1928, a priest in Belinyu began a Dutch-Chinese School. The Sisters of Providence took over the school in 1930. They asked Fermont-Cuypers to design a building complex. The firm presented them with a very ambitious plan, with more than eleven buildings on a site of about 100 by 100 metres. It was a rectangular configuration, containing a boys' boarding school, a girls' boarding school, a building with a kitchen unit, a dining room, numerous classrooms, two dormitories for 55 people, a convent and a church. Each building consisted of one floor with a generous roof. Covered galleries connected the buildings together. Most of them were situated along enclosed gardens, which, depending on their location, served as playground for boys or girls, or as a convent garden. Everything was given standard dimensions. The regular classrooms had a floor area of 7 by 8 metres, the special ones were 8 by 8 metres.
On Monday June 22, 1931 a large number of visitors attended the festive opening of the convent and the school. Han de Jongh spoke on behalf of Fermont-Cuypers. The complex apparently satisfied a large demand.
'Private Dutch-Chinese School' has recently reappeared on one of the façades in large letters. The website of the school draws attention to the original furniture with positive astonishment: 'The school desks made of the best quality teak are equipped with a drawer, the top is foldable and there is a hole for an ink pot'. In the nuns' former bedrooms, there are still the steel tanks for the collection of rainwater. These were installed during the construction of the school, so that the use of groundwater could be kept to a minimum.

Belinyu, original school buildings in 2017, shortly before being replaced by new buildings CON

29 | 1931 Pangkal Pinang: Catholic boarding school

CITY: Pangkal Pinang
ADDRESS: Kerkstraat/Jl. Budi Mulia No. 107
ARCHITECT: Th. Taen, L. Logemann
YEAR: 1931
CLIENT: Fathers of the Sacred Hearts
CURRENT SITUATION: Gedung Sekolah SD Budi
SOURCES: *Koloniaal Missie Tijdschrift* 1935 p. 140; CEK AR-Z167; Ethelbert (1986), pp. 67-84

Pangkal Pinang became the new capital of the island of Bangka in 1913. The Catholic Church then decided to make this town their main centre on the island. The location of the boys' boarding school, designed by Fermont-Cuypers, stemmed from that policy decision. The building was inaugurated on June 23, 1931. It was T-shaped with the temporary chapel and the classroom in one wing and the dining areas, kitchen and bathroom in the other wing. The sleeping quarters were on the first floor. In the brochure designed to recruit students it was stated that no school was yet connected to the boarding school. Sufficient enrolments could change this because the new building would then be enlarged and reclassified. The brochure shows a drawing, made by Laurent Logemann on May 20, 1930, with the addition of an extension of the main building with additional classrooms, a presbytery and a small church. Among the 150 attendees at the opening on 23 June there were many clergy from Bangka, Billiton and Singapore. Han de Jongh represented Fermont-Cuypers. A day earlier he had attended the consecration of the Convent in Belinyu one hundred kilometres north. In 1934, the Brothers of Dongen, a different order, took over the school. They also started a school in Sungialat, which is located nearby in the north. Perhaps this ambition contributed to the fact that the vision of Fermont-Cuypers never became reality, because in the end there were not enough pupils at Pangkal Pinang. The church, designed by Fermont-Cuypers, did not materialise either. On the proposed site there was a temporary church building for years, which later made way for an extension of the school. To date, the school is still there and provides education for hundreds of children every year.

Pangkal Pinang, a drawing of the intended complex with from left to right: presbytery, church, and boarding school and school buildings. Because funds were lacking for such a large project, the construction of half of the rightmost building was started, but was not continued CFC

Pangkal Pinang, the school in 2015 WEBSITE SD BUDI

Pangkal Pinang, front of the boarding school annex school shortly after completion in 1931 CFC

30 | 1931 Semarang: British American Tobacco factory

CITY: Semarang
ADDRESS: B.A.T. weg/Jl. Manisharjo Raya/-
ARCHITECT: A. Dikstaal, H. de Jongh
YEAR: 1931
CURRENT SITUATION: demolished in 2018
SOURCES: Gemeente Semarang 1906-1931, p. 103, report city council 1929; *De Telegraaf*, January 25, 1929; *De Indische Courant*, May 2, 1929; *Het Nieuws van den Dag voor Nederlandsch-Indië*, December 27, 1929; *Algemeen Handelsblad*, May 15, 1931; *De Indische Courant*, September 8, 1939; Coté (2017) p. 204; Archive of Fermont-Cuypers

Before the stock market crash of 1929, Fermont-Cuypers was commissioned to design and build a large cigarette factory in Semarang for the British American Tobacco Co. The company must have been satisfied with the factory that the firm had produced for this client five years earlier in Cirebon. 'It is a pity, in a way,' sighed a local newspaper, 'that British American Tobacco could not find another location to build its factory'. The company chose to build the factory on a football field that was completed four years earlier with much effort and expense. 'The local football association will lose a field, as there is hardly another on Java', the newspaper noted.
The new name for the street where the plant was planned, also posed difficulties. The management of British American Tobacco opted for B.A.T. Road (*weg*). The city council did not want to use that name because of fear of the bastardisation of the street name, but the management stood firm. A journalist wrote: 'It is unwise to begrudge those who bring a new and large company to the municipality such a relatively small amount of pleasure'. And so it indeed became the B.A.T. Road (now: Jl. Manisharjo Raya). At Fermont-Cuypers, the design drawings in 1930 were prepared for one of the largest and most modern cigarette factories of that time with a production capacity of fifteen million cigarettes a day. 'If things go well, the factory will be expanded within the foreseeable future, so that the monthly production will increase proportionately', according to a newspaper article. The Hollandsche Beton Maatschappij started the construction in 1930. The factory was 118 metres long by approximately 36 metres wide. It had a hipped roof in spite of the presence of air conditioning. This was therefore primarily introduced to keep the tobacco at a constant temperature, so that changes caused by the outdoor climate did not affect the quality of the tobacco. Constructively, the flat slab floor was unique for Semarang. Thomas Karsten was often mentioned in the context of the flat slab floor, but Karsten's projects with such a floor were utilised in Semarang seven years later. (Pasar Jatingaleh and Pasar Johar). During the building process in May 1931, a newspaper stated that the company had to drastically cut its expenditure and therefore the construction was stopped. A photograph from the second half of 1931 indicates that the building was indeed completed in that year, but without the usual festive opening. In 1939, the firm was commissioned for additional business development on the site. In the remarkable architecture, along the floors there are open galleries, special, outward protruding corner sections give the building a characteristic appearance. A tower rises up out of one of these extensions, as a true eye-catcher.
Unfortunately, the Gudang Sampoera building no longer exists since 2018.

The factory in 2013 CON

Semarang, an aerial photograph of the British American Tobacco factory built in 1931 KNILM/CFC

Semarang, British American Tobacco shortly after the completion in 1931 CFC

31 | 1931 Jakarta: Carolus Hospital, main building, convent and chapel

CITY: Jakarta
ADDRESS: Salemba 41/Jl. Salemba Raya No. 41
ARCHITECT: Th. Taen
YEAR: 1931
CLIENT: Sisters of Mercy of St. Carolus Borromeo from Maastricht (the Netherlands)
CURRENT SITUATION: Rumah Sakit Carolus
SOURCES: *d'Oriënt*, December 6, 1930, p. 8; *Bataviaasch Nieuwsblad*, October 9, 1930; *Koloniaal Missie Tijdschrift* (1931), p. 196; *Koloniaal Missie Tijdschrift* (1931), pp. 251-252; *Koloniaal Missie Tijdschrift*, (1931), pp. 283-284; *De Tijd*, July 25, 1931

In 1930 Fermont-Cuypers built a new front building, with a chapel, a convent and an X-ray and electro-medical department on the grounds of the Carolus hospital on Salemba in Jakarta. The chapel's construction drawings are dated from October. It was built behind the new convent and replaced the emergency chapel from 1920. The villa that stood on the site was maintained during the construction of the chapel. The first foundation stone for the chapel was laid on November 26, 1930. Matthias Kaptijn attended the ceremony on behalf of the firm. With ecclesiastical songs, the location was dedicated, where the altar would be built. As it turned out, the chapel did not stand on the spot where in the 1920s the chapel was planned as part of the main building. An important reason must have been that the original central location for the chapel lent itself better for expansion of the main building in combination with a parking area. The ceremony ended with the usual custom of bricking in a lead cylinder with charter and the foundation stone. One of the speakers pointed out that this simple ceremony was an important next step for the hospital. However, several outbuildings and a separate children's hospital still had to be built. A speaker summarised the situation as follows: 'as long as it lasts, we can move forward', because the growth continues. In 1931, the 12.5-year jubilee of St. Carolus Hospital was festively celebrated in the presence of the chief pastor of Jakarta, many doctors and sisters and numerous former patients. Some stained-glass windows were gifted to the new chapel, which would be consecrated on July 20, 1931.

Jakarta, construction drawing of the convent and chapel dated October 23, 1930 and signed by Philip Wijsman CAA

Jakarta, new entrance building of the Saint Carolus Hospital in 1931, designed by Fermont-Cuypers CFC

Jakarta, the new sister house of the hospital from 1931, designed by Fermont-Cuypers CFC

Jakarta, the chapel of the Saint Carolus Hospital in 1931 with the sister house behind it CFC

Jakarta, the chapel at the Carolus Hospital (Rumah Sakit Carolus) in 2015 CON

Jakarta, the new hospital pavilions of the Saint Carolus Hospital CFC

Jakarta, the new sister house with in the back ground the chaple of the Saint Carolus hospital CFC

32 | 1931 **Banjarmasin: Escomptobank**

CITY: Banjarmasin
ADDRESS: Resident de Haan/Jl. Lambung Mangkurat/-
ARCHITECT: Th. Taen, H. de Jong
YEAR: 1931
CLIENT: Nederlandsch-Indische Escompto Maatschappij
CURRENT SITUATION: Bank Bumi Daya (in the 1980s), now demolished
SOURCES: *Algemeen Handelsblad*, December 15, 1926; *Soerabaijasch Handelsblad*, August 26, 1931; *De Indische courant*, September 29, 1931; *Algemeen Handelsblad*, January 10, 1934; *Het Nieuws van den Dag voor Nederlandsch-Indië*, January 16, 1934

The agent of the bank was photographed at his desk on Friday September 25, 1931, the day of the festive opening of this branch of Nederlandsch-Indische Escompto Maatschappij. On the desk stood an Art-Deco ink set and on the wall behind him hangs the certificate of the foundation stone which was laid on April 17, 1931 by the agent's daughter. At the same time, the agent's own home was completed. Both the certificate and the ink set were designed and offered by Fermont-Cuypers. The construction took less than six months. Almost all of Banjarmasin's dignitaries attended the opening. The agent was the first speaker, followed by Han de Jongh, then the Resident, the Mayor and the chairman of the Trade Association. Many emphasised the courage of the Escompto Maatschappij, which had pursued this project despite the gloom of the economic malaise. Despite all optimism, the Escompto branch in Banjarmasin had to close its doors after two years due to the crisis. The building was completely in the tradition of smaller bank branches designed by the firm. It consisted of a basement, a bell-floor and a hipped roof with overhang. The front façade had three axes with the entrance in the more pronounced central axis with stairs under an awning. For Banjarmasin this was something out of the ordinary. A newspaper observed: 'Almost all houses here are made of wood, because stone is almost impossible, with a view to the swampy soil. The Escompto, however, has had a magnificent office of reinforced concrete built here.'
The construction corresponded with that of the Javasche Bank, which the office built in 1923 in Banjarmasin. Theo Taen also played an important role. Another newspaper reported on an up-to-date bank building with an elegant home for the agent. All rooms of the bank bordered on the spacious public hall: the agent's room, the accounting, the securities department and the money counter. This ensured an efficient operation while the bank staff also had a lot of space because of the long length of the counters. Work could be done quietly and unhindered. The agent's room and the space for money transactions were completely closed, in contrast to the other rooms, which formed a well-ventilated whole with the public hall. Under the fire-proof vault of reinforced concrete was a water reservoir, also of reinforced concrete, the bottom plate of which served as a foundation plate. A covered path was included from the bank to the agent's home. The building on Jalan Lambung Mangkurat disappeared at the beginning of this century.

Inkwell, offered by Fermont-Cuypers at the opening of the bank in Banjermasin CFC

Banjarmasin, the Escomptobank on the day of the opening on September 25, 1931 CAA

Banjarmasin, the agent of the bank, Mr. Spitsbergen, with an inkwell donated by Fermont-Cuypers on his desk and a copy of the charter on the wall as it was bricked in on the day the first stone was laid CAA

Banjarmasin, the cashiers' department CAA

Banjarmasin, the Escomptobank and the agent's residence on September 29, 1931 CAA

Banjarmasin, the Escomptobank and the agent's residence on the day of the opening CAA

Banjarmasin, the former bank in the late 1970s CON

33 | 1931 Jakarta: 'The Good Shepherd' Girls' boarding school

CITY: Jakarta
ADDRESS: Pasarstraat 122/Jl. Jatinegara Barat Raya No. 122
ARCHITECT: Th. Taen
YEAR: 1931
CLIENT: Sisters of the Good Shepherd from Leiderdorp (the Netherlands)
CURRENT SITUATION: SD Santa Maria Fatima
SOURCES: *Onze Missiën in Oost- en West-Indië, tijdschrift der Indische Missie-Vereeniging*, 12, 1927, p. 190; *Het Nieuws van den Dag voor Nederlandsch-Indië,* March 29, 1930; *Bataviaasch Nieuwsblad,* April 4, 1930; *Bataviaasch Nieuwsblad*, November 16, 1939; Brochure of Robert Deppe Batavia, 1938; Vetter (1997), p. 67

In 1926, the Sisters of the Good Shepherd ('De Goede Herder') arrived in the Dutch East Indies. Within a few year, the nuns had to look for a new accommodation with expansion possibilities. Through a foundation, they bought a plot of land on Pasarstraat 122 in July 1928, the location of a regent's former home. The site covered approximately 25,000 square metres, of which approximately 4,600 square metres had to be left undeveloped as a riverbank. There was a problem with the purchase: the council of the municipality of Meester Cornelis (now: Jatinegara) had drawn up a road plan with a road intersecting the site. Before a decision on the sale was taken, Arthur Fermont acted on behalf of the foundation and contacted the mayor, who said that the road plan was subject to change and that the projected transverse route could, in theory, be cancelled. With this commitment, the foundation bought the land for Fl. 50,000. Then the council turned against the mayor's promise and after many discussions, both the municipality and the foundation had to adjust their plans. For example, the home of the regent had to fit in and the construction of the road had to be taken into account until further notice. At that time, a local newspaper printed a bird's-eye view with the original plan of Fermont-Cuypers. The drawing shows an extensive building complex surrounding enclosed gardens with a chapel on the site of the regent's old home. Two-storey buildings would be built under one roof along the river. Along the road, the plan provided for the construction of a one-storey building under a roof. Behind the intended chapel, a covered gallery had to bridge a height difference of three metres. As a result of the troubles with the municipality, the chapel had to be relocated in order to save the old house. Construction of the modified plan commenced in March 1931. The refurbished home was to serve as a convent. On November 5, 1931, the new girls' boarding school could be inaugurated. Shortly after completion, Matthias Kaptijn took some photos of the straightforward design of the buildings around a courtyard with lots of trees.

Construction of the chapel did not start until 1940 and was located closer to the road than in the first plan. From 1945 on, the complex temporarily served as a provisional hospital for people from the internment camps. For many years now, is has served as a school.

Jakarta, the relief of 'de Goede Herder' (Good Shepherd), designed in the studio of Robert Deppe CFC

Jakarta, the main building of the extensive complex of the Sisters of 'de Goede Herder' (Good Shepherd) with the relief above the entrance CFC

Jakarta, the lower buildings along the water, with the courtyard filled with the many trees that all survived because of the shade they provided CFC

34 | 1931 **Solo: Catholic Church and presbytery** (design)

CITY: Solo
ADDRESS: unknown
ARCHITECT: C.Th. Nix
YEAR: 1931
CLIENT: Jesuit Fathers
CURRENT SITUATION: not built
SOURCES: *De Indische Courant*, September 8, 1931; *De Maasbode*, December 24, 1931; Schlömer (1934); Groenen (1940); HNI CUYZ 0353377; Archive of Fermont-Cuypers

On October 31, 1931, Thomas Nix completed the bird's eye view of a church building in Solo 'intended for Catholic services in Javanese'. Was it a competition or did Fermont-Cuypers make himself more noticeable after they discovered that Van Oyen was being considered by the client. Two months later, *De Maasbode* announced in the Netherlands on December 24, 1931: 'Solo, almost the most important city of the Vorstenlanden, has developed in recent years into an important place, and for the Catholics too. The time has come for us to see how the church building in Solo, which was still too large a decade ago for the number of churchgoers, now offers insufficient space. An expansion of church space had to be found; and the solution will have to be found by establishing several church buildings. The old church building was not eligible for expansion, so Father Koch S.J. bought another site. The architect J. Th. van Oyen designed a truly beautiful church building' according to *De Maasbode*. 'The Van Oyen church should have provided space for 300 seats and 750 squatting places'. Sadly, the church was never built. Thomas Nix's design was also never used.

Solo, a bird's-eye view of the design for a Catholic church signed by Thomas Nix CFC

35 | 1932 **Jakarta: Hotel des Galeries**

CITY: Jakarta.
ADDRESS: Molenvliet-east 1/Jl. Hayam Wuruk No. 1
ARCHITECT: A. Dikstaal, C.Th. Nix
YEAR: 1932 (design 1930)
CLIENT: Sajid Saleh bin Obeid bin Abdat
CURRENT SITUATION: unrecognisably converted
SOURCES: *Bataviaasch Nieuwsblad*, July 1, 1930; *De Indische Courant*, October 4, 1930; *De Sumatra Post*, October 13, 1930; *Bataviaasch Nieuwsblad*, October 22, 1930; *Het Nieuws van den Dag voor Nederlandsch-Indië*, October 22, 1930; *Het Vaderland*, November 11, 1930; *d'Oriënt* (1932), no. 3; *Bataviaasch Nieuwsblad*, September 24, 1931; *Algemeen Handelsblad*, October 23, 1931; *Het Nieuws van den Dag voor Nederlandsch-Indië*, April 22, 1932; *Het Nieuws van den Dag voor Nederlandsch-Indië*, May 3, 1932; *Het Nieuws van den Dag voor Nederlandsch-Indië*, May 6, 1932; *Algemeen Handelsblad*, August 27, 1932; *Algemeen Handelsblad*, October 23, 1932; Bergeijk (1995), p. 177; Archive of Fermont-Cuypers

On July 1, 1930, *Het Bataviaasch Nieuwsblad* had the headline: 'Shopping gallery on Noordwijk', 'The Fermont-Cuypers firm has already produced a complete design for the shopping gallery'. *Het Nieuws van den Dag voor Nederlandsch-Indië* wrote in response to the drawings: 'Batavia is gradually becoming a big city', to write a year later: 'This new building is a jewel for the Harmonieplein (now: Harmoni) and gives the capital more the cachet of a truly big city. Everyone who visits Batavia comes to this building, which stands out on the Harmonieplein since its opening on January 1, 1932.' This was once the location of Hotel Wisse, which fell into disrepair and was bought by an Arab named Sech Saleih bin Obeid bin Abdat. He wanted a hotel annex shopping centre, and so in 1932 not only the largest apartment building, but also Jakarta's largest shopping gallery was created. On the ground floor there were 15 retail units; on the first and second floor, each 24 flats. The shop on the corner, visible on both Noordwijk (now: Jl. Ir. H. Juanda) and Molenvliet (now: Jl. Hayam Wuruk), was particularly well-positioned. Above this was a large café/restaurant with terrace on the first floor. On the second floor there were the offices and the home of the manager, while on the third floor there was a terrace for the residents. Two lifts and three staircases gave access to the upper floors. It was said that the café-restaurant could certainly be one of Jakarta's busiest places, thanks to the terrace. The houses were very spacious and fully equipped. On the ground floor, the garages had been built behind the shops. A newspaper writes: 'The design leaves nothing to be desired architecturally, as our photo shows. We have found the building to be solid and excellently appointed during a visit this morning.'

The building had sculptural qualities due to the wrap-around, horizontally rounded horizontals in the form of the parapets under the horizontal window strips and accompanying frames. As sculptors, Dikstaal and Nix added two towers to the Harmonieplein as vertical elements, a low one at the Molenvliet side (now: Jl. Hayam Wuruk)), a high one on the busy Noordwijk (now: Jl. Ir. H. Juanda) as an eye-catcher. It thus guided the traffic flows at this junction in the city. It formed a visible link between the north and the south of Jakarta. Dikstaal brought the spirit of the famous Dutch architect Dudok to the firm, for whom architecture could take on the character of three-dimensional composition. Just half a year after the opening of the now architecturally famous city hall of Hilversum in the Netherlands, Jakarta welcomed this unique Hotel des Galeries.

It is a loss for Jakarta that this building has been stripped of everything that was special and timeless.

Jakarta, a photo of Hotel des Galeries, seen from the Harmonieplein (now: Harmoni), shortly after the completion in 1932 CAA

Jakarta, Hotel des Galeries seen from Molenvliet (now: Jl. Hayam Wuruk) towards Harmonieplein (now: Harmoni).
The advertising mast, which stood since 1933, generated some income CAA

Jakarta, view from Hotel des Galeries in 1935 CON

Jakarta 1933, Hotel des Galeries with a rented shop unit and a well-paved footway CFC

Jakarta, Hotel des Galeries and surroundings on an aerial photo from around 1935 KNILM/CFC

< Jakarta, Hotel des Galeries in 1935, now fully operational KITLV 45052

36 | 1932 Muntok: Catholic church, school, convent, boarding school

CITY: Muntok
ADDRESS: /Jl. Basuki Rachmat No. 208
ARCHITECT: Th. Taen, C.Th. Nix
YEAR: 1932
CLIENT: Poor Sisters of the Divine Child from Amsterdam
CURRENT SITUATION: church and school TD-SD-SMP Santa Maria
SOURCES: *De Indische Courant*, January 12, 1932; *Het Nieuws van den Dag voor Nederlandsch-Indië*, June 16, 1931; *Het Nieuws van den Dag voor Nederlandsch-Indië*, January 29, 1932; *De Sumatra Post*, January 29, 1932; *Koloniaal Missie Tijdschrift* (1932), p. 339; *Het Nieuws van den Dag voor Nederlandsch-Indië*, August 1, 1932. Archive of KDC: various photos

Muntok, the capital of Bangka until 1913, consisted mainly of an old compact residential core called the Chinese Camp. This was close to the harbour with a harbour pier that was also used by the ships of the K.P.M. ('Koninklijke Pakketvaart Maatschappij': Royal Packet Shipping Company, now: Pelni). Further inland, there was an area with detached colonial buildings on country roads in lush green surroundings, with a hotel, hospital, post office, a few schools and various 'luxury' homes of the local dignitaries. On Monday January 11, 1932, the Resident, the chief of the Bangka Tin Winning and other authorities attended the inauguration of the new buildings of the Roman Catholic mission a school, convent and boarding school. A church was later added, also designed by Fermont-Cuypers. The complex is on the corner of the road to the Lieutenant's residence and the road to the residential office, because street names were not known in Muntok in the 1930s. Fermont-Cuypers based their design on a global urban plan of a civilian civil servant. The available grounds were divided up functionally. The programme included a monastery annex convent, a school with four classrooms, a girls' boarding school and various outbuildings, including a toilet, laundry facilities, recreation rooms, all served by covered connecting paths. The boarding school was positioned by Fermont-Cuypers in one of the corners of the complex, where both the building mass and the roof met. As the firm often did, they used a damp-proof course of river pebbles with white plaster applied above it. The parish church was erected next to the boarding school, its foundation stone was laid on February 14, 1932. After a construction period of less than six months, this building could also be consecrated on July 24, 1932. It is a charming church building, not only because of the architecture that with the combination of Art Deco and expressionism is typical for Fermont-Cuypers, but also because of the care devoted to the entire project. The large, composite roof, from the front a composition with triangles, reveals the spatial layout inside. The church hall of 9 by 15 metres offers space for 130 seats, all with a view of the altar. The colourful high-placed stained-glass windows show geometric patterns relating to Biblical symbols in the colours green, blue, red, pink, purple, orange, yellow and white. They were, like the furniture, also designed by Fermont-Cuypers.

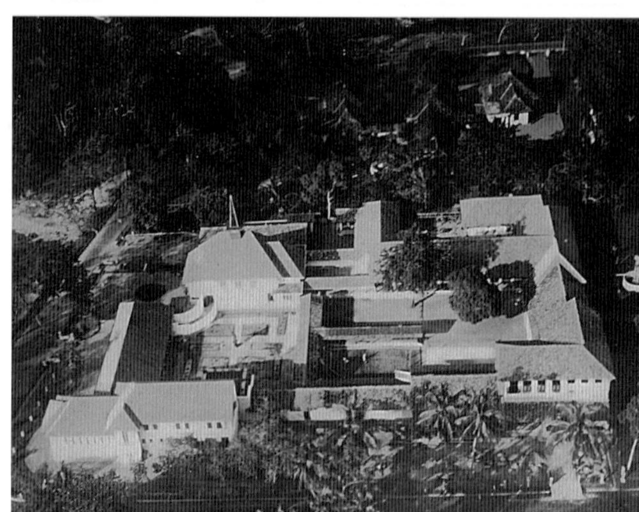

Aerial photo from the thirties, with from left to right; the monastery, the church and the school complex KDC TF6A4223

The eighty-five year-old church and school in Muntok photographed in 2017 CON

37 | 1932 **Semarang: Franciscan Sisters' school**

CITY: Semarang
ADDRESS: Pendrikan/Jl. Imam Bonjol No. 98
ARCHITECT: Th. Taen, C.Th. Nix
YEAR: 1932
CLIENT: Franciscan Sisters from Heythuysen (the Netherlands)
CURRENT SITUATION: SMP Maria Goretti
SOURCES: *Koloniaal Missie Tijdschrift*, (1932), p. 303; Hoof (1934), p. 370; Polman (1935); HNI: CUYZ 0353370

On December 27, 1931, Father Van Kalken S.J. laid the first stone for this school. Han de Jongh was present, representing Fermont-Cuypers. Van Kalken became familiar with the firm during the construction of the Saint Joseph Church (1924) and the Saint Louis Institute (1930) in Ambarawa. He appears to be as ambitious as Fermont-Cuypers. The architecture firm set a long-term vision on paper for the development of a large building complex with a teacher training school, a boarding school, a primary school, a Fröbel school, a convent and a chapel. The complex was to be erected on a site between Bodjong (now: Jl. Pemuda) and Pendrikan (now: Jl. Imam Bonjol) and was meant for pupils and teachers who used the school building in Semarang-Bangkong, which was considered less suitable due to new insights from 1908. At the office they were happy with this commission from a city where their colleague J. Th. van Oyen was dominantly present. On the drawing that Thomas Nix produced, the convent and boarding school are projected along Bodjong and the school complex is located along Pendrikan. Both complexes consist of buildings surrounding an enclosed garden, in which the large trees were maintained. The front of the main building had to be on the street with an evocative turret with bell. The chapel was to form the link between the two complexes. The architecture can be described as an Indies interpretation of what is known as the Delft School in the Netherlands. Nix adapted his Delft theory into Indies practice here. New for Fermont-Cuypers were the round vents and the small round window above the main entrance.

After the inauguration of the school on June 26, 1932, the three departments of Bangkong moved to the new building, enabling new beginnings for the Fröbel and primary school with 400 pupils, the MULO school (junior secondary school) and the teacher training school.
The monastery and the other buildings on Bodjong (now: Jl. Pemuda), as designed by Fermont-Cuypers, were never built.

Semarang, the stained-glass windows in the stairwell of the school CVN

Semarang 1932, the new school building from the courtyard CFC

Semarang, the school in 2016 CVN

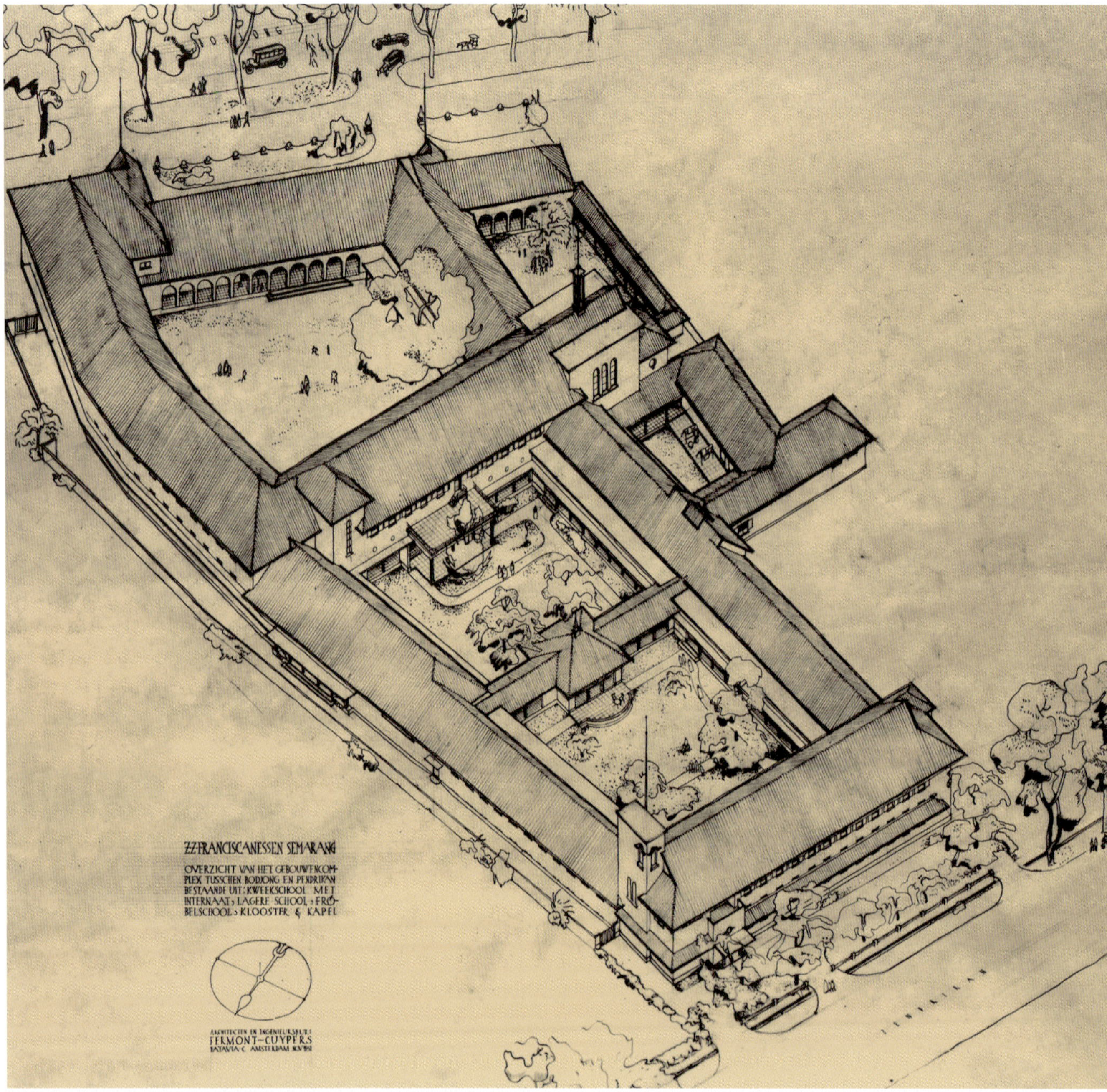

Semarang, a bird's-eye drawing by Thomas Nix of the school and convent complex, where, partly as a result of the crisis, only the front part of it was built CFC

Semarang 1932, the school building with the remarkable bell tower seen in 1935 from the Pendrikanstraat (now: Jl. Imam Bonjol) CFC

Semarang, an aerial photograph from 1935 of the entire complex seen from Bodjong (Jl. Pemuda) KNILM/CFC

38 | 1932 **Jakarta: Van Lith school with chapel**

CITY: Jakarta
ADDRESS: Tanah Njonja 2/Jl. Gunung Sahari Raya No. 91
ARCHITECT: Th. Taen
YEAR: 1932
CLIENT: Brothers from Dongen (the Netherlands)
CURRENT SITUATION: SMP Van Lith Jenjang
SOURCES: *Bataviaasch Nieuwsblad*, March 30, 1932; *Koloniaal Missie Tijdschrift* (1932), p. 179; CEK: AR-B004 photalbum 11604, p. 37: CEK: AR-B004-1483. *60 jaar missiewerk in Indonesië, 1926-1986*, pp. 31-34. Archive of Fermont-Cuypers

At the end of August 1930, an auction was held in a house on Tanah Njonja 2. The residents wanted to sell off their things, which usually signalled a relocation. The building was located near a school of the Brothers from Dongen. Fermont-Cuypers was instructed to check what was going on with the house. After research they let it be known that the building was for sale. On September 3, the Brothers from Dongen became the owners of the building with a large piece of land. Fermont-Cuypers was asked to design a school complex, with a monastery in the old building. The Dutch East Indies Department of Education was initially unwilling to grant a subsidy for a new school, 'which would be too far from the road', but in January 1931, after some urging, a positive decision followed. The firm's design was for seven classes with galleries and a pavilion structure (*pendopo*) for Fl. 41,800. Construction started on November 2, 1931. On March 30, 1932, the school, named after Frans van Lith S.J. (1863-1926), was completed. Afterwards, the interested attendees were given a tour of a simple but efficient building. The main building connected a number of work and living rooms of the Brothers, the sacristy, kitchen, seven classrooms and a bicycle shed, grouped around a courtyard garden, where a small chapel was built shortly afterwards next to the pavilion structure. The chapel was, also designed by Fermont-Cuypers. The chapel still exists. The current school buildings are new.

Jakarta, the SMP Van Lith school and chapel in 2017 CON

39 | 1932 Pekalongan: Primary school, Fröbel school

CITY: Pekalongan
ADDRESS: Heerenstraat 13/Jl. Progo No. 16
ARCHITECT: Th. Taen
YEAR: 1932
CLIENT: Ursuline Sisters from Weltevreden
CURRENT SITUATION: SD Pius Pekalongan
SOURCES: *De Indische Courant*, May 8, 1931; *De Tijd*, May 22, 1931; *Bataviaasch Nieuwsblad*, March 19, 1932; *Het Nieuws van den Dag voor Nederlandsch-Indië*, March 19, 1932; *Koloniaal Missie Tijdschrift* (1932), p. 165. Archief CEK: AR-Z117. Inventaris Ursulinen van de Romeinse Unie: 10425; CKD: LARC2744, *Archieven van Weltevreden*

On May 8, 1931 Fermont-Cuypers, on behalf of the Ursuline Sisters of the Little Monastery in Jakarta, filed an application with the municipal administration of Pekalongan for the construction of a St. Joseph convent. To this end, the Sisters had purchased a piece of land with three dwellings located on the Heerenstraat (now: Jl. Progo) for Fl. 50,000. The intention was that one of the existing buildings be renovated and expanded to create a convent and school. A newspaper described the commission as follows: 'The renovation consists of converting the old residence into two classrooms, a consulting room, dining room, linen room and sitting room. In addition, the outbuildings on both sides of the present house are to be converted on one side into a chapel, sacristy and confessional room, while the outbuildings on the other side will be converted into a Fröbel classroom annex storage, kitchen and bathroom. The expectation is that the entire complex will certainly enhance the cityscape.' However, everything turned out to be temporary. The intention was to start building soon after acquiring the necessary permits from the municipality. On March 19, 1932, the first stone was laid for the First European Primary and Fröbel School in Pekalongan, the St. Joseph school. The pastor of Purworejo performed this ceremony on the first Friday in August 1932. Two years later the complex expanded with a Dutch Chinese School and a domestic school would be added. Until well into the 1940s, the school and monastery complex lay between the Heerenstraat and the Residentweg (now: Jl. Diponegoro and Jl. Progo). The current buildings are new.

Pekalongan, the small school complex around a courtyard CFC

Pekalongan, galleries of the school complex CFC

40 | 1932 **Jakarta: Sancta Ursula convent**

CITY: Jakarta
ADDRESS: Postweg 2/Jl. Pos No. 2
ARCHITECT: Th. Taen
YEAR: 1932
CLIENT: Ursuline Sisters of Weltevreden
CURRENT SITUATION: Santa Ursula
SOURCES: Archive of KDC: LARC2744 *Archieven van Weltevreden*; Hoof (1934), pp. 369, 375

The existing buildings of the so-called Little Convent ('Kleine Klooster') stood just north of the cathedral, wedged between the Waterlooplein (now: Taman Lapangan Banteng) and the Postweg (now: Jl. Pos). On both sides were grounds and buildings of the Post Office. To make the construction of a new convent possible, a piece of land from the post office had to be purchased. Fermont-Cuypers designed three buildings that were positioned around a garden in the form of a U. The longest structure, of about 85 by 15 metres, consisted of two high floors with a generous roof. One of the buildings at right angles to it, included a ground area of about 15 by 25 metres, had two storeys, a roof and small roof turret. The third building with a comparable surface area is too low to be connected to the two old villas on the Postweg. Almost all rooms in the buildings open out onto an open gallery with a view of the garden. The first stone was laid on December 8, 1931. The building complex was consecrated on October 21, 1932.
An effective extension was to be created, using a light and airy design, without sophisticated details, although the eye was definitely drawn to the round vents when viewed from the beautifully landscaped convent garden. The new building provided space for a dining room, various rooms, hospital rooms and many bedrooms on the first floor. From the Postweg the project is now hidden behind the villas and the chapel dating from 1889, once designed by Father Dijkmans S.J. (1851-1922) who also made the cathedral design. That chapel came with this expansion in the middle of a complex, of which the oldest buildings still date from 1859.

Jakarta, gallery of the monastery in 2015 CVN

Jakarta, the Little Convent seen from the north with the U-shaped new building surrounding the convent garden in the 1930s KNILM/CFC

Jakarta 1934, the Little Convent seen from the cathedral, in the foreground is the new building for, among other things, the sister house KNILM/CEK

41 | 1932 **Rangkasbitung: Regency Council of Lebak**

CITY: Rangkasbitung
ADDRESS: Aloen Aloen/Jl. Alun Alun Selatan No. 2
ARCHITECT: Th. Taen
YEAR: 1932
CLIENT: Regency Board of Lebak
CURRENT SITUATION: Kantor Bupati Lebak
SOURCES: *Het Nieuws van den Dag voor Nederlandsch-Indië*, December 8, 1932; Perron (1956), p. 7

'In January 1937, more than 80 years after the Lebak case, I travelled to Rangkasbitung, with the idea of writing a commemorative article. I chose a train that brought me there in 3 hours from Jakarta. One is inclined to think of the town of Lebak, which is by no means along the railway, but whose name is immortalised by Multatuli as the administrative department [...] Rangkasbitung where the Regent and the assistant-Resident could see each other's lamps on the Alun-Alun in the evening. This Alun-Alun is spacious and beautiful, and next to the regent's residence (*kaboepatèn*) a brand new building has been erected bearing the name 'Regentschapsraad'. By the way, Rangkasbitung is now a sweet, clean Indies town, consisting of that Alun-Alun as a centre for shopping, a small Chinese shopping district and two long streets, one of which is named after Multatuli', wrote Eddy du Perron.
He will not have realised that the new building he saw was a product of Fermont-Cuypers. The regency council of Lebak officially opened it on December 8, 1932. Han de Jongh attended the opening ceremony on behalf of the firm. The Regent held a speech on that occasion, in which he described the long and painful process preceding the building creation. The initial, agreed amount of money for the government construction, ended with a 'no'. As a result, a loan of Fl. 35,000 was required. One of the speakers expressed the hope that the building would instil the zest for work of the members of the Regency Council and of course a portrait of Queen Wilhelmina was presented. Finally, the Regent of Lebak thanked those present for the interest shown with the words: 'I hope that the bond between the Netherlands and the Dutch East Indies can continue for years to the benefit of the land and the people'. With the cutting of a ribbon, a cannon shot and fireworks, the opening took place. De Jongh organised a tour in which 'visitors discovered the efficient and neat finish of the new building', a newspaper summed up. Then drinks and refreshments were offered. The party ended with the ritual burial of the water-buffalo head, after which peace returns. This was the peace that Du Perron described.
The building indeed fits in with the firm's effective approach, with a one-storeyed, long, symmetrical façade on the street with an overhanging roof. In the wide middle axis is the entrance with stairs and awning. The façade consists of a damp course of a natural glazed tile and white plaster. Above the wide windows there are smaller ventilation openings and, on the roof, the well-known ventilation tower, now equipped with a bell.

Rangkasbitung, the building in 2017 COF INTERNET

› Rangkasbitung 1932, photographs of the building for the Regency Council in the completion phase CFC

Rangkasbitung, the almost completed building for the Regency Council in 1932 CFC

42 | 1933 Rangkasbitung: Hospital

CITY: Rangkasbitung
ADDRESS: Multatuliweg 38/Jl. Multatuli No. 41
ARCHITECT: Th. Taen
YEAR: 1933
CLIENT: Franciscan Sisters of the Missionaries of Mary
CURRENT SITUATION: RS Misi Lebak
SOURCES: *Het Nieuws van den Dag voor Nederlandsch-Indië*, February 28, 1933; *Het Nieuws van den Dag voor Nederlandsch-Indië*, March 2, 1933; DE SUMATRA POST, March 6, 1933; Schlömer (1934), p. 64

On March 1, 1933, Fermont-Cuypers handed over the hospital to the Lebak Hospital association. There was only a small group present at the ceremony with the Regent van Lebak, as Honorary Chairman of the board. The plans for the establishment of the hospital dated from 1927. The execution encountered objections and postponements time and again, until finally the first phase of the construction started. This resulted in a very small hospital that looked more like a house than a hospital, which was the intention. Only when there was enough money could the construction of the actual hospital begin. Fermont-Cuypers had the plans ready. The buildings from phase 1 could then serve as the director's residence. The small building offered room for fifteen patients. The operating room was in the front of the building. In a specially constructed section, six sisters had their residence Those sisters were missing at the opening. And there were other logistical problems. The instruments for nursing also had yet to arrive. Three weeks later, six Franciscan Sisters arrived from a congregation that still had to gain experience of working in the tropics. They had collected a lot of money in the Netherlands. Patients were not there yet, but the sisters had their hands full getting everything organised. Moreover, they had to get used to the climate, according to a journalist. Shortly thereafter, the hospital underwent an extension and the sisters could make use of a brand new convent with a small chapel, both also designed and built by Fermont-Cuypers.

It was built according to the tried and tested approach, finely finished: a plinth of *batu-lempeng*, a natural stone, with white plaster, wide window openings with small ventilation grates above, a large roof overhang, awnings in front of the entrance with open galleries to the garden.
A new hospital building has recently been added to the small old hospital from 1933.

Rangkasbitung, Multatuliweg (Jl. Multatuli) near the hospital in 1934 CFC

Rangkasbitung 1933, the final touches are put to the small hospital, awaiting the arrival of the nursing staff CFC

Rangkasbitung, on the right the small chapel and on the left the hospital building that, on further growth of the hospital, later had to serve as a doctor's house CFC

43 | 1933 **Jakarta: Dutch-Chinese Primary school**

CITY: Jakarta
Address: Prinsenlaan 135/Jl. Raya Mangga Besar No.135/-
ARCHITECT: Th. Taen
YEAR: 1933-1936
CLIENT: Brothers from Dongen (the Netherlands)
CURRENT SITUATION: new construction: Yayasan Budi Mulia Lourdes (PG / TK-SD-SMP-SMA)
SOURCES: *Het Nieuws van den Dag voor Nederlandsch-Indië*, June 27, 1933; *Koloniaal Missie Tijdschrift* (1933), p. 286; Hoof (1934), p. 386; CEK AR-B004-1586, CEK AR-B004-1483; *60 jaar Missiewerk in Indonesië 1926-1986*, pp. 34 -37

After the Brothers from Dongen became owners of the grounds on the Prinsenlaan (now: Jl. Mangga Besar Raya), they approached Fermont-Cuypers for the construction of a school with four classes to begin with, for a maximum amount of Fl. 20,000. In addition, the firm had to arrange the building permit; set up an investigation because of the Public Nuisance Act (*Hinderwet*) in connection with the adjacent hospital; and they had to take care of the relocation of two graves on the site. Construction started on January 31, 1933. On June 27, 1933 the inaugural ceremony took place of the Dutch-Chinese School. A few clerics, the Major of the Chinese and representatives from various Chinese associations, attended the event. Arthur Fermont represented the firm. After the attendees had taken their places in the indoor play area behind the classrooms, a pastor spoke to them. 'What did not succeed in the golden age has now succeeded in this silver period', said the speaker, without the support of the Government. The pastor wished the Brothers good luck with their beautiful school and the Chinese residents with this opportunity to let their children learn and the Fermont-Cuypers firm success with the construction work. Arthur Fermont pointed out that the concrete school building had been kept as simple as possible. The firm was complimented that it had done all that with limited cash. Fermont-Cuypers was also thanked for the bell, which was given to the school board as a gift and for the photo album containing a map and some 15 photos, made shortly after completion. The school consisted of a pre-school class, a first and a second class and a fourth room, which was put into use in 1934. The four school classrooms that stood in a straight line along the Prinsenlaan (now: Jl. Mangga Besar Raya), were airy and built under a generous roof. The assembly hall had a roof construction, with open ends for ventilation. The school furniture was also designed and produced by Fermont-Cuypers.
The complex was replaced by another school building.

Jakarta, Yaysan Budi Mulia Lourdes school in 2015 CON

Jakarta 1933, classrooms of the 'Hollandsch Chinese School' (Dutch-Chinese School) around a green playing field CEK

Jakarta 1933, buildings including the covered playground of the 'Hollandsch Chinese School' (Dutch-Chinese School) CFC

44 | 1933 Jakarta: Sancta Maria Teacher Training School

CITY: Jakarta
ADDRESS: Waterlooplein/Jl. Lap.Banteng Utara or Jl. Pos No. 2
Architect: Th. Taen, C.Th. Nix
YEAR: 1933
CLIENT: Ursuline Sisters from Weltevreden
CURRENT SITUATION: SMA Santa Ursula
SOURCES: *Soerabaijasch Handelsblad* 16-03-1931; *De Tijd*, May 22, 1931; Hoof (1934) p. 386; KDC: LARC2744 Archieven van Weltevreden

The decision to lengthen the three-year H.B.S. secondary school into a five-year course meant that the old Juliana school (now: Santa Ursula Junior High School) had to undergo a reorganisation and an expansion. The old building, opened on July 4, 1910 and designed by civil servants of Burgerlijke Openbare Werken' (Civil Public Works) in the so-called 'Dutch East Indies Building Style', had to be left intact as much as possible. In addition, a teacher training school had to be built on the site. Fermont-Cuypers was asked to execute this complicated integration plan. By purchasing a narrow strip of land on the east side of the Juliana school, the entrance to the teacher training school could be created on that side, accessible from the public road. New two-storey buildings appeared with a roof and the entrance on the ground floor, behind the old school. A stairwell and hallways had been created in order to access the new classrooms, a drawing room, a craft room and a gym with rubber floor. An assembly hall and a few Fröbel classes were located on the ground floor. In order to increase the visibility of the new access from the Waterlooplein, the new building jutted forward even though it was behind the school. Unlike in the old building, no arched windows were used. The round element only returned in the ventilation openings above the five high rectangular windows. This created some affinity with the more than twenty-year-old building. The building still exists. Inside, the tiled floors stand out, as do the robust stairs. On June 30, 1933, the school was consecrated in church, and officially opened a day later. The five-year H.B.S. secondary school was given the name 'Sancta Ursula', while the teacher training school was called Sancta Maria. Years later, all buildings are still unchanged and in use under that name, only no longer accessible through the doors on the former Waterlooplein (now: Taman Lapangan Benteng).

Jakarta 1933, the large hall in the building with staircase and tiled floor
CFC

Jakarta 1933, the hall and staircase between the teacher-training school, the convent buildings and the Juliana school (SMA Santa Ursula) CFC

Jakarta, the entrance of the Sancta Maria teacher-training school shortly after the new building is put into use CFC

Jakarta 1933, on the left the school building from 1910 with in the background the new entrance to the teacher-training school CFC

45 | 1933 **Ambarawa: Chapel at St. Louis Institute**

CITY: Ambarawa
ADDRESS: road to Magelang/Jl. Mgr. Sugiyapranata No. 191
ARCHITECT: Th. Taen, A. Dikstaal
YEAR: 1933
CLIENT: Brothers from Maastricht (the Netherlands)
CURRENT SITUATION: chapel SMP Pangudiluhur
SOURCES: *Koloniaal Missie Tijdschrift*, (1933), p. 286; Hoof (1934), p. 386; *Het Nieuws van den Dag voor Nederlandsch-Indië*, July 6, 1933; Christinus (1940), pp. 210-211; Interview with Mrs. M Dikstaal-van der Bijl on May 23, 2014

At less than 400 metres from the St. Josef College and St. Josef's Church, the Saint Louis Chapel of Saint Stanislaus came into use on Sunday, July 2, 1933. A chapel was still missing at the building complex that had developed around an existing house, with Father Van Kalken S.J. as a driving force from 1927 onwards . The priest was inspired by the successes of Muntilan and wanted to train young Javanese at this boarding school. In that sense, the formula was unique in that, besides Javanese, young people of European descent were also eligible. Dikstaal and Taen took into account from the outset the existing U-shaped ensemble of buildings. In it were the sleeping quarters, study places and other living quarters, adjacent to an open gallery. The chapel had to be built immediately behind the main entrance, making it visibly the centre of the total complex. The first stone was laid on February 11, 1932 in the presence of Arnold Dikstaal, who supervised the building process on behalf of the firm. A photo taken during the construction shows that building methods in 1932 are little different than in the time of Hulswit, about thirty years earlier. Arthur Fermont attended the inauguration, who as a newspaper notes, had come over from Jakarta especially. Arnold Dikstaal and his wife were also present.
The entrance was located behind the façade, in a gallery with an awning in front. On the outside, awnings were placed along both side walls over a great length, covering the buildings at the level of the choir as a type of spacious tent roof. On the roof there is a carefully detailed roof turret just behind the façade, with a nice structure for a clock. As with the church in Bandung East, the designers opted for a wooden construction without horizontal beams. The trusses were still clearly visible on the inside, probably on the advice of Dikstaal. The chapel was not as wide as the church in Bandung East, but it has a comparable height, which makes it appear much more slender.

Arnold Dikstaal's son, who, as a small child with his mother in St. Louis, was locked up in the Ambarawa internment camp during the war, later revisited the church in his old age and said: 'this was the building my father was most devoted to'.

Ambarawa, the chapel of the St. Louis Institute shortly before the consecration on July 6, 1933 CNJ

Ambarawa, 'This was the building my father was most devoted to', said the son of Arnold Dikstaal during a visit to this chapel CON

46 | 1933 **Purworejo: Catholic church**

CITY: Purworejo
ADDRESS: Heerenstraat 7/Jl. KH Wahid Hasyim No. 1
ARCHITECT: C.Th. Nix
YEAR: 1933
CLIENT: MSC Missionaries from Tilburg (the Netherlands)
CURRENT SITUATION: Gerja Katolik St. Perawan Maria
SOURCES: *De Limburger Koerier*, February 8, 1928; Archive of Brothers from Dongen; Archive of Fermont-Cuypers.

De *Limburger Koerier* of February 8, 1928 wrote: 'The missionaries of the Sacred Heart of Jesus from Tilburg started a new mission in central Java and settled provisionally in Purworejo at the end of October, because there was just a very small church and a presbytery already present. It will be difficult to work there. After all, communism is gaining a strong foothold in this region, and it is unfortunate that so little has been achieved among a population of 5 million. There is only one Dutch Indonesian School with over 300 pupils; and then there is a *schakel* school (connecting or link school), where two Javanese teachers teach the studious youth in Dutch'. On March 12, 1933, the first stone was laid for the new Catholic church of Purworejo. Fermont-Cuypers sent the design drawing of Thomas Nix to the editorial board of the *Missie* journal's jubilee number which was to be published in 1934. This, of course, was used as an advertisement.
On August 13, 1933, the church could be consecrated.
The building is located in northwest-southeast direction, near the Alun-Alun and the post office. The construction had to remain simple, as the building costs of approximately Fl. 28,000 left little room for more. The construction corresponded with the church in Purwokerto that had been created three years earlier with identical module sizes. The tight budget still had to produce as many seats as possible here. The total length of the church is about 36 metres, with a width of 16 metres. The main entrance on the southeast side stands out with a large awning. As in Purwokerto, the church has a low and narrow side aisle on both long sides, which is not intended for seating. The middle aisle has a hipped roof with a large overhang, covered with roof tiles. The simple roof turret is located a short distance from the front façade, so that it serves as an eye-catcher. Still, this was a less expensive option compared to the larger tower of the church in Purwokerto. Inside, the church breathes modernity in the furniture, the columns and the light, and the light ceiling frame with square plates, which were also applied to the walls. In the light aisle, there are windows in the form of horizontal rectangles with again a quadratic row distribution. The windows in the side aisles have been kept relatively small with a round opening here and there.
The building still exists and is gratefully used.

Purworejo, the entrance side in 2013 CON

Purworejo, a drawing by Thomas Nix from 1933 of the new church CFC

Purworejo, the consecration of the church on August 13, 1933 CFC

Purworejo, one of the aisles of the generously proportioned church from 1933 CFC

Purworejo, the Gereja St. Perawan Maria in 2013 CON

Purworejo, the interior of the church in a sober and unfussy architectural style shortly before the consecration CFC

Purworejo, the entrance of the church a few years after construction CFC

47 | 1933 Palembang: Boarding school and Fröbel school

CITY: Palembang
ADDRESS: Talang Djawa area 19/Jl. Kol. Atmo 132/-
Architect: Th. Taen, C.Th. Nix
Year: 1933
CLIENT: Sisters from Moerdijk (the Netherlands)
BUILDER: Hollandsche Beton Maatschappij N.V.
CURRENT SITUATION: SMA Xaverius (original buildings have been rebuilt)
SOURCES: *Bataviaasch Nieuwsblad*, June 2, 1933; *Bataviaasch Nieuwsblad*, December 8, 1933; *Koloniaal Missie Tijdschrift* (1935), pp. 143-145.

In June 1933, the Fermont-Cuypers firm in Weltevreden had completed the plans to bid on a school with a girls' boarding school in Palembang. This was to be built in phases, because not enough money was available for the entire project. The initiative and the money came from the sisters of the Most Sacred Heart of Jesus from Moerdijk. Thomas Nix made a design for a modern-looking main building, which was to stand at right angles to the Talang Djawaweg (now: Jl. Kol. Atmo), directly behind an old wooden school building. That would make way for an expansion of the main building, as soon as there was money available The Hollandsche Beton Maatschappij was awarded the tender with the lowest bid and completed the building on 15 November of the same year, which was as agreed, half of the project. The inauguration took place on December 8, 1933. Behind the main building was the Fröbel school, which until then, had been very poorly housed. The new boarding school had the living areas, dining room, reading room and a few classrooms downstairs. On the first floor was the dormitory with required bathrooms and toilets. In the dormitory, each child had his or her own space by arranging simple room dividers. It was cool inside, thanks to a well-ventilated roof, which the firm consciously chose. A few years later the main building was extended, towards the road, so that the length of the building was approximately 64 metres and the width was 12 metres. Behind the fresh-looking, modern building was the Fröbel School, where tropical hard-wood defined the look.
The complex made way for new construction in the 1970s.

Palembang, the school building annex boarding school in the 1930s CFC

48 | 1934 **Jakarta: Mater Dei vocational school**

CITY: Jakarta
ADDRESS: Noordwijk 29/Jl. Ir. H. Juanda No. 29/-
ARCHITECT: Th. Taen
YEAR: 1934
CLIENT: Ursuline Sisters of the Roman Union on Java
CURRENT SITUATION: SMP Santa Maria
SOURCES: *Koloniaal Missie Tijdschrift*, (1933), p. 286; Goumans (1935), p. 163; Hoof (1934), p. 386

Throughout the many years that the Ursuline Sisters lived and worked in the Great Convent, conditions changed drastically. On Java, schools and boarding schools opened here and there, which made them increasingly 'competitive' with other congregations. Moreover, they were told by their Catholic leadership that, unlike in the past, they were only allowed to offer training to Catholic students. In 1931, the government demanded that they cancel the teacher training school and that the three-year HBS secondary school had to be converted into junior secondary school (MULO). 'A lot of unpleasant bother', according to one of the sisters in her contribution to the memorial book *Gedenkboek 1535-1935*, 'but by the fearless zeal and ingenuity of one of them', a new vocational school was begun on July 3, 1933. This two-year form of education was so successful that they had to ask Fermont-Cuypers to build a new school complex. The inauguration took place on July 30, 1934. 'The new building is a jewel for the Maria park', the nun wrote. Behind the buildings on Noordwijk and thus behind the chapel, once designed by Eduard Cuypers in 1926, were the 'objective' style of school buildings that met the demands of the tropical climate in the open space, which sisters called 'the old coconut garden' up until then. Almost 100 pupils received schooling there annually.
In later years these buildings made room for new ones.

Jakarta 1936, aerial photo of the Great Convent on Noordwijk (now: Jl. Juanda) with the buildings of the vocational school centre top KNILM/CFC

49 | 1934 **Bengkulu: Schools, convent and chapel**

CITY: Bengkulu
Address: Aloon-Aloon/Jl. Todak No. 119
ARCHITECT: Th. Taen
YEAR: 1934
CLIENT: Sisters of the Holy Carolus Borromeo of Maastricht (the Netherlands)
CURRENT SITUATION: TK St Carolus Bengkulu
SOURCES: *Bataviaasch Nieuwsblad*, June 22, 1934; *De Indische Courant*, June 23, 1934; Gorris (1937)

In Amsterdam, Laurentina de Sain (1891-1970) joined the order The Sisters under the Arches. In 1931, she arrived as a sister in Bengkulu, where she became head of a school with 80 pupils. The school had a good reputation and it was also recognised by the Department of Education in the Dutch East Indies, so that three years later, student numbers had swelled to 200 pupils. She managed to build a convent, a boarding school and a new school with funds from the Congregation. Fermont-Cuypers had the job of designing it. She knew the firm through her sister Lies, Theo Taen's wife. Under the direction of Mr. H.G. Beelen, overseer at Fermont-Cuypers, construction began in 1933. During the inauguration on June 17, 1934, Fermont and Taen were in the Netherlands and so Matthias Kaptijn spoke on behalf of Fermont-Cuypers.

Furthermore, the Monsignor of Palembang later wrote: 'In Bengkulu in the period 1933-1934, a convent, a girls' boarding school, new buildings for the Fröbel teaching and a Dutch-Chinese school were all completed. Because the old school had disappeared, there was space for a church as well as for the housing of the missionaries and a boys' boarding school'. For Laurentina de Sain, the new building was not the most important, but with the government's approval, 'her' school was on a par with the other schools in Bengkulu and she could therefore count on financial support. 'On a Saturday morning, the first meeting with an Inspector', is written in the Yearbook of the Order. 'After a month of waiting, a letter is delivered with a very positive answer. It is April 25, 1935. The school now has 285 pupils and there is great joy', according to the Yearbook.

The architecture again displays the Dutch East Indies, airy variant of functionalism, visible in, among other things, the high, unobstructed (well-ventilated) roofs, the open classrooms and the verandas. Only at the main entrance is the architecture more decorative and more in the spirit of the so-called 'Delftse school'.

Despite tsunamis and earthquakes, the school still exists as an institution. Most buildings still exist, now in between other buildings along Jalan Todak.

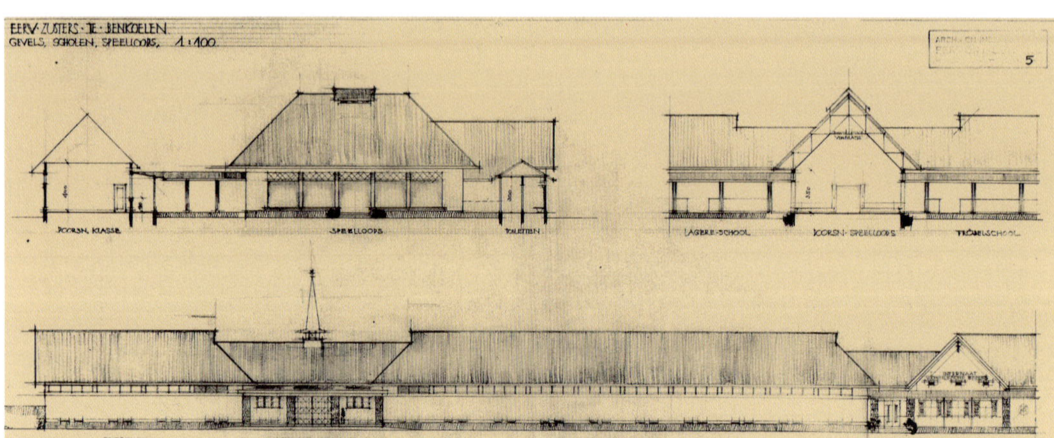

Bengkulu, the building plans of the school complex dated April 13, 1933 CFC

Bengkulu 1934, the main entrance of the complex of the Sisters of the Saint Carolus Borromeo CFC

Bengkulu, the inside of the school complex near the entrance of the school in 1934 CFC

50 | 1934 **Surabaya: Vincentius hospital**

CITY: Surabaya
ADDRESS: Reinierszboulevard 136/Jl. Diponegoro No. 51
ARCHITECT: Th. Taen, C.Th. Nix
YEAR: 1934
CLIENT: Mission sisters of Steyl (the Netherlands)
CURRENT SITUATION: Rumah Sakit Katolik St. Vincent de Paul (RSK)
SOURCES: *Bataviaasch Nieuwsblad*, August 7, 1920; *Bataviaasch Nieuwsblad*, July 20, 1933; *De Indische Courant*, August 14, 1933; *De Indische Courant*, August 15, 1933; *Soerabaijasch Handelsblad*, November 21, 1933; *De Indische Courant*, September 25, 1934; *Soerabaijasch Handelsblad*, October 26, 1934; *Soerabaijasch Handelsblad*, October 27, 1934; *De Katholieke Missiën*, (1935), p. 100; *Nieuwe Courant*, April 28, 1950

In October 1919, the first plots for the new hospital were purchased, located in what was to be known as the Darmo district. However, it would take more than 15 years before the new Vincentius hospital in Surabaya was completed. Fermont-Cuypers was not responsible for this, according to Matthias Kaptijn in his speech on Sunday, October 28, 1934, the day of the official opening. They had the plans ready for years. In 1930 they underwent an adaptation based on a sketch by Laurent Logemann.
The hospital was built on a site of approximately 35,000 square metres. The built surface area amounted to approximately 20,000 square metres. The 60-metre-wide front building, including a steep turret, is parallel to the boulevard. In front of the entrance is the awning, where cars to drop off and pick up patients and visitors could stop for a moment. The hospital, designed in a clear Indies functionalist style, is still there. The front doors, with coloured glass, open into the hall with the waiting room on the left and the office with the counter on the right. Several rooms for the treatment of patients adjoin the hall, including an x-ray room, operating room, sterilisation room and dressing room. According to a newspaper, the operating room was the 'first refrigerated' facility in the Dutch East Indies. All doors in the hospital complex had a special sound-absorbent construction.
The central hall still leads to a green courtyard of 120 by 40 metres, criss-crossed by covered footpaths that interconnect the various pavilions. 'All pavilions consist of a front gallery with rooms with a sink and smooth cupboards with a sloping top,' reported a journalist,
After the opening, there was still plenty of room on the grounds for the expansion of a number of pavilions and service buildings according to a rectangular layout, which was ideal for flexible interpretation. The aerial drawing made by Laurent Logemann from 1930 showed that. Indeed, all conceivable extensions took place within this framework. Nobody could have conceived in 1934 that car ownership would become as common as it did. Moreover, at that time there was a tram stop in front of the main entrance.

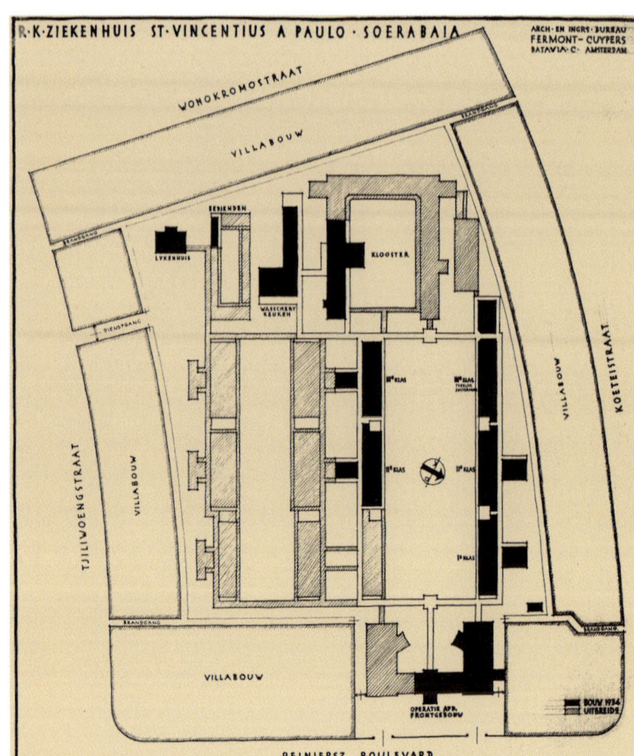

Surabaya, the main building on the Reinierszboulevard (Jl. Raya Diponegoro) shortly after the opening in 1934. Expansion on the left was ultimately an option, mirroring the right side CFC

‹ Surabaya, the zoning map for the Vincentius Hospital of Fermont-Cuypers from 1930 CFC

Surabaya 1934, the back of the main building on the left the window of the operation CFC

Surabaya 1934, the pavilions in a recently landscaped garden CFC

Surabaya 2017, some pavilions of Rumah Sakit St. Vincentius a Paulo in a beautiful garden CON

51 | 1934 **Yogyakarta: Seminary expansion**

CITY: Yogyakarta
ADDRESS: Telemajalaan/Jl. Ahmad Jazuli No. 2
ARCHITECT: Th. Taen
YEAR: 1934
CLIENT: Jesuit Fathers
CURRENT SITUATION: Universitas Sanata Dharma
SOURCES: *Soerabaijasch Handelsblad*, July 12, 1934; *De Tijd*, October 21, 1937; Archive of Jesuits in the Low Countries, Kadoc Leuven (B)

In 1934, the Seminary announced an expansion. Fermont-Cuypers had built it seven years earlier. *Het Soerabaijasch Handelsblad* reported: 'the work for this expansion has been entrusted to Fermont-Cuypers. The plan involves the construction of two wings, housing the new chapel, while space will also be created for classrooms and dormitories. These new wings will have a first floor. The "now slightly shabby architecture" will be significantly enhanced by the new building', the newspaper predicted. In 1934, the two ends of the main building were extended. Most space was available on the south side. A building section of approximately 24 by 15 metres was installed against the façade which was then closed. It had two storeys and a roof, overflowing into the existing roof. This was the location of the new chapel. This created space in the rear of the grounds by reusing the old, small chapel. The façade on the north side did not lend itself to the same architectural solution. Here, the solution was to build a two-storey extension of about six metres under one roof. The main building was therefore given the desired symmetry. ‹By rearranging the existing and new volume, a few additional classrooms will be created. The entire project is thoroughly refurbished inside and can last for years›, a newspaper reported.

Today, the decor still remains of the Fermont-Cuypers building, hidden between later buildings.

Yogyakarta, the seminary late 1930s CON

Yogyakarta, the seminary after the extensions at both ends of the building and at the rear in 1934 KNILM/CFC

Yogyakarta, rear of the seminary after the extensions in 1934. In the foreground the St. Anthony Church built in 1926 KNILM/CFC

52 | 1934 **Jakarta: Tan villa/Italian Consulate**

CITY: Jakarta
ADDRESS: Burgemeester Bisschopplein 6/Jl. Taman Suropati No. 6
ARCHITECT: C.Th. Nix, A. Dikstaal
YEAR: 1934
CLIENT: Mr. Tan Tjoan Keng
CURRENT SITUATION: India House
SOURCES: *Bataviaasch Nieuwsblad,* February 17, 1934; Voorneman (1937), p. 175; Temminck Groll (2002), p.156; Passchier, (2016), p. 84; Archive of Fermont-Cuypers.

'The Fermont-Cuypers firm, acting on behalf of a principal, has requested the city council to consider selling a building plot at a reduced price on the Burgemeester Bisschopplein', *Het Bataviaasch Nieuwsblad* stated, 'The plot covers an area of 3,950 square metres and would normally cost Fl. 47.400, but it is an unfortunate shape and the rear of the plot is on a quite steep incline . The Mayor and City Council Members would therefore sell the site for Fl. 36,600, also because the plans indicate that a sizable residence will be built; according to the said Members, no better buildings can be desired.' The client Tan Tjoan Keng, wanted the building as a villa for himself. At Fermont-Cuypers they made a design inspired by the latest developments in the field of modern architecture, with which Mr. Tan strongly identified. He was a great lover of cars and western technology. For such a person, Fermont-Cuypers was happy to design a modernist home. That was reflected in the horizontal articulation, the flat roof with terrace, large expansive windows and curves that were inspired by the latest trend of building in a streamlined way. Realising that pure modernism, whatever that may be, did not lend itself to the tropics, they introduced in the design, among other things, large awnings above the windows, cavity constructions under the flat roofs, numerous ventilation grilles and a few loggias, including a particularly large loggia on the first floor and a wide roof terrace. Nix and Dikstaal made a scale model of the design. Pictures of the design were sent to the Netherlands, where Fermont and Taen were on leave. A photo series was made of the construction process with the end result photographed from all possible points of view. Yet the Tan family did not move in. The building was admired enormously by the Italian Consul in the Dutch East Indies, Mr. L. Cenzi, who wanted to rent it if there would be some structural adjustments made. He wished to establish his consulate on the ground floor and wanted to live on the first floor. Fermont-Cuypers was given the assignment to alter the building in that way.
The building underwent an extension on the side of the Van Heutszboulevard (now: Jl. Teuku Umar) and received an extra entrance there. Above the door came the coat of arms of Mussolini's Italy. The Italian flag was hanging on a mast in the garden. In 1936, the municipality published her promotion book *'Batavia als Handels- Industrie- en Woonstad'* with a photograph of this building, but without mentioning the architects behind it. In the years that followed, photos of this building were frequently published, always with praise about the architecture, but omitting Fermont-Cuypers' name. This building is a beautiful example of the 'International Style' as this modern architectural style was first mentioned, two years earlier, at a major exhibition on the 'Moderns' in New York. That was precisely the accusation frequently levelled at Fermont-Cuypers: 'they could not build Modern'.

At the expense of the form, loggias were later closed off and windows reduced, proving that the 'International Style' was less suitable for the tropics.

Jakarta, facing brick with the name Fermont-Cuypers CON

Jakarta, the front of the Italian consulate on Burgemeester Bisschopplein (now: Jl. Taman Suropati) designed by Fermont-Cuypers and photographed after the ‘second completion’ CFC

Jakarta, the façade of the Italian consulate at the Van Heutsz Boulevard (now: Jl. Teuku Umar) shortly after the completion of the building in 1934 CFC

Jakarta, the modern monumental house with outbuildings CFC

Jakarta, the Italian consulate with its flowing lines seen from the Van Heutszboulevard (now: Jl. Teuku Umar) CFC

Jakarta, the consulate with upstairs residence viewed from the back garden shortly before completion in 1934 CFC

Jakarta, the former Italian consulate, 'India House' in 2015 CON

53 | 1934 **Jakarta: Brother house**

CITY: Jakarta
ADDRESS: Koningsplein east 2/Jl. Medan Merdeka Timur / -
ARCHITECT: C.Th. Nix.
YEAR: 1934.
CLIENT: Brothers of Oudenbosch (the Netherlands)
CURRENT SITUATION: demolished in 1977
CURRENT USE: land used by the Indonesian oil company Pertamina
SOURCES: *Berichten uit Nederlandsch-Oost Indië van de Claverbond* (1912), p. 227; *Bouwkundig Weekblad* (1912), 591 image 3; *De Indische Courant*, September 19, 1934

The story of the oldest boys' school run by Catholic brothers in Jakarta began in 1905, in a rented house. Four years later, on June 20, 1909, the brothers moved into the school on Koningsplein (now: Medan Merdeka), designed by P.A.J. Moojen (1879-1955) in the Dutch-Indies style of architecture, with characteristics such as the symmetrical design, masonry, windows with rods and Dutch spout gables. Hulswit-Fermont and Ed. Cuypers may have expanded the complex in 1922 and provided it with a small chapel to the rear. The real renovation, with a major expansion, which took place in September 1934 was carried out by Fermont-Cuypers. The drawing made by Thomas Nix from November 1931 shows a square building with the entrance in a forward extension. Downstairs is an open gallery with columns with an awning in front. There are round openings in the plastered façade above it. Despite the modest dimensions, a monumental effect was created. Preconsultation with the client led to changes. The original roof terrace above the developed portal turned into a loggia. The round ventilation openings were exchanged for semi-circles. The building had twelve rooms, five on the ground floor and seven on the first floor. The entire building came under a tent roof with a large overhang. A newspaper was very positive about the effective ventilation and modern conveniences in all rooms.

The building, including the school, made way for office development of Pertamina, the former 'Bataafsche Petroleum Maatschappij'.

The stairs in the building shortly after completion in 1934 CFC

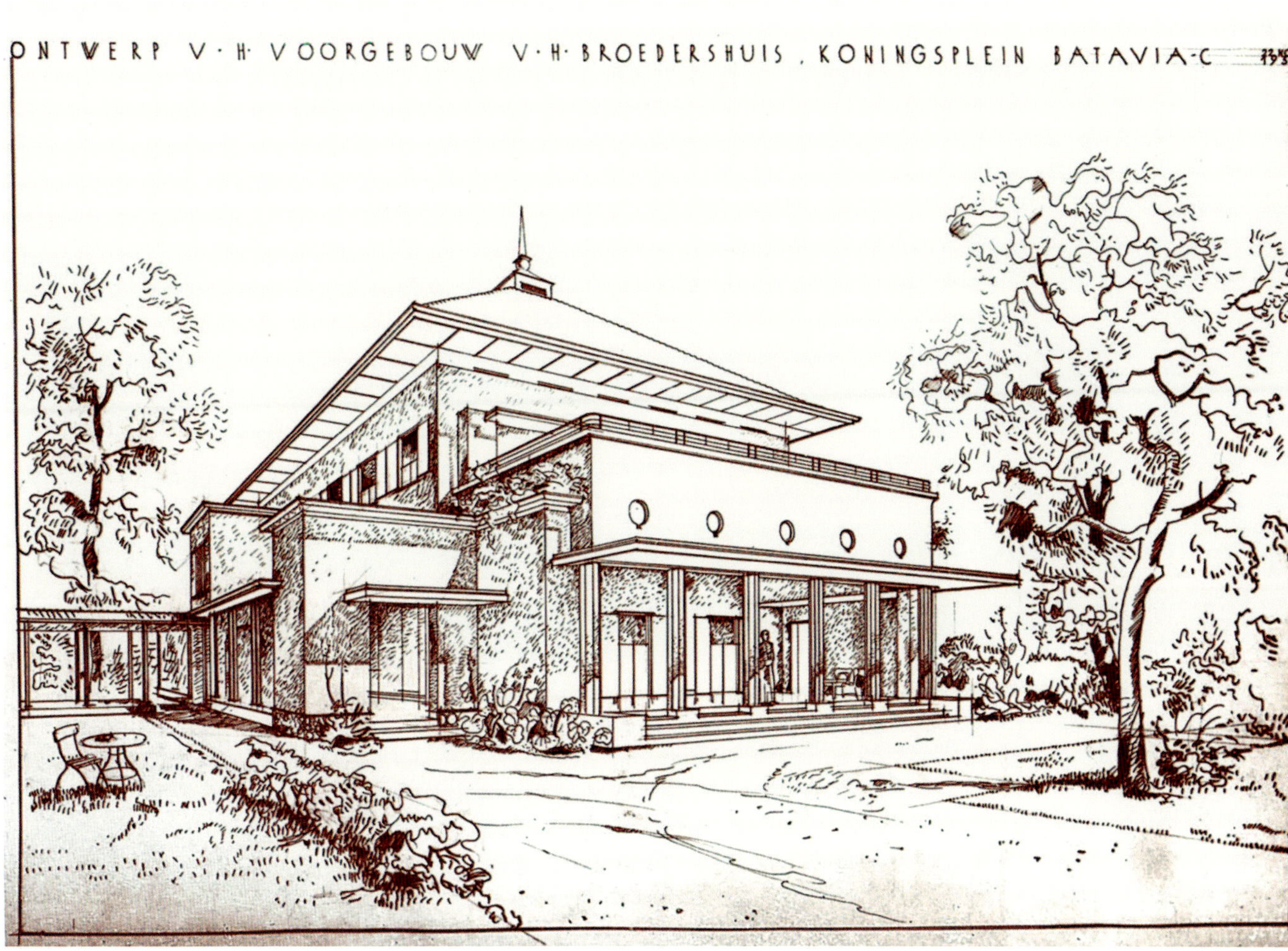

Drawing by Thomas Nix for the planned new building behind the school, dated November 22, 1931 CFC

Jakarta 1934, the new building behind the school of the Brothers of St. Aloysius. Parts of the end result differ visibly from the drawing CFC

54 | 1935 Cirebon: Dutch-Chinese Primary School

CITY: Cirebon
ADDRESS: Pesisir/Jl. Sisingamangaraja No. 22
ARCHITECT: Th. Taen
Year: 1935
CLIENT: Ursuline Sisters from Weltevreden
CURRENT SITUATION: SD Santa Maria (Most original buildings have disappeared)
SOURCES: *Het Nieuws van de Dag voor Nederlandsch-Indië*, June 29, 1933; *Kruistriomf* (1933-1934), pp. 104-107; *Het Nieuws van de Dag voor Nederlandsch-Indië*, January 24, 1935; *Bataviaasch Nieuwsblad*, February 20, 1935; KDC: LARC2744 *Archieven van Weltevreden*

Fermont-Cuypers appeared to be the regular architect of the Ursuline Sisters of the 'Kleine Klooster' from Weltevreden (the convent on Jl. Pos). The firm built both the new building for their convent and their Sister house. As a result, they became involved in the construction of the first school of the same sisters in Cirebon, the Saint Joseph school, which was inaugurated on June 28, 1933. A newspaper referred to a building that 'makes a simple but very solid impression, also with regard to the layout of the classrooms'. It was no more than a Chinese house transformed into school. Behind it was a vast garden, large enough for future new construction. That must have motivated Fermont-Cuypers to do their utmost for the small renovation. In January 1935, a newspaper reported that the number of schools in Cirebon had steadily increased: 'In addition to the existing educational establishments, a private secondary education course is set up to prepare students from the 7th class for the HBS secondary school or other equivalent secondary schools. There is also an evening course for adults at this school, for those who want to learn Dutch more intensively and who also want to follow the course in English and Accounting. The school is run by the Ursuline Sisters who also intend to establish a Dutch Chinese School. They will start with a Fröbel first class, which was opened on February 1, 1935 and was called the Maria school. Fermont-Cuypers designed it. Because the number of pupils of the St. Joseph school was also growing steadily, the existing building underwent an expansion, for which on February 27, 1935 the first stone was laid. The newspaper followed the development closely: 'At the start of the new school year, the easily erected building is ready for the new school year'. All buildings later disappeared.

Cirebon: The 'Hollandsch Chineesche School' (Dutch-Chinese School) with sisters and pupils in 1935 CFC

55 | 1935 **Jakarta: Pek villa**

CITY: Jakarta
ADDRESS: Oranjeboulevard 51/Jl. Pangeran Diponegoro No.51
ARCHITECT: C.Th. Nix, A. Dikstaal
YEAR: 1935
CLIENT: Mr. Pek
CURRENT SITUATION: unrecognisably changed
SOURCE: *Het Nieuws van den Dag voor Nederlandsch-Indië*, February 25, 1935

Very little data remains on the design of this house and of the client. The Fermont-Cuypers archive mentions the Pek family, who must have been rich. They purchased the land in cash which was a reason to ask for a discount. The subsidy amounted to a discount of 5%, granted to candidates for unissued plots of land with cash payments. Upon acceptance of this subsidy, in the present case the purchase price of the land would be Fl. 14,240. What the new owner earned with this deal was probably invested in the new house. It had to be a modern home, which showed that the first owner felt akin to the European avant-garde and the 'International Style'. In a sculptural way, a tower-like, vertical volume contrasts with the horizontal accents of the continuous awnings and framing of the two-storey main volume. The house has a roof terrace, smaller but identical to that of the Italian consulate. The unsuitability of this building style for the tropics was reflected in the comparatively small windows in this design, which the family closed with shutters to keep sun and heat out as much as possible in a time without air conditioning.
The house still exists but has unfortunately changed beyond recognition due to later renovations and modifications.

Jakarta, Pek villa on Oranjeboulevard (now : Jl. Sisingamangaraja) 51 in Menteng in 1935, designed by Fermont-Cuypers CFC

56 | 1935 **Jakarta, Bank vault building of Javasche Bank**

CITY: Jakarta
ADDRESS: Binnen Nieuwpoortstraat/-
ARCHITECT: Th. Taen, C.Th. Nix
YEAR: 1935
CLIENT: The Javasche Bank
CURRENT SITUATION: Museum Bank Indonesia (this building became part of the entire bank building in 1937)
SOURCES: *Bataviaasch Nieuwsblad*, November 3, 1933; *Soerabaijasch Handelsblad*, November 8, 1933; *De Indische Courant*, January 13, 1934

At the beginning of January 1934, the first pile was ceremonially driven into the ground for an extension of the Javasche Bank in Jakarta - the bank vault building. It was built on the still vacant terrain between the Javasche Bank on the Binnen-Nieuwpoortstraat and the just completed new building of the 'Nederlandsche Handel-Maatschappij', the Factorij. The Dutch flag hung at the top of the pile driver and hundreds of firecrackers hung on the 18-metre-long piles, which produced deafening levels of noise for those present, including the management of the Javasche Bank, the members of the board of the Factorij and the construction companies that did the job. After Han de Jongh and Mr. Dr. G. G. van Buttingha Wichers, the President of the Javasche Bank, uttered some appropriate words, the latter operated the pile driver for the first of 170 piles. A newspaper said that the execution was under the management of Fermont-Cuypers. The 'Nederlandsche Aanneming Maatschappij' (NV NEDAM) took care of the substructure. The superstructure was carried out by the firm Selle & de Bruyn. The newspaper concluded that the building had to be ready by September 1, 1935. It was in all respects an extension of the main building in the same architectural style. The old building with its representative appearance received a relatively austere, closed wing with ten Greek columns, which, unlike the old building, did not fulfil a supporting function, but only served as a façade ornament. They were manufactured in such a way that they were relatively easy to move. Before construction, it had already been decided that a completely new front building would be erected in the short term, which would incorporate the new bank vault.

Jakarta, the bank vault building next to the bank is ready in 1935, but will only be visible for three years CFC

57 | 1935 Jakarta: Tarcisius Primary School

CITY: Jakarta
Address: Chaulanweg/Jl. KH. Hasyim Ashari No. 26
ARCHITECT: Th. Taen, C.Th. Nix
YEAR: 1935
CLIENT: Missionaries of Tilburg (M.S.C.), the Netherlands
CURRENT SITUATION: new building of Tarsisius School
SOURCES: *Soerabaijasch Handelsblad*, April 24, 1935; *De Indische Courant*, April 25, 1935; Goumans (1935)

On the morning of Easter Monday in 1935, the first stone was laid for a school building in the west of Jakarta on the Chaulanweg (now: Jl. KH. Hasyim Ashari). The building was located behind the old building of the Saint Tarcisius school and had two storeys with four classrooms on each floor. The school was ready in the course of 1935. Two classrooms on the ground floor served as a chapel for the time being, the other two as playrooms.

In 1938, Fermont-Cuypers built the Our Lady of the Sacred Heart Church on this spot. Of the consecration on September 18, 1938, a newspaper reported: 'The church was crowded to capacity and it promises much for the future, among the attendees we noticed Mr. Fermont, with almost his entire staff.' Later renovations made the school unrecognisable and the church building was replaced.

Jakarta, the Tarcisius school photographed in 1936 CFC

58 | 1935 Bandung, Pandu Church, presbytery, club-building

CITY: Bandung
ADDRESS: Pandoeweg 2a/Jl. Pandu No. 4
ARCHITECT: C.Th. Nix.
YEAR: 1935
CLIENT: Crosier Brothers from St. Agatha (the Netherlands)
CURRENT USE: Gereja Santa Perawan Maria Bunda
SOURCES: *Het Nieuws van den Dag voor Nederlandsch-Indië*, February 5, 1935; *De Indische Courant*, October 24, 1935; *Soerabaijasch Handelsblad*, October 25, 1935; Goumans (1935); *Kruistriomf* 15 (1935-1936), pp. 26, 154, 207-209

The construction of this church in Bandung with a presbytery and a building for the 'Catholic Social Union' (K.S.B.) was a challenge for the firm. This project enabled Thomas Nix to redeem himself and the firm after missing the opportunity to build the Theresia Church in Jakarta, a commission that went to the architect J. Th van Oyen a year earlier. They designed a somewhat similar church, with steep saddle roofs in two short steps above the entrance, as an expressive gesture. The church was constructed in the west of Bandung on a vacant parking area along the Pandoeweg (now: Jl. Pandu), creating a veritable eye-catcher The building of the 'Catholic Social Union' was behind it, with the presbytery situated behind that. This resulted in an architecturally beautiful ensemble. On February 22, 1935 the specifications and drawings for the church, the presbytery and Catholic Union building were ready for the tender. On Friday, May 10, 1935, the first stone was laid for the Our Lady of Seven Sorrows, which rapidly became known simply as the Pandu Church. An enthusiastic pastor De Rooy O.S.C., who briefly worked in Bandung, regularly contributed to the magazine of his congregation and also placed photographs of 'his church' under construction. The three projects were completed shortly one after the other. The church building was put into use on October 25, the official consecration took place on November 17, 1935. Afterwards, the churchgoers, including Arthur Fermont, went outside to take pictures in front of the main entrance, surrounded by young people.

The church building has a clearly configured cross shape within a ground area of 30 by 30 metres. The high roof is automatically enhanced due to the low side façades. A slender roof turret marks the crossing of the transepts. Inside, columns were not allowed to obstruct the view of the altar. Therefore, a truss construction was used for which no intermediate supports were required. The walls and ceiling are predominantly white. Only the frame where the ceiling boards are laid in is dark, as are some of the rafters. Due to the high placement of the windows under the overhang of the roof, there was never any direct sunlight. There was no stained glass, possibly due to lack of money. The presbytery stood right behind the church, so that it formed unity together with the church. The K.S.B.'s union building was more austere than the beautifully designed presbytery. In the second half of the last century, the ecclesiastical ensemble became completely wedged in between dwellings and other buildings.

It now takes some effort to find the church. Inside, the church continues to look beautiful. Renovations have made the presbytery and the K.S.B. building unrecognisable.

Bandung, the Pandu church in 2017 CON

Bandung, the church of 'Onze Lieve Vrouw van Zeven Smarten' (Our Lady of Seven Sorrows) on the Pandoeweg (now: Jl. Pandu), which was therefore almost immediately called Pandu church. The building is still under construction in 1935, the roof turret is being finished off CFC

Bandung, the Pandu church with the presbytery shortly before the consecration in 1935 CFC

Bandung, the club building and Pandu church in the late 1930s CFC

Bandung 1935, the more elevated presbytery behind the Pandu Church with beautiful stairway CFC

Bandung, an interior photo of the church made in 2017 CON

59 | 1935 Semarang: Javasche Bank and staff residence

CITY: Semarang
ADDRESS: Bodjong/Jl. Pemuda No. 3
ARCHITECT: Th. Taen, L. Logemann
YEAR: 1935 (design 1930)
CLIENT: The Javasche Bank
CURRENT SITUATION: Bank Jateng
SOURCES: *Soerabaijasch Handelsblad*, August 30, 1930; *Bataviaasch Nieuwsblad*, November 3, 1933; *De Indische Courant*, November 4, 1933; *Bataviaasch Nieuwsblad*, July 18, 1934; *Het Nieuws van den Dag voor Nederlandsch-Indië*, July 26, 1934; *Het Nieuws van den Dag voor Nederlandsch-Indië*, November 29, 1935; *De Indische Courant*, November 29, 1934; *Het Nieuws van den Dag voor Nederlandsch-Indië*, December 13, 1935; *De Locomotief*, December 14, 1935; Borsi (1987)

On June 17, 1934 the first stone was laid for the new building of the Javasche Bank on the site on Bodjong (now: Jl. Pemuda). The president and commissioners of the Javasche Bank, representatives of the Hollandsche Beton Maatschappij attended the ceremony, as well as Han de Jongh and Arnold Dikstaal from the firm. They all put their signatures on the customary certificate. The agent of the bank gave a short speech, after which Han de Jongh thanked the bank's management for the important commission. The designer of the building, Laurent Logemann, who had left Fermont-Cuypers in the meantime, remained unmentioned. Four years earlier he drew three variations, from which the management of the Javasche Bank chose one. The new bank building was built just outside the old town along the road that runs into Bodjong, the extremely long, straight street to Semarang-south and Candi. Because the Blakan-Kebon Road was extended to Bodjong, a very small park was created in front of the new bank.
The building consists of a simple main building mass with, on the left, a relatively low tower with the main entrance. The plinth, the parapet above the substructure and the eaves form clear horizontal accents, but more characteristic are the narrow, vertical windows. On the main building is a steel roof construction, covered with roman glazed tiles. The tower is unusual for the architecture of Fermont-Cuypers. The heavy, flat, blunt characteristics of the architecture matched the latest trends in Europe. The 'Monumental Era' started in the early 1930s and this is evident in this building with marble, copper and gold-coloured glazed tiles. Behind the entrance, a staircase leads up to the main floor with the porter's lodge on the left and a heavy revolving door straight from Europe on the right. Behind this door there is a waiting area, entirely executed according to Logemann's sketch from 1930. Behind the counters there are large office areas, a meeting room and the room of the bank's agent. Next to it are the stairs to the basement with the safe, which is 'sealed off with an eight-ton door from Europe', according to the newspaper. At the back of the building are the toilets and a dining room for the staff. The simple service residence was built behind that, it was also designed by Fermont-Cuypers.
At the opening of the bank on December 14, 1935, the Gas Company offered 'floodlights', shining a light on Semarang's new acquisition.

Semarang, the former Javasche Bank, now Bank Jateng in 2013 CON

Semarang, the new Javasche Bank on Bodjong (now: Jl. Pemuda) just outside the old town in 1935, with the accompanying bank residence on the right CFC

Semarang 1936, an aerial photo of the recently completed Javasche Bank KNILM/CFC

Semarang, the design chosen by the management for the new Javasche Bank building from 1930. The drawing was made by Laurent Logemann CFC

Semarang, a drawing by Laurent Logemann of the public hall in the new building for the Javasche Bank CFC

The bronze fence in the former Javasche Bank CSL

Semarang, the entrance via a staircase to the higher public areas of the bank CFC

Semarang, the tiled hall with counters shortly after it was opened to the public in 1935 CFC

60 | 1935 **Pekalongan: St. Peter's Catholic church and presbytery**

CITY: Pekalongan
ADDRESS: Bridge Lodji/Jl. Blimbing 1/-
ARCHITECT: Th. Taen, C.Th. Nix
YEAR: 1935
CLIENT: Missionaries (M.S.C.) from Tilburg (the Netherlands)
CURRENT SITUATION: buildings have been replaced by new buildings
SOURCES: *De Indische Courant*, August 7, 1935; Archive of Fermont-Cuypers

On August 4, 1935, the first stone was laid for the St. Peter's Church in Pekalongan. An initiation took place whilst prayers were softly spoken and holy water was liberally doused, ending at the spot where the first stone was laid. The pastor gave a speech full of superlatives: 'At a crossroads where four ethnic families reach out to each other: European, Javanese, Chinese and Arab; on a square where two cultural circles intersect: the Western and the Eastern; near a bridge, which has two riverbanks and as a symbol reminiscent of the bridging of time to eternity, we have come together today to cement the memorial stone of a new church building. For all citizens, the new church is a cultural monument, an enhancement of the cityscape, an elevation of the spirit, an increase of civilisation. The present generation will be helped by the church building in its pursuit upward. In order to achieve this, art and competence of the Fermont-Cuypers firm remain our guarantor.' Many of those present then put their signatures on the usual certificate, which, together with a few coins, disappeared into a lead cylinder to be bricked in.

The church had to accommodate about 300 people. The construction consisted of an iron frame, combined with reinforced concrete. There was a little church tower with a clock to top it off. After a little more than three months, the church could be consecrated on December 15, 1935. Partly prefabricated trusses and other modern techniques made it possible to build quickly, thus creating a church hall under a gable roof, covered with wood shingles. The simple roof turret looked suspiciously similar to the Pandu church in Bandung. The presbytery on the banks of the Pekalongan River next to the church was given a half-hipped roof, with open ends for ventilation. Both buildings, with their lower course of river pebbles, formed a harmonious ensemble in a building style that later is called 'De Delftse School' in the Netherlands. The design betrayed the hand of Thomas Nix, who honed his profession at Delft Technical University in the late 1920s under Professor M.J. Granpré Molière.
The friendly ensemble of buildings on the river made way for a larger church building with presbytery years later.

Pekalongan, sketch of the church and presbytery by Thomas Nix CFC

Pekalongan 1935, the front of the church under construction with the presbytery to the right CFC

Pekalongan 1935, the presbytery on the river with the church under construction behind CFC

61 | 1936 Bandung: 'Maria Sterre der Zee' schools and convent

CITY: Bandung
ADDRESS: Waringinweg 149/Jl. Kebon Jati No. 209
ARCHITECT: Th. Taen, C.Th. Nix
YEAR: 1936
CLIENT: Sisters of Divine Providence from Steyl (the Netherlands)
CURRENT SITUATION: Sekolah Dasar Maria Bintang Laut
SOURCES: *De Indische Courant*, May 8, 1936; *De Limburger*, September 25, 1936; *De Tijd*, September 28, 1936.

On April 26, 1934, seven Sisters of Divine Providence from Steyl set foot for the first time in Bandung, where they immediately started a school for 16 children in their home on the Residentsweg 23 (now: Jl. Otto Iskandar Dinata). Within three months there were 54 pupils. At that moment they started informally with the Fröbel school. In June 1935, the Ministry of Education and Worship informed them that they could start a Dutch Chinese School. Within a year and a half, they had bought a large building plot and Fermont-Cuypers received the contract for an extensive complex consisting of a convent, a boarding school and two schools. On February 24, 1936 Emiel Schedler, a draftsman at Fermont-Cuypers, designed the plans and Thomas Nix finalised the watercolour of a bird's-eye view of the desired final situation. The primary school had to be ready for the start of the new school year and the boarding school ready at the end of September. In anticipation of the construction, discussions took place with the sisters from Steyl, leading to some modifications to the plan. For example, the simply designed columns in the two main buildings had to be classical arches, which had become popular again in Europe. *De Indische Courant* reported on May 8, 1936, 'On the corner of the Waringinweg (now: Jl. Kebon Jati) with the Chineese kerkweg (now: Jl. Kelenteng) in Bandung, the construction agency Lim A Goh is currently working on the construction of a Chinese Catholic convent, following the design of the architects Fermont-Cuypers in Batavia'. In July 1936, just five months after the design was finalised, the two school buildings were already in use. The children entered the building through a remarkably well-designed main entrance with river pebbles. It was a primary school with seven classes and two Fröbel classes. The first floor of the main building offered space for a boarding school, another part of the 'Maria Sterre der Zee' convent ('Maria star of the sea'). After completion, the building looked fresh and airy and extremely business-like. Hidden away between buildings of a later date, the complex is still in full operation and little children play between beautiful stained-glass windows, in what once was the convent.

Bandung, school and 'Maria Sterre der Zee' convent complex shortly after completion in July 1936 CFC

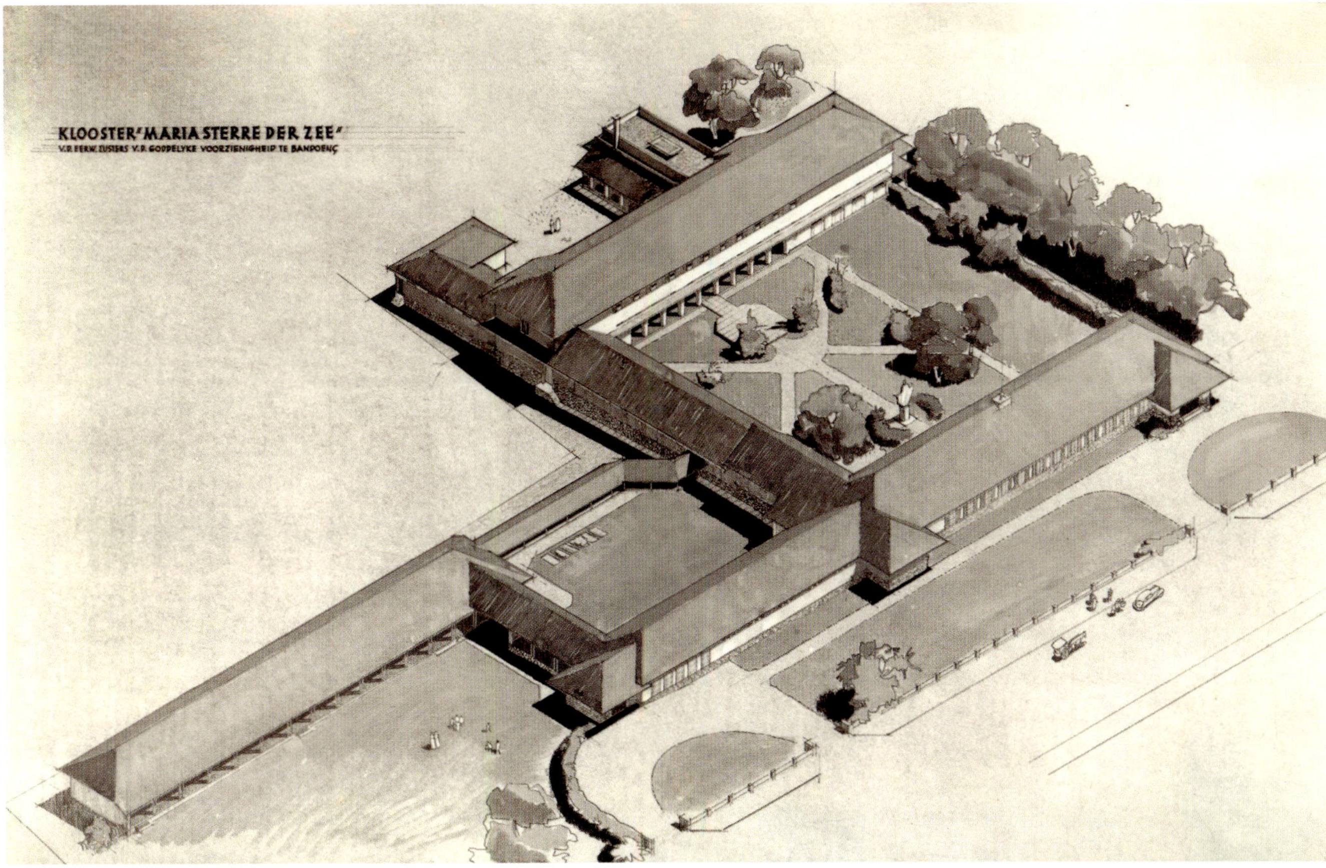

Bandung, bird's-eye view of schools and 'Maria Sterre der Zee' convent complex, made by Thomas Nix CFC

Bandung, stained-glass windows in the school complex and sister house in 2017 CON

62 | 1937 **Tegal: Textile factory**

CITY: Tegal
ADDRESS: Tegal-oost/Jl. Pala Raya/-
ARCHITECT: H. de Jongh, Th. Taen
YEAR: 1937
CLIENT: N.V. Java Textiel Maatschappij
CURRENT SITUATION: Pabrik Texin Tegal, has been demolished recently
SOURCES: *De Indische Courant*, August 24, 1936; *De Indische Courant*, September 1, 1936; *Soerabaijasch Handelsblad*, May 22, 1937; *Bataviaasch Nieuwsblad*, June 21, 1938

On Saturday morning, May 22, 1937, a procession of cars drove over the main road from Semarang to Tegal and turned right past the border of the municipality of Tegal on a road to the new factory laid by the Textiel Maatschappij. *Het Soerabaijasch Handelsblad* considered it newsworthy: 'Less than a year ago, there were still paddies here, and now there is the 'Proeftextielbedrijf' of the N.V. Java Textiel Maatschappij'. The establishment of this company took place on March 24, 1936 by a group of Dutch Industrialists and three major Dutch East Indies banking institutions, together with three well-known shipping companies and some Dutch East Indies import companies. The supremacy of the Dutch textile industry had come to an end. Free trade led to major Japanese competition in the textile market. The economic crisis caused more and cheaper textiles from Japan to be purchased at the expense of Dutch products. In response, the Dutch parties joined forces and a textile committee was set up, which in 1934 undertook a trip to Java with the aim of starting a broad-based textile industry aiming at the Dutch East Indies as a market. In the second half of 1935 negotiations took place for the purchase of a terrain in Tegal for the creation of a 'mechanical test weaving mill'. Fermont-Cuypers delivered the design. Lindeteves-Stokvis provided the steel construction together with Selle & de Bruyn the civil construction. Most machines came from the Netherlands, a small number from Japan. It started as a pilot company with two hundred mechanical looms. On the day of the opening, the management welcomed the many guests. Among those present were the Governor of Central Java, a number of other government officials, the Regent of Tegal, the mayor of this city, but also Mr. J.H. van Mook, chief general economic officer. Arthur Fermont represented Fermont-Cuypers, as well as the overseer Beelen. The Governor turned on the main switch, and the looms began to rattle. A glass of champagne sealed the best wishes for the well-being and prosperity of this new company. *Het Bataviaasch Nieuwsblad* reported on June 21, 1938 that the factory would be expanded according to Fermont-Cuypers' plans. The company was in production until the beginning of this century, followed by closure, vacancy and demolition. The factory was housed in some large warehouses with an industrial appearance. Some low office buildings designed by Fermont-Cuypers belonged to the complex as well.

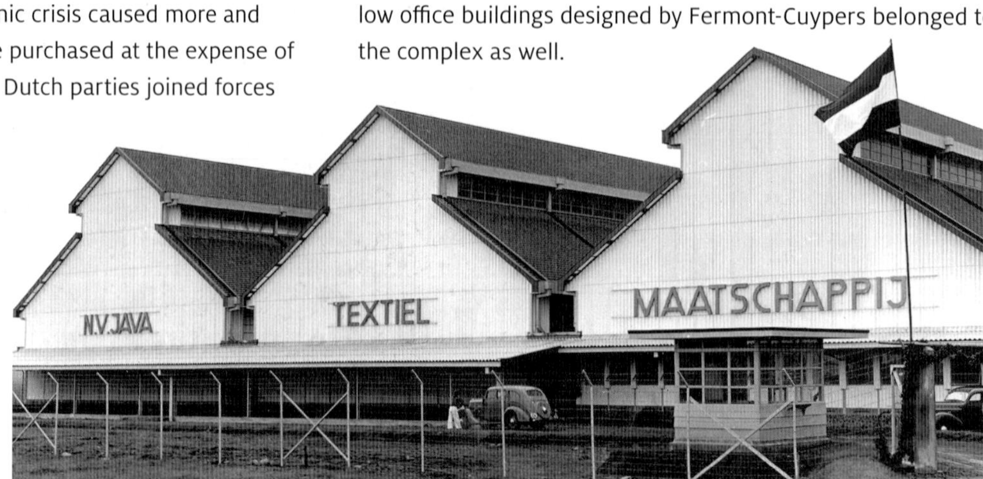

Tegal, factory complex of 'Java Textiel' company shortly after the opening in 1937 CFC

63 | 1937 **Tegal: Ursuline schools**

CITY: Tegal.
ADDRESS: Kraton-west/Jl. Kapt. Ismail 120
ARCHITECT: Th. Taen
YEAR: 1937
CLIENT: Ursuline Sisters of Weltevreden
CURRENT SITUATION: BKK SMK SMA Pius Tegal (most original buildings are gone)
SOURCES: *De Broeders van liefde in de missie van Java vanaf 1929*; Koopmanschap (1996) p. 20; COH, photo albums; KDC photo AFBK-6a3951

On October 3, 1934, the first stone was laid for the St. Paul's convent and the Brother's school. The school formed a simple complex in a leafy environment consisting of a Dutch Chinese School, a Dutch Indonesian School and an intermediate school. Later on, the Sisters arrived and began their projects: a European Fröbel School, a Chinese Fröbel School, a Dutch Chinese School and a School for Primary Education, all designed and built by Fermont-Cuypers, completed in 1937. There are some photographs of the European primary school made after completion.

After the war, the apostolic vicariate of Purwokerto, which included Tegal, made up the balance. All Catholic schools, the convents and a chapel were almost completely destroyed, and so everything that Fermont-Cuypers built there had disappeared. In 1950 one of the Brothers sighed: 'Our buildings in Tegal have become victims of the scorched-earth tactic in the freedom struggle'. They were not rebuilt. The Brothers decided to move to Wonosobo. The Sisters took over the terrain from them and had a new school complex built under the name Piusschool.

Tegal 1937, the building of the girls' primary school and the European Fröbel school. In the background classrooms for the other forms of education, including the 'Hollandsch-Chineesche School' (Dutch-Chinese School) and the 'Hollandsch-Inlandse School' (Dutch Indonesian School) COH

64 | 1937 **Jakarta: Front building of Javasche Bank**

CITY: Jakarta
ADDRESS: Binnen Nieuwpoortstraat/Jl. Lada No. 3
ARCHITECT: C.Th. Nix, Th. Taen.
YEAR: 1937
CLIENT: The Javasche Bank
CURRENT USE: Museum Bank Indonesia
SOURCES: *Bataviaasch Nieuwsblad,* March 3, 1936; *Bataviaasch Nieuwsblad*, March 10, 1936; *Bataviaasch Nieuwsblad,* June 12, 1937; *Het Nieuws van den Dag voor Nederlandsch-Indië,* June 12, 1937; *De Telegraaf,* June 17, 1937; Brochure Robert Deppe Batavia 1938

On June 12, 1937, Fermont-Cuypers presented the key of the completely renovated main building of the Javasche Bank to the management, after completion. It was erected in front of the original building from 1913, designed by Eduard Cuypers. A bank vault building was added shortly before. The new façade was designed as a whole with a total length of 105 metres. The foundation consists of 19-metre-long reinforced concrete piles. These support a skeleton of reinforced concrete with cavity walls, resulting in optimal insulation against the heat. The main entrance with *porte cochère* (covered drive-through porch) is in the middle part. Three doors lead to the portal, where a wide staircase of polished granite and black marble leads up to the bell-floor. The passage to the left provides access to the wing along the Kali Besar with the boardrooms. The open view through the large hall creates an impressive spatial effect. The vaulted ceiling rises approximately 14 metres above the floor of the portal. In the central hall, opposite the entrance, are the cash desk counters. Bronze turnstiles left and right lead to the large cash room (*kashal*) and the hall of the securities department. At the front, on the right side, there is a room for the doorman and on the left a consulting room for the public with a telephone booth. Sixteen lofty columns, covered with ceramics, support the richly carved concrete dome, incorporating a strip of light with glass building blocks over the entire length. The walls of the portal and the three public spaces are clad with ceramics. The upstanding partitions contain ceramic grates, ending in consoles with the various coats of arms of the cities, where the Javasche Bank had branches. Above the entrance doors, there are six high window strips with eighteen stained-glass windows. These provide a subdued light in the central hall. Some windows originate from the former front building, while matching windows are fitted in the central strip designed by Fermont-Cuypers with depictions of theatre, literature, painting, film, architecture, sculpture, indigenous industry, pottery, weaving, music, dance, sports and radio. In the long wall, where the cashiers used to be, so-called cages were installed, while on the side of the Javabankstraat (now: Jl. Pintu Besar Utara) the counters of the exchange department and the consulting room are placed. In the former securities department, the room for the chief of the department was fitted with a panelling with inlays from various Indies wood.
The floors are covered with double-fired tiles in a simple pattern. The large cash hall on the right and the public hall for the securities department on the left, are executed in the same materials as the central hall. All new stained-glass windows were designed by Fermont-Cuypers and were manufactured by Bogtman from Haarlem. The De Lint company from Delft produced the ceramics on the walls. The different city coats of arms came from the studio of Robert Deppe from Jakarta. The Wiener company in Amsterdam supplied the bronze work, the Mesman Schultz company in Jakarta manufactured the other metalworks, such as the glass partitions. The stained-glass windows of the large cash hall are a Fermont-Cuypers design, made by the Dutch East Indies Grid Work Factory. The roof was covered with glazed European tiles from Van Oordt in Alphen aan den Rijn (the Netherlands), identical to those of the old building. The iron roof construction was carried out by the Machinefabriek Batavia. The electrical lighting installation, as well as the alarm and safety installations, were supplied by Siemens and installed under the direction of Van der Veen & Vis. All furniture was produced by the Furniture Industry Andriesse in Semarang and by the firm De Canton in Jakarta, according to the design by Fermont-Cuypers.

Jakarta 1937, the recently completed front building of the Javasche Bank in the 'spotlight', with the head office of the 'Nederlandse Handelmaatschappij' in the background, photographed by Matthias Kaptijn CFC

Jakarta 1937, the front building over the entire width of the façade in 'floodlights', photographed by Matthias Kaptijn CFC

The A. de Hoog firm supplied the memorial plaque, as well as many other smaller bronze works. The lamps in the office spaces came from the 'Industriële Maatschappij Gebroeders Van Swaay'. The construction of the construction took place under the direction of Fermont-Cuypers by the 'Hollandsche Beton Maatschappij N.V.'
The newspapers in the Dutch East Indies responded positively to the transformation with reports such as: 'The building meets the most modern requirements. With regard to design and layout, the building can compare positively with most of today's modern bank buildings. For the exterior, of course, the architecture of the already built part has been followed. The generous proportions of the front and bays make it much more monumental 'The more monumental the better because that fits seamlessly with the 'monumental era' that Europe was in the midst of. In the Netherlands, with the exception of *De Telegraaf*, no newspaper or trade journal paid attention to this project. That may say more about the disinterest in the Netherlands about what was going on in the colony than about the architecture of the building.

The main staircase in the new building CFC

Jakarta, stained-glass window from 1937 in the stairwell, partly reused from the original building from 1913, partly designed by Fermont-Cuypers (the bottom row on the photo) CON

Employees at their new workplaces in the Javasche Bank shortly after the opening in 1937 CFC

Jakarta, Museum Bank Indonesia in 2017, with the counters for the former Javasche Bank in the hall CON

Jakarta, the former bank building is now used as a museum CMB

Jakarta, decorations of the façade from 1913 were reused in the new front CGD

65 | 1937 Jakarta, Urban plan for Koningsplein (Medan Merdeka)

CITY: Jakarta
ADDRESS: Koningsplein/Medan Merdeka
ARCHITECT: Fermont-Cuypers
YEAR: 1937
Client: own initiative
CURRENT SITUATION: plan not implemented. Monas Jakarta
SOURCES: *Het Nieuws van den Dag voor Nederlandsch Indië*, June 12, 1934; *Bataviaasch Nieuwsblad*, September 25, 1937; *d'Oriënt*, September 25, 1937; *Bataviaasch Nieuwsblad*, October 2, 1937; *De Ingenieur. Weekblad gewijd aan de techniek en de economie van openbare werken en nijverheid* 52 (1937), no. 49; *Bataviaasch Nieuwsblad*, March 4, 1938; *De Indische Courant*, March 17, 1938; *Bataviaasch Nieuwsblad*, May 10, 1938; Brochure Robert Deppe Batavia 1938; Roosmalen (2008) pp. 130-132, 140-143.

The municipality of Batavia (Jakarta) presented a plan with its town hall in 'that large open space', in the very heart of the Koningsplein. It was made by Thomas Karsten. The municipality then asked professionals, including Fermont-Cuypers, to respond to the proposals. At Fermont-Cuypers, the employees wondered how the municipality could be so pretentious to position itself so centrally in a place that belonged to the whole country, with a palace and a national museum on the edge. They made an alternative plan and had a scale model made by Robert Deppe (1902-1943) with the following explanation:
'In our design, our guiding main principle is not to undermine the thoughts and ideas of those who created this large open space. That is only achieved by leaving the middle part completely undeveloped and not divided by buildings. As the eastern part was cut off by the railway line and the station from the original larger public space, a 'dead' side was thus created and therefore ideally the location for the desired buildings in accordance with the programme, all the more because it can hide the unsightly railway yard. For the Stadium, a central location on the east side seems the most favourable, both technically, access to and from the station- and aesthetically, because it allows for clear grouping of buildings including the new town hall with a representative appearance that is in keeping with the buildings around this unique square This cluster of buildings is accessible via a new road, which forms the new eastern boundary of the remaining large green space. The intended town hall is on the axis of the extended Museum avenue. An underpass formed by five generous gates underneath the town hall ensure access to the front and rear of this building that has yet to be designed. Due to the north-south orientation of the building, its location is favourable in terms of light and temperature. The north and south wing of the town hall can be expanded with numerous services, which are easily accessible by car and by train. In the south-east corner of the Koningsplein, space remains for a new museum complex with future expansions. The grounds to the front and the enclosed gardens can be arranged as an open-air museum.
In the northeast corner of the Koningsplein, plenty of room remains for Government Buildings. As a counterpart to the existing Telephone Office which will be maintained, a new building has been conceived for the Police Headquarters. A lively monumental closure of the square will be created by the concentration of the buildings on the eastern edge of the Koningsplein'.

The municipality was 'not amused' about the interventions of Fermont-Cuypers and, to the annoyance of some local newspapers, pushed forward with its own plan. In the meantime it was 1938. On May 10 of that year the final meeting took place in the city council with the result that a majority was against town hall on the square. With the intervention of the Second World War and the Indonesian independence struggle, it took until 1961 before the Koningsplein, which in the meantime was called Medan Merdeka, was redesigned. The National Monument was erected at the heart of the square, surrounded by greenery. A lay-out that, apart from the monument, is reminiscent of the sketch plan Dr. M. Treub made in 1892, and that Eduard Cuypers in 1909 firmly supported.

Jakarta 1937, Fermont-Cuypers choose for a monumental road in the west-east direction with a substantial building in the form of the new town hall as a termination. Behind it lies the intended stadium. In the background is the Willemskerk (now: GPIB Immanuel) with dome CFC

Jakarta, with its alternative plan in 1937, Fermont-Cuypers recommended leaving the open space of the Koningsplein (now: Medan Merdeka) as large as possible. All the buildings foreseen in their plan will be situated as far as possible on the edges, such as a new city hall and the stadium. Both form the centre of this photo of the scale model. Both are thus within walking distance of the train station. In the foreground the station and the Willemskerk (now: GPIB Immanuel) with dome CFC

Jakarta, Koningsplein ((now: Medan Merdeka) in 1937 formed the green heart of a city, which would grow enormously. For Fermont-Cuypers a reason to leave it as empty as possible CON

Jakarta, scale model of the plan as proposed by Fermont-Cuypers from 1937 CFC

Jakarta, detail photo of the model with the tower belonging to the stadium in the middle and the location for the intended town hall next to it CFC

Jakarta, the Koningsplein is called Medan Merdeka after independence. The open space, stripped of buildings such as the telephone office, offers space for the National Monument surrounded by greenery COF

66 | 1938 **Bandung: Bank vault at Javasche Bank**

CITY: Bandung
ADDRESS: Pieterspark/Jl. Braga No. 23
ARCHITECT: F. Dicke
YEAR: 1938
CLIENT: The Javasche Bank
CURRENT SITUATION: Bank Indonesia (bank vault)
SOURCES: *Het Vaderland*, September 9, 1937

'People are working on the construction of a large, blast-resistant bank vault behind the building of the Javasche Bank in Bandung', *Het Vaderland* reported on September 9, 1937 in the Netherlands, 'This expansion was anticipated in the construction of the bank in 1918. It was then already the intention to store all major securities and gold in Bandung'. In 1918 the idea of making Bandung the capital of the country was being considered. Now, the bank building in Jakarta was at risk of aerial bombardment. 'Therefore, a few other works are now being carried out on the Bank's premises in Bandung', according to the Dutch newspaper. In the Dutch East Indies, the press did not pay any attention to this event, in order to prevent unrest. Early September 1937, a large hole was dug to accommodate a bomb-proof vault between the bank and the home of the agent of the bank. Mr. I.M. van Lidth de Jeude, received several people involved in the building process. In the presence of his wife and children and the project builders, he toasted the smooth running of the works and expressed the hope that the vault would never have to be used.

Bandung: The work on the vault at the Javasche Bank in Bandung is in full swing in 1937 CFC

67 | 1938 **Jakarta: Kolff printing works**

CITY: Jakarta
ADDRESS: Petjenonganweg 72/Jl. Pecenongan/-
ARCHITECT: C.Th. Nix, F. Dicke
YEAR: 1938
CLIENT: Kolff & Co
CURRENT SITUATION: new buildings
SOURCES: *d'Oriënt*, December 1937; Terweij (1948)

In 1937's Christmas issue of the *d'Oriënt* family magazine, Kolff & Co printers announced the refurbishment of their printing works, located at Petjenongan (now: Jl Pecenongan), a side street of Noordwijk (now: Jl. Ir. H. Juanda), where the company had been established for some time. Fermont-Cuypers were commissioned to do the work. Thomas Nix made a colourful sketch of the desired situation, including a new office building and several industrial buildings with an impressive steel structure. This was because of the large span and with the ventilation openings that are necessary in the Dutch East Indies. The printers, which has been known as 'Royal' since 1930, informed the reader that since its inception in 1848, it had grown into one of the largest private printers in the Dutch East Indies, and that an expansion was necessary anyway: 'to bring the management and administration together in a modern office building. The high demands placed on modern printing nowadays require spacious and airy workshops.' 'The artist and copywriter, can now, work together to create something beautiful', according to the publisher. The construction and the opening attracted little publicity in 1938. The printing activities were conducted in the large new halls, printing books, newspapers and a magazine as *d'Oriënt*. The new office, according Fermont-Cuypers design, was never built.

Jakarta, drawing of the new office building for Kolff & Co made by Thomas Nix *D'ORIËNT*, DECEMBER 1937

68 | 1938 **Palembang: Charitas Hospital**

CITY: Palembang
ADDRESS: Talang Djawa 123/Jl. Jendral Sudirman No. 1054
ARCHITECT: Th. Taen
YEAR: 1938
CLIENT: Franciscan Sisters of Charitas from Roosendaal (the Netherlands)
CURRENT SITUATION: Rumah Sakit RK. Charitas
SOURCES: *Het Nieuws van den Dag voor Nederlandsch-Indië*, April 5, 1937; *Het Nieuws van den Dag voor Nederlandsch-Indië*, June 4, 1937; *Nieuwsblad voor de Residenties Palembang, Djambi en Banka*, January 18, 1938; CFR, photos, drawings

The terrain measuring approximately 40,000 square metres where the hospital was built, lays along what then was called Talang Djawa, which crossed Palembang's projected ring road (now: Jl. Kapten A. Rivai and Jl. Veteran) near the construction site. This road was completed almost simultaneously with the construction of the hospital. The very uneven building site exhibits height differences of up to nine metres. Many trees had to remain where possible for shade. The programme consisted of a main building, a few hospital pavilions for the first, second and third classes and a children's pavilion. In addition, they had to build a pavilion for infectious diseases, a service building with a kitchen, laundry facilities and a small mortuary. The complex also included a convent with a chapel and lodgings for the resident staff. Fermont-Cuypers positioned the main building in the southeast corner of the site, taking into account the expansion of both wings. The terrain was partially excavated, so that a number of buildings were located on the same level. Gentle embankments overcame the difference in height between the hospital pavilions, 'so that the food trolleys and patients for surgery can be pushed everywhere', according to the description.

The hospital pavilions and the convent were located parallel to the ring road. 'It is the intention to maintain the small hill with a very large tree near the convent, precisely because that place offers beautiful views in all directions'. The construction of the pavilions was kept as simple as possible. Concrete plastered brick walls were erected on foundations of reinforced concrete. Merawan wood was chosen, because jati or teak had to come from Java and that made it costly. The merawan roof constructions were given a deck of indigenous tiles, made locally.

'NV Volkers Aannemingsmaatschappij' presented the lowest bid of Fl. 157,000 and completed the job in seven months, from the moment the first stone was laid on June 4, 1937. Arthur Fermont attended this special moment, accompanied by his colleagues Beelen and Van Loon, who had been involved as supervisor and overseer. On January 15, 1938 the festive opening took place in the presence of 'all civil, military and municipal authorities'. Theo Taen was among the speakers. A day later, the building was consecrated by the church. From that moment on Palembang owned a hospital that 'was allowed to be', according to a newspaper.

Palembang, the first stone is laid on June 4, 1937 with a ceremony CFR

Palembang 1939, aerial view of the entire hospital grounds KNILM/CFC

Palembang, main building of the Charitas Hospital on the morning of the opening, January 15, 1938 CFC

Palembang, the laundry and kitchen of the Charitas Hospital in 1938 CFR

Palembang, the buildings of Charitas Hospital in 1938 CFR

Palembang, one of the hospital pavilions in 1938 CFC

69 | 1938 **Semarang: Bataafsche Petroleum Maatschappij**

CITY: Semarang
ADDRESS: Bodjong/Jl. Pemuda No. 114
ARCHITECT: C.Th. Nix
YEAR: 1938
CLIENT: Bataafsche Petroleum Maatschappij (Shell)
CURRENT SITUATION: PT. Pertamina Persero MOR IV
SOURCES: *Het Nieuws van den Dag voor Nederlandsch-Indië*, January 23, 1937; *De Indische Courant*, May 14, 1938; *Soerabaijasch Handelsblad*, May 14, 1938; *De Telegraaf*, October 19, 1938; Robert Deppe Batavia; CBN: photo album. Archive of Fermont-Cuypers.

These offices were officially opened on May 14, 1938. The building stands on 136 concrete piles, each with a length of 20 metres. The property has double external walls for better insulation. Furthermore, the large roof overhang of two metres contributes to a pleasant indoor climate. An 'air conditioning' installation could be installed in the future if and when 'these methods of air treatment are applied on a larger scale in these regions', reported a newspaper. The building was designed in the form of a right angle, with the rear wing providing the necessary extension possibilities. A higher ascending volume interrupts the main wing to the left of the centre. This volume, including the entrance and the special stairway, forms a vertical interruption in the horizontally layered building. This sort of vertical volume behind the entrance had already been used by the firm during the time that Ed. Cuypers was still a driving force at the firm. An example was in 1925, at the building of the H.V.A the Amsterdam Trade Association in Surabaya. In these earlier examples, however, the main entrance was always in the middle. The plinth of the building is finished with green-grey granite. Forged ironwork serves to protect the windows of the cash department, which is located on the corner. A generous *porte cochère* in front of the entrance gave access to the hall which, according to a newspaper, made a refined impression through the simple, yet tasteful finish. A beautiful showcase on both sides of the door displays the company products. 'The walls of the hall are clad with a polished travertine from Italy, which had not yet been used in the Dutch East Indies' according to the newspaper. Above the travertine there are several sculptures by the sculptor Louis van der Noordaa, who had settled in Bali for some time. Above the middle door on the back wall is the symbolic figure of a woman rising from a shell, the trademark of the company. On the right side is an image of a tank of a refinery and drilling towers. On wall on the righthand side there is a tanker and above it a Hermes figure, symbol of trade. On the other side, the Dutch East Indies as portrayed by a Dajak. In the bay, several ships are anchored, with oil installations in the foreground as could be seen on Borneo. The right wall bears a commemorative plate with the words: 'Eerste steen gelegd door Mevr. J.S. Cornelisse-Van Eendenburg 10 Juli 1937. Uitvoering: Nedam, Architecten: Fermont-Cuypers.' ('First stone laid by Mrs. J.S. Cornelisse-Van Eendenburg July 10, 1937. Execution: Nedam, Architects: Fermont-Cuypers) The staff and agency for Central Java donated the four stained-glass windows above the main entrance, made in Robert Deppe's studio. They portray very colourful actions concerning the use of fuel. In the public hall the walls covered in Delft turquoise ceramic tiles are an eye-catcher. Behind the portal is the stairwell, where the circular staircase attracts special attention in combination with tiled slender columns and the colourful stained-glass that is installed in the narrow windows in the ceiling. The stained glass in the dome window is also by artist Robert Deppe. Underneath the building is a cellar where employees could shelter in case of air strikes. 'This office building is the first in the Dutch East Indies, where such a provision is immediately included', according to a newspaper.

The building itself was still beautiful in 2015, thanks to Pertamina. It is a pity that the large new shopping centre next to it has been built so closely to this colonial jewel.

Semarang, the new office of the 'Bataafsche Petroleum Maatschappij' seen from the air KNILM/CFC

Semarang, design sketched by Thomas Nix, made for the office of the 'Bataafsche Petroleum Maatschappij/Shell' CFC

Semarang, front of the B.P.M. shortly after completion of the building, May 14, 1938 CFC

Semarang, an edited photo of the building in 2015 CON

Semarang, the entrance to the office from the inside in 1938 CFC

Semarang, the layout of the office space in 1938 CFC

Semarang, the remarkable staircase in the building CFC

Semarang, the boardroom in the office of the BPM in 1938 CFC

Semarang, the restaurant in the office of the BPM CFC

70 | 1938 **Jakarta: N.K.P.M. building ('Koloniale')**

CITY: Jakarta
ADDRESS: Koningsplein-Zuid 18/Jl. Medan Merdeka Selatan No. 18
ARCHITECT: C.Th. Nix
YEAR: 1938
CLIENTS: N.K.P.M., K.P.V.M., Socony
CURRENT SITUATION: Departemen Energi dan Sumber Daya Mineral
SOURCES: *d'Oriënt*, January 22, 1938, pp. 28, 29; *Soerabaijasch Handelsblad*, January 17, 1938; Breuning (1954), p. 143

On January 15, 1938 three partner companies officially occupied their new offices on Koningsplein-Zuid (Medan Merdeka Selatan). These were the sister companies: 'Nederlandsche Koninklijke Petroleum Maatschappij' (N.K.P.M.) and the 'Koninklijke Petroleum Verkoop Maatschappij' (K.P.V.M.), which worked closely with the American parent company Socony since 1933. They acquired joint offices, designed by Fermont-Cuypers. In large letters on the façade was: 'De Koloniale'. The façade extends over more than 65 metres and the guttering height is almost 12 metres. The building has two storeys with an Indian roof and a number of toilets above the main entrance and central staircase. The plinth was clad in locally sourced trachyte, Indonesian natural stone of volcanic origin from Cirebon. The ground area is approximately 65 by 18 metres. Behind the main building, there are two short side wings. The layout is simple with a central corridor on both floors from which the rooms can be accessed on either side. The first floor provided space for the N.K.P.M.'s management, communications department and research bureau. The ground floor was predominantly occupied by the K.P.V.M.'s executive departments such as the Accounting Department, a laboratory and cycle parking for sixty bicycles.
The 'Hollandsche Beton Maatschappij' laid steel foundations. The superstructure consists of masonry with a skeleton of reinforced concrete. The outer shell consists of cavity walls as they provided good insulation against the heat. The narrow, vertical windows in the deep recesses ensure uniform subdued light. *Het Nieuws van den Dag voor Nederlandsch-Indië* wrote about the air conditioning on December 5, 1936: 'We were told that this N.K.P.M. building will be the first in the Dutch East Indies, where the design already includes provisions for the installation of an air-conditioning unit. However, these plans are still being reviewed, as it has become apparent that different people react differently to temperature changes resulting from air conditioning'.
As far as architecture is concerned, it is noticeable that the façade is completely symmetrical with a protruding and more elevated central section. Above each of the four pillars in the middle section, there is a supporting sculpture group, made by Louis van der Noordaa. They symbolise Labour, Technology, Trade and Prosperity. (They are nowadays somewhat weathered by wind and air pollution) Above the main entrance hang the emblems of the three companies. Fermont-Cuypers made that visible with three doors above which gargoyles were incorporated, forming unity. These sculptures are also made by Van der Noordaa. Upon entering, the visitor enters a hall with a light brown travertine panelling and a double staircase executed in black and red terrazzo. The stairway leads to a landing where light enters through eight narrow, tall, stained-glass windows, in which Robert Deppe colourfully has shown the nature of the company. a derrick, a tank, a ship and an airplane and further kegs, barrels and similar objects. At the top of the windows Deppe placed the coats of arms of the cities where the companies had branch offices: Bandung, Palembang, Jakarta, Surabaya and Semarang. Moreover, one window contained the coat of arms of the Netherlands.
At the busy reception at the official opening, the three companies received their guests in the vestibule on the first floor. In his speech, the director focused on the cooperation between the companies, which from now on were under one roof.
The director finished his speech with the words: 'Should the Municipality of Batavia be able to implement its long-standing wish to create the road connecting with Koningsplein-West, this office building will undoubtedly form a worthy building along this new road. In this connection, I express our hope

Jakarta, a design sketched by Thomas Nix for the 'Koloniale' on the Koningsplein (now:Jl. Medan Medeka Sel.)' CFC

Jakarta, stained-glass windows from the studio of Robert Deppe CON

One of the four sculptures incorporated into the façade, called 'Prosperity' by the sculptor Louis van der Noordaa *D'ORIËNT* JANUARY 22, 1938

of having access to the spacious strip of land along the new road. We will give it a suitable purpose to further enhance this important future road'. This connecting road was a consideration that Fermont-Cuypers kept in mind from the start. In 1934, the architecture firm had already built a few structures for the N.K.P.M. on this plot, and in such a way that the building in question would form an architectural unity with the new building that was being created.
H.A. Breuning, a retired civil servant from the Jakarta municipality, wrote in 1954 that he thought this was a 'gaudy building'. Whether he was right or not could not be judged in the Netherlands as his book *Het voormalige Batavia* did not contain photographs of the building.

Currently the building has become the representative front building of a number of high office towers behind it. The whole building complex is in good condition. The three gargoyles above the doors are painted gold now. The present owner is considering making it a museum.

Jakarta, the new head office called the 'Koloniale' of the 'Nederlandsche Koninklijke Petroleum Maatschappij' (N.K.P.M.) and 'Koninklijke Petroleum Verkoop Maatschappij' (K.P.V.M.). The building was put into use on January 15, 1938 CFC

Jakarta, the main entrance with three doors of the former 'Koloniale' (now: Departemen Energi dan Sumberdaya Mineral) with a gargoyle above each door made by Louis van der Noordaa, those have been painted gold now CON

71 | 1938 Jakarta: 'Bataafsche Petroleum Maatschappij' (B.P.M.)

CITY: Jakarta
ADDRESS: Koningsplein-Oost/Jl. Medan Merdeka Tim 1A
ARCHITECT: C.Th. Nix
YEAR: 1938
CLIENT: 'Bataafsche Petroleum Maatschappij'/Shell
CURRENT SITUATION: Koperasi Karyawan Pertamina Dana Ventura and Bank Mandiri
SOURCES: *De Indische Courant*, August 13, 1937; *Bataviaasch Nieuwsblad*, October 8, 1938; *De Indische Courant*, October 8, 1938; *Het Nieuws van den Dag voor Nederlandsch-Indië*, October 12, 1938; *Soerabaijasch Handelsblad*, October 10, 1938; Brochure of Robert Deppe Batavia 1938; Breuning (1954), p. 143; Nix (1949) p. 114

In 1936, the Board of the 'Bataafsche Petroleum Maatschappij' (B.P.M.) decided to build new offices. Fermont-Cuypers made the design based on a construction plan drawn up by the Technical Department of the company. It was determined in advance that the building should not only be suitable for the management of B.P.M., but also for the B.P.M Agency in West Java and for the 'Koninklijke Nederlandsch-Indische Luchtvaart maatschappij' (K.N.I.L.M.: Royal Dutch-Indies Airways). The first stone was laid on August 12, 1937, after which the construction company N.V. Nedam finished the works in 14 months. The official opening took place on Saturday morning, October 8, 1938. In a short speech Arthur Fermont said that the assignment to make one building for three parties put a stamp on the building, because each party asked for its own separate entrance, whilst one architectural unit had to be created. 'As far as architecture is concerned, we strove,' says Fermont, 'to give the building an air of strict functionality and simplicity'. The building was erected as a skeleton structure in reinforced concrete in between brick masonry. Virtually all materials used came from the Dutch East Indies, with the exception of a few bronze works, metal windows, the roof covering and the marble floor and the wall coverings of travertine. 'It is gratifying,' says Fermont, 'that many of the works of art such as the sculpture, the bronze memorial plaques, the stained glass and ceramics, for which people used to rely on Europe, were designed and executed in this country.' Fermont continued, 'I hereby express my gratitude for the trust of this important client. I hereby hand over to you the building that I hope will meet your future requirements and be a symbol of the growth and prosperity of the B.P.M.'

The building was on the corner of the Willemslaan (now: Jl. Perwira) and Koningsplein-Oost (now: Medan Merdeka Tim). A façade of 105 metres stood along the Willemslaan. The design, with this wall length and with the 32-metre-high corner tower was in response to a little green triangular square of similar dimensions that the municipality wanted to create in front of the building, in accordance with its plan for the Koningsplein from 1934 and 1937. The little square was not to be, there are however countless roads from where you can barely see the building now. The building has a depth of 20 metres and a guttering height of about 19 metres. The façade along the Koningsplein-Oost was 32 metres and is thus in proportion to the height of the tower. The tower was crowned with a 'light lantern', with the letters B.P.M. visible from all sides. Two generously proportioned *portes cochères* marked the two entrances of the building on the Willemslaan. There were display cases on both sides. In the design of the building, the Dutch East Indies climate was taken into account as much as possible with extra attention to coolness, air circulation and minimal direct sunlight. This is visible on the outside in the roof and the horizontal window strips with the vertical partitions. These prevent direct sunlight. All windows and exterior doors are made of steel, similar to the roof construction, while the roof covering of the building is made of European glazed tiles. The plinth of the building is made of natural stone, namely trachyte from Cirebon, which Fermont-Cuypers also used in other projects. Entirely in the spirit of time, a bomb shelter was created in the building.

The left entrance along the Willemslaan provided access to the stairs of the office of the main representative of B.P.M.,

Jakarta, an aerial photo from 1938 with the new headquarters of the B.P.M. on the corner of Willemslaan (now: Jl. Perwira) and Koningsplein (now: JL. Medan Medeka Tim.). Next to the new building is the Brother school from 1906, with the Brothers' house behind it, which was also designed by Fermont-Cuypers KNILM/CFC of which all rooms were on the first floor. These boardrooms occupied the entire wing up to the middle section. The walls of the entrance hall are covered with polished travertine, white marble is used on the floor and to line the stairs. In front of the back wall, the staircase is situated with a bronze balustrade to the first floor. A bronze relief hung above the stairs, designed and executed by the sculptor Louis van der Noordaa. Elsewhere in the hall hung a bronze plaque of Sir Henry Deterding, the founder of the firm. Above the main entrance, light was projected through stained-glass windows. Across the stairs, a hallway with a beautiful vertical Art-Deco lamp reaches the hall on the first floor where travertine also features. Above the staircase, daylight enters through six high stained-glass windows, which were installed in the end of the hall in the building. The windows were made in the studio of Robert Deppe and show images related to the company, namely: the extraction, transport, processing, distribution and use of the various products made and distributed by the company. In the lower windows on the stairwell landings there are depictions of local residents from Java, Sumatra, Kalimantan and West Irian, the islands where the exploitation of petroleum took place. In the upper windows, the artist incorporated the emblems of the important companies of the group. The hall on the first floor is also clad in travertine. The main rooms were covered with jati-kembang wood.

The middle section on the Willemslaan granted access to the B.P.M.'s agency for West Java that took up most of the building. In order to separate public and staff in this office, there is a double hall on the ground floor, the foremost part of which is mainly intended for the public. This hall is covered with travertine with some bronze reliefs above the cladding from Van der Noordaa with symbolic representations of Europe and Asia. The inner hall on the ground floor provided access to the various rooms, such as the agent, legal representatives, secretary, statistics department, archives and sales department. To the right were the purchasing department, technical department and shipping. A monumental staircase leads from the hall to the first floor. On the first floor were accounting and mechanisation. The walls of the lower hall and the staircase hall were tiled with European ceramics, while the floor and stairs were made of polished decorative concrete. A bronze plaque of Queen Wilhelmina, designed by the Dutch sculptor Toon Dupuis (1877-1937), was hung on the landing in the stairway.

Behind the 32-metre-wide façade on Koningsplein-Oost (now: Medan Merdeka Tim.) was the K.N.I.L.M., which rented its office space from B.P.M. The façade was very appealing because of the seven-metre high windows overlooking the square, the entrance on that side and an open gallery on the first floor. On the right side there was a display case on the ground floor against the façade, in which the company presented itself to the visitors. A bronze plate showed the departure hours of aircraft to the different destinations. The visitor was received in a large, very modern room with contemporary counter functions. Here people came with commissions for aerial photography and orders were picked up. A large ceramic tableau was installed in the stairwell, showing all the airlines of the K.N.I.L.M. The light entered the hall through stained-glass windows, designed in the studio of Robert Deppe, with representations of the most important airports which the airline visited, such as Sydney, Bangkok, Manila, etc. The hall opened out into the offices of the management and accounting, which were on the first floor and of course the public hall for the passage office on the ground floor.

Jakarta 2015, bronze relief above the stairs designed by Louis van der Noorda (1894-1945) PHOTO: JOEP WALTER

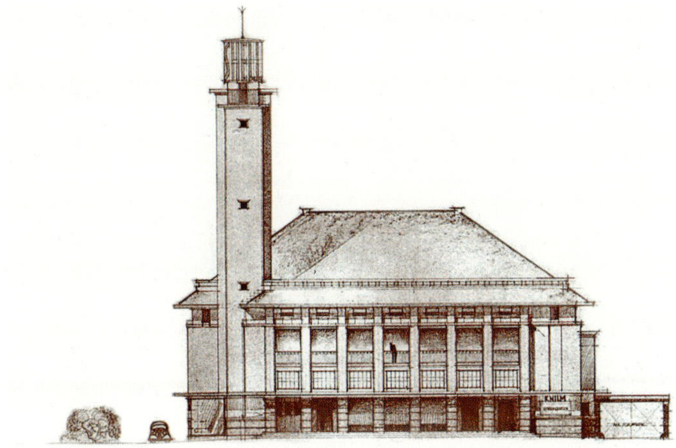

Jakarta, façade of K.N.I.L.M. on Koningsplein (now: Jl. Medan Merdeka Tim). Drawing by Thomas Nix from 1937 CFC

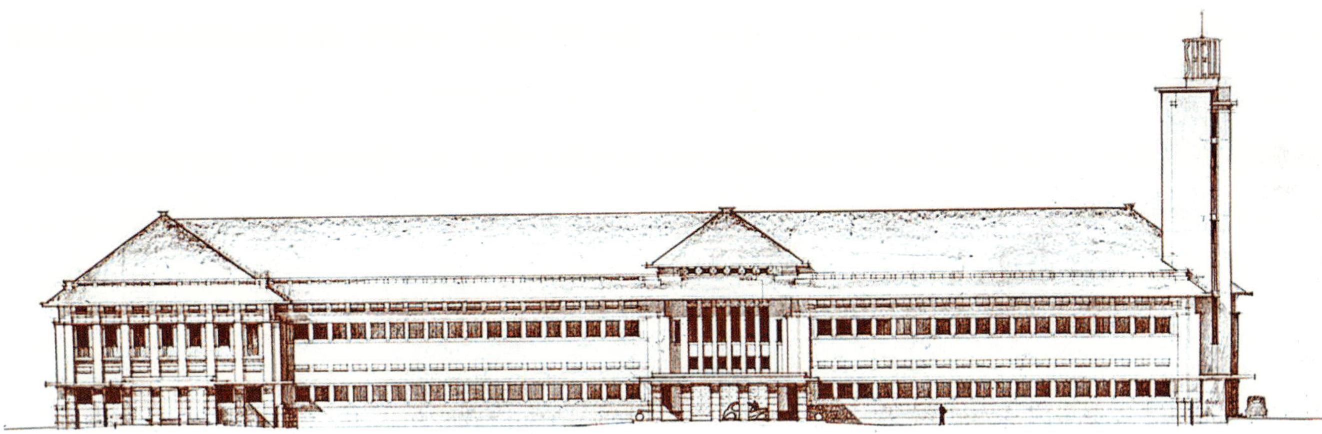

Jakarta, B.P.M. façade on Willemslaan (now: Jl. Perwira). Drawing by Thomas Nix from 1937 CFC

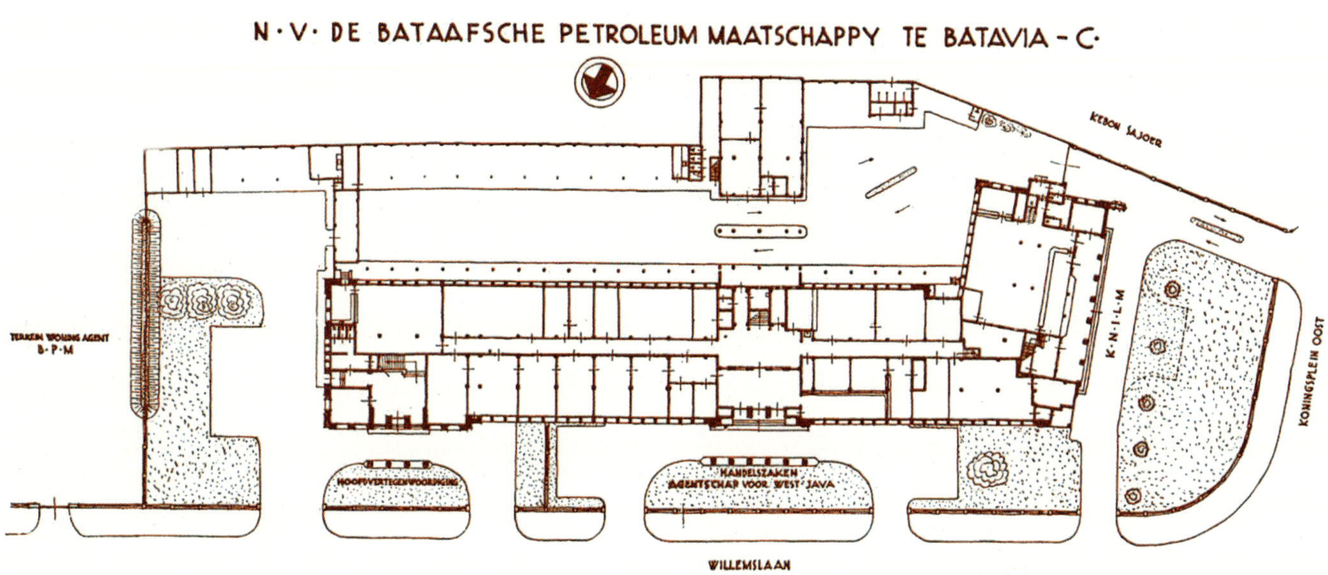

Jakarta 1938, B.P.M. ground floor with from left to right, Head representation B.P.M, agency West-Java and K.N.I.L.M. Drawing by Thomas Nix CFC

Jakarta, tower on the corner of Willemslaan (Jl. Perwira) and Koningsplein (Jl. Medan Merdeka Tim.) in 1938 CFC

The entrance for the board of the B.P.M. shortly after the opening on October 8, 1938 CFC

The tower, viewed in 1938 with light lantern with company logo CFC

The south façade of the headquarters in 1938 CFC

The still empty display case of the passage office of the K.N.I.L.M. CFC

The entrance for the board of the B.P.M. CFC

The main entrance of the B.P.M. shortly after the opening CFC

The accounting department of B.P.M. CFC

The hall with stairs to the boardrooms on the first floor CON

B.P.M., stairwell to the first floor CFC

72 | 1938 **Palembang: Escomptobank and Volkscredietbank**

CITY: Palembang
ADDRESS: Passarstraat -Tenkoeroekkade/Jl. Bumi Sari/-
ARCHITECT: A.A. Fermont
YEAR: 1938
CLIENT: Escomptobank and Algemeene Volksverzekeringsbank
CURRENT SITUATION: demolished during construction of Ampera bridge
SOURCES: *De Sumatra Post*, October 9, 1937; *Soerabaijasch Handelsblad*, December 3, 1938; Brochure of Robert Deppe, Batavia 1938

For many years, the Nederlandsch Indische Escompto Maatschappij had a plan for the construction of an office building in Palembang, but it was only in 1937 that the plan became more concrete. Fermont-Cuypers was commissioned. The previous bank building that the firm had created for the Escompto was in 1931 in Banjarmasin. But it had been forced to close its doors as a result of the economic crisis a few years later. What made this build in Palembang so special was that the Escompto bank was working together with the 'Algemeene Volksverzekeringsbank'. The building had to accommodate both banks and had to be built on the plot where the Escompto was already located. This was near the ferry landing over the Musi river. The building site offered more space than needed, for the compact programmes of both banks. This left room for another company. (the Nederlandsche Handel Maatschappij built a small modern building there in 1938, architect J.Th. van Oyen)
Many interested parties attended the opening on November 25, 1938. Arthur Fermont informed those present that the dual formula meant that several entrances were needed. Both banks wanted to keep their own standing. The building rested on a foundation of concrete piles and was erected as a frame construction in reinforced concrete with an intermediate filling of brick masonry. The cavity walls provided extra insulation. The large, shady roof, the awnings and the windows with deep reveals, provided maximum protection from the sun and kept the building cool. The architecture of the building was characterised by a Dutch-East-Indian, business-like character with small windows, horizontal awnings and the Indian roof with overhang. The entrance to the Escomptobank was on the corner of the Schoolweg and the Tengkoeroekade. Behind the entrance there was a large public hall, bordered by the office spaces, including a room for the agent, the administration and a cashier's room. Behind the main building were the safes, the garage and sanitary facilities with a fireproof archive space upstairs, which could be accessed via stairs from the office. The reinforced concrete pile foundation was carried out by the Volkers Aanneming Maatschappij. The doors of the vault and archives came from Lips in Dordrecht (the Netherlands), Lindeteves Stokvis supplied the steel windows. The ceramic wall covering in the hall was designed by Robert Deppe. Deppe also made a ceramic model with the coat of arms of the Volkscredietbank. The tiles on the floors came from Czechoslovakia. The Mesman Schultz company in Jakarta supplied the ironwork. The interior and furniture were designed according to Fermont-Cuypers design by Sin Hap Lie from Palembang. On the roof were improved Dutch tiles, delivered from the tile setting works in Palembang.
Sadly, because of the construction of the approach road to the Ampera Bridge, the building had to be demolished, as well as the neighbouring building of Nederlandsche Handel-Maatschappij and the Javasche Bank of Eduard Cuypers from 1922.

Palembang, the Escomptobank on November 25, 1938, the day of the opening CFC

Palembang 1938, the Fermont-Cuypers bank building (right) and the Nederlandsche Handel-Maatschappij. Both buildings are demolished in 1962 during the Ampera bridge works CFC

Palembang 1938, behind the new building, the Javasche Bank from 1922, which was also demolished for the construction of the new bridge over the Musi river CFC

73 | 1938 Jakarta: Dutch East Indies Tourist office (NITOUR)

CITY: Jakarta
ADDRESS: Rijswijkstraat 2/Jl. Majapahit No. 2A
ARCHITECT: C.Th. Nix
YEAR: 1938
CLIENT: Lissone-Lindeman and Oger Frères
CURRENT SITUATION: shop premises
SOURCES: *Bataviaasch Nieuwsblad*, July 27, 1934; *De Indische Courant*, February 26, 1938; *Bataviaasch Nieuwsblad*, March 18, 1938; *Bataviaasch Nieuwsblad*, November 9, 1938

'For a country such as the Dutch East Indies, which is only on the threshold of its further development, tourist traffic is of great significance. Because a visit to the country itself more than what is written in the books about the archipelago, will teach the visitor that in addition to a fairy-tale of natural wealth, other riches are to be found. Knowledge of a country such as Insulinde must generate appreciation and interest. This means that the Indies can occupy a worthy place among the other countries around the Pacific, where the centre of gravity of the world is moving towards' according to Nitour, as the travel agency Lissone-Lindeman in the Dutch East Indies was known as after July 1, 1934.

The travel agency occupied the new building from November 14, 1938, which, with a very modern look, radiated confidence in the future at one of the most striking locations in Jakarta. Nitour was already at this location, together with Oger Frères. This tailor's retail business also occupied part of the new building designed by Fermont-Cuypers on the Rijswijkstraat (now Jl.Majapahit) and the Djaga Monjet (now: Jl. Suryopranoto). On March 18, 1938, *Het Bataviaasch Nieuwsblad* published the news of the planned new building: 'We have heard of plans to remodel the building at the beginning of the Rijswijkstraat, where the Nitour and Oger Frères are now located'. Another newspaper expressed the expectation that the building, as a counterpart of Hotel des Galeries, will significantly enrich the cityscape around the Harmonieplein (now: Harmoni). It was what the papers called a 'two-storey building' with all the qualities of a modern building, which was carefully integrated into the existing situation. On the side of Djaga Monjet (now: Jl. Suryopranoto) the gradualpassage of architectural styles was visible from the clean lines of the flat-roofed corner building further along to a single-storey toko with a roof. Although all three façades in sight show an architectural similarity, they showed visible differences in the openings on the first floor, which resulted in a pleasantly varied picture within the tight pattern. The travel agency itself occupied the retail space on the corner of the Harmonieplein (now: Harmoni) and was present on all sides in its shop windows, displaying its selection of trips, alternating with photos and models of seagoing vessels. The ground floor was arranged for the public, where interested persons could find information. Above was the documentation department, where travel plans were created and calculated, and the hotel rates and the like were tracked. There was also the archive and the administration. The clothing store Oger Frères had its main entrance and shop window on the Rijswijkstraat (now: Jl. Majapahit), but also had earlier access to Djaga Monjet. The company's chief lived above this shop. The building was indeed a successful counterpart to the Hotel des Galeries, which was completed six years earlier. 'The Harmonieplein has undergone a significant improvement in six months', a newspaper wrote the day after the opening. Because of its crucial location, the building served as a backdrop for many important moments in the history of Indonesia. Maintenance of the building is therefore not only of architectural interest, but of historical importance as well.

Jakarta 2017, the former NITOUR building on Harmoni, which many pass by every day without knowing that it is a modern monument of the city CON

Jakarta, the NITOUR building on Harmonieplein (Harmoni) on the corner of Rijswijkstraat (now: Jl. Majapahit) and Djaga Monjet (now: Jl. Suryopranoto), with a slightly different façade architecture on each street CFC

Jakarta, the rear of Oger Frères on Djaga Monjet (now: Jl. Suryopranoto) in 1938 CFC

Jakarta, the NITOUR building shortly after the opening on November 14, 1938, the Rijswijkstraat (now: Jl. Majapahit) on the left CFC

Jakarta 1938, the attractive link between the NITOUR building and the Oger Frères building on Djaga Monjet (now: Jl. Suryopranoto) CFC

74 | 1938 **Jakarta: St. Carolus Hospital, children's pavilion**

CITY: Jakarta
ADDRESS: Salemba 41/Jl. Salemba Raya No. 41/-
ARCHITECT: Th. Taen
YEAR: 1938
CLIENT: Sisters of Mercy of the Holy Carolus Borromeo from Maastricht (the Netherlands)
CURRENT SITUATION: new building for Rumah Sakit Carolus
SOURCES: *Het Nieuws van den Dag voor Nederlandsch-Indië,* December 10, 1938

On December 10, 1938, Mrs. Tjarda van Starkenborgh Stachouwer, the wife of the Governor-General, opened the new children's pavilion of the St. Carolus hospital on Salemba. She was presented with the key to the pavilion from Arthur Fermont on a velvet cushion, inviting her to open the new building. The structure was T-shaped. The design was characterised by an Indian functionalism with small windows, a large lofty roof and a plinth of river pebbles. The pavilion contained eighteen separate rooms for children. One wing was intended for babies, the other for older children. 'We consciously opted for separate rooms, so that the risk of contamination in the event of outbreaks of disease was kept to a minimum, Fermont said. 'All these rooms were painted in soft white and light green colours, which are particularly pleasing to the eye, as is the white lacquered furniture', wrote *Het Nieuws van den Dag voor Nederlandsch-Indië* and continued, 'Each room has its own bed and bath, with hot and cold running water and a dressing table. The night lighting in the hallway and in the rooms consists of a so-called 'skirting-board lighting', whereby lighting has been installed along the skirting boards in order not to disturb the children with sudden flashing light'. Each room also had its own front gallery, where the beds of the patients could be placed in good weather. The entire pavilion was mosquito-free. It had excellent ventilation that excluded draft and provided sufficient cooling due to the high roof. The leg of the T shape housed rooms, such as the kitchen, the milk-bottle sterilising and extra-bathrooms. On the other side, there were extra toilets and bathrooms and the sisters' bedrooms were so situated that there was an overview of all sleeping quarters. By using marble and ebonite everything was easy to keep clean. *Het Nieuws van den Dag voor Nederlandsch-Indië* continued on December 10, 1938, 'The children all have an unobstructed view of a large garden that they can enjoy in the shade of the trees on summer days'.

The building was located along Salemba next to the main building. The pavilion made way for high-rise buildings of the hospital, whereby the characteristic masonry wall with lighting along Salemba also disappeared.

Jakarta, the new children's pavilion on the grounds of the Sint Carolus Hospital in 1938. An attractive fence formed the border on Salemba (now: Jl. Salemba Raya) CFC

75 | 1939 **Wonosobo: Institute for the Deaf and Mute**

CITY: Wonosobo
ADDRESS: /Jl. Mangli No. 10
ARCHITECT: Th. Taen
YEAR: 1939
CLIENT: Sisters of the order Daughters of Maria and Joseph from 's Hertogenbosch (the Netherlands)
CURRENT SITUATION: Lembaga Bisu Tuli
SOURCES: *Nieuwe Venlosche Courant*, May 28, 1938; *Koloniaal Missie Tijdschrift*, March 15, 1939, p. 95; *Soerabaijasch Handelsblad*, February 9, 1939

On Tuesday February 7, 1939, an institute for the deaf and mute opened its doors. It had been commissioned by the sisters of the Daughters of Mary and Joseph, an order based in 's Hertogenbosch, that was in the Dutch East Indies for only a year, with the aim of achieving something meaningful for the deaf and mute in that country. Attendees included the Governor of Central Java, the Resident of Kendu, the regents of Wonosobo and Bandjarnegara. In his speech, Fermont said that in order to carry out this project properly, he had visited a similar institute in Sint Michielsgestel in the Netherlands to create a scheme for design and layout. Then Fermont-Cuypers designed a complex that offered space for 100 pupils. As the budget was insufficient for this, only part of the planned middle and left wings, with an intermediate kitchen and a toilet building, were carried out. The front of the centre wing, which could be used as a boarding school in the future, housed three classrooms on completion, while the office and storage space were at the entrance. The play area was located behind the main building and formed the connection between the boarding school and the school building. The school had ten classrooms. Each classroom offered space for ten pupils. Because these were always seated in a semi-circle around the teacher, only a relatively small number could be in a class. A maximum of light was an absolute requirement for an institution like this. In the south wing, the front section served as chapel and dining room. The back section contained the dormitory for the sisters. Between both wings stood the service building with a kitchen. This kitchen complex was situated in such a way that a direct connection was possible between the children's and the sisters' dining rooms. The future chapel was projected in the extension of the south wing onto the forecourt and could seat 100 people. The buildings consisted of a concrete skeleton, its walls were sealed with plastered brick. This construction offered the best guarantees against collapse by earthquakes. The architecture conformed practically and functionally to Indies functional design.

Wonosobo, the front of the institute for the deaf, which was opened on February 7, 1939 CFC

76 | 1938 **Sungailiat: Primary school and Brother house**

CITY: Sungailiat
ADDRESS: /Jl. Maria Goretti No. 7
ARCHITECT: Th. Taen
YEAR: 1938
CLIENT: Brothers from Dongen (the Netherlands)
CURRENT SITUATION: SMP Maria Goretti
SOURCES: *Nieuwe Tilburgse Courant*, January 19, 1938; *Charitas*, February 15, 1938; Ethelbert (1986), pp. 99-106; CEK AR B004 1483

'In 1934, Sungailiat was a shabby station', according to Charitas of the Brothers from Dongen. After a number of difficulties were overcome, the Dutch Chinese School was established in a house in August 1935. The number of pupils grew steadily and the house became too small. That is why the brothers decided to build a new school with a brother house. They discovered a large plot for both the brother house and a school complex. At the end of 1937, the favourable message from Dongen in the Netherlands was conveyed that enough money had been raised for the project. Fermont-Cuypers was commissioned for the design. One of the brothers carried out the construction. There was money for two thirds of the project. The remaining amount followed shortly thereafter, so that the building was completed in September 1938. The official inauguration of the spacious school complex took place on November 25, 1938. The result is a classic-looking, symmetrically-designed Brother house of one storey with a roof. The main entrance is situated in the middle axis of the façade, with small windows and shutters on both sides, which could keep the heat out. The school's covered assembly hall to the right of the brother house is close to the street. On the other side, it opens to the school garden. There are several connected classrooms, around an open playground, all covered with a generous roof.
On January 23, 1954, the brothers decided to close the school due to lack of staff. On July 15, 1954 the sisters took over the complex, which is still in use today.

Sungailiat, the covered play area/assembly hall from 1938, still in use in 2017 CON

Sungailiat, classrooms interconnected around a large space, which still has to be planted with greenery in 1938 CFC

Sungailiat, the covered playground seen from the public road with the Brother House to the rear in 1938 CFC

77 | 1939 **Lahat: Schools and convent**

CITY: Lahat
ADDRESS: Goenoeng Gadjah/Jl. Sekolah No. 13
ARCHITECT: Th. Taen
YEAR: 1939
COMMISSIONER: Sisters of St. Carolus Borromeo from Maastricht (the Netherlands)
CURRENT SITUATION: SMP Santo Yosef, Susteran
SOURCES: *Nieuwsblad voor de Residentiën Palembang, Djambi en Banka,* March 2, 1939

In 1933, the priest in Lahat started a school that attracted so many pupils that the sisters had to take the school over three years later. One of them was Laurentina de Sain, who had been present at the beginning of the large school complex in Bengkulu. She had set up a primary school, a school for advanced elementary education and a Dutch Chinese School in Lahat and had ensured that in 1936 new buildings could be considered, even though the funds were still lacking. The fact that Laurentina looked again to Fermont-Cuypers was not surprising, because she was Theo Taen's sister-in-law. However, it was not Taen, but Fermont who was present on Wednesday morning March 1, 1939, the day that countless visitors were received by Laurentina for the opening of the new school complex with adjoining convent. In his speech, Arthur Fermont said that at the end of 1936 they were asked to make a sketch, which led to the purchase of a suitable terrain. The primary school, the school for advanced elementary education and the St. Joseph convent were situated on it with a projected access road. Fermont frankly stated that the structure of the convent and boarding school largely corresponded to the buildings in Bengkulu. As in Bengkulu, the complex here was characterised by an Indies objective style with a touch of traditionalism, in the spirit of what is known in the Netherlands as: 'Delftse School'.

Lahat, the opening of the school building and convent complex on March 1, 1939 CFC

Lahat 1939, on the right the convent with two sisters in the main entrance, access to the schools on the left CFC

Lahat, the convent including the chapel, photographed on the day of the consecration, 1 March 1939 CFC

78 | 1939 **Bandung: Ciumbuleuit Villas**

CITY: Bandung
ADDRESS: Tjioemboeleuit/Ciumbuleuit (unknown address)
ARCHITECT: Th. Taen
YEAR: 1939
CLIENTS: Tan Tjoan Keng and Tan Tjoan Hong
CURRENT SITUATION: unknown
SOURCES: *Bataviaasch Nieuwsblad*, February 13, 1933; Interview with Hwan Tan on July 14, 2016

The clients of this project were Tan Tjoan Keng and his brother Tan Tjoan Hong. Fermont-Cuypers had been commissioned six years earlier by Tan Tjoan Keng to build the villa in Menteng, which soon became the Italian consulate. The man was erudite, studying first in Jakarta at the Dutch Chinese School and then the H.B.S. secondary school, so that he could go on to study Indies law in Leiden (The Netherlands). He had a penchant for architecture, photography and was a car fanatic. During and after his studies he frequently participated in car rallies in Europe and in the Middle East. Streamlined design was what he and his brother wanted to see reflected in the architecture of their two houses. The houses were built on a large estate, known as 'theeland Tjioemboeleuit', just outside the municipal boundary of Bandung. One of the houses called 'Huize Olga' was featured on the photos in the Fermont-Cuypers archive. Olga was Tan Tjoan Hong's wife. Her name was mentioned on the left of the driveway. Houses like these were popular in the Dutch East Indies, but most of them consisted of a substructure, a roof, a bay window and the like. These distinguish themselves as one sculptural whole, partly through the use of *batu-lempeng*, natural stone slabs, in the plinth and the walls around the porch. Whether they still exist could not be traced.

Bandung 1939, the two villas in Ciumbuleuit with the names of the two brothers at the communal entrance: Tan Tjoan Hong and Tan Tjoan Keng CFC

79 | 1939 Makassar: Brother school

CITY: Makassar
ADDRESS: Komedielaan 12/Jl. Thamrin No. 3
ARCHITECT: Th. Taen, F. Dicke
YEAR: 1939
CLIENT: Brothers from Tilburg (the Netherlands)
CURRENT SITUATION: SMP Brother
SOURCES: *Het Vaderland*, November 2, 1939; *De Tijd*, November 3, 1939; *Maasbode*, November 7, 1939; *De Indische Courant*, November 7, 1939

There was great interest on November 1, 1939 when the Apostolic Prefect of Makassar blessed the new brother school of St. Rafael. Among the attendees were the Mayor of Makassar, representatives of the Interior Board, the Inspectors of Education, the Director of the HBS secondary school and many others. The blessing was followed by the handover of the building by Theo Taen. He outlined the origins and execution of the plans and expressed the hope that the building would meet all expectations after completion. The mayor congratulated the brothers wholeheartedly. The Inspector of Education said he could ensure that this school was not only the most beautiful in Makassar, but even in the 'Groote Oost' (Great East). He also congratulated the management and staff with this great result. Then two boys from the upper class came forward, presented a congratulation in rhyme and offered the Director a flower arrangement. A newspaper wrote: 'All residents of Makassar have seen this building on the Komedielaan (now: Jl. Thamrin) rise out of nowhere.
A visit to the property confirms the impression you obtain from outside'.
For years, a small hall gave access to two spacious, well-ventilated rooms on both sides. Behind the hall, the stairwell led upstairs to four more spacious classrooms. Each classroom offered room for 30 students and in some cases, it was easy to add another row of seating for ten pupils.
The school underwent numerous expansions. The principal's office is now located in the former hall of this thriving school. On the outside next to the old front door, which is now closed off, there is still the stone displaying the name 'Fermont-Cuypers'.

Makassar, the recently opened Brother school, November 1, 1939 PHOTO THEO TAEN CFC

80 | 1940 **Makassar: Stella Maris Hospital**

CITY: Makassar
ADDRESS: Standweg corner Arendsburgweg/Jl. Somba Opu No. 273
ARCHITECT: Th. Taen
YEAR: 1940
CLIENT: Sisters of the Holy Virgin from 's Hertogenbosch (the Netherlands)
CURRENT SITUATION: RS Stella Maris
SOURCES: *De Indische Courant*, October 21, 1938; *Het Nieuws van den Dag voor Nederlandsch-Indië*, January 10, 1940; *I.B.T. Locale Techniek* 9 (1940), pp. 133-135

Until well into the twentieth century, Makassar was little more than a port with a row of warehouses along the beach. After a tsunami, a seawall was constructed, so that building plots were created on the land side where land had been reclaimed. One of these plots became the official residence of the mayor. The large plot next to it was bought by the Roman Catholic mission for the construction of a hospital. Arthur Fermont discussed a first concept with the municipality with one-storey pavilions with a roof, as the firm had previously built in Surabaya and Palembang. The municipality itself thought of some modern buildings with two storeys. Fermont convinced the municipality to refrain from doing so. The first stone was laid on December 8, 1938. The terrain was 160 metres wide and

Makassar, new Stella Maris Hospital in 1939, the new seafront on the right CFC

had an average depth of 115 metres. Two existing houses were kept for the time being as a sister house and nurses' home. The distance between the pavilions had to be kept to a minimum Fermont-Cuypers placed the general service buildings as centrally as possible. The main building stood with the front façade to the beach promenade. It contained the administration and an operating room with all the accessories. On either side of the main building, space was left for a future hospital pavilion and a maternity hospital. In the extension of the main entrance, a gallery served as a connection for all existing and future galleries. The hospital pavilions were on either side of a communal service entrance with the service rooms behind them. On the east side of the site were the laundry and kitchen. All buildings, except the front building, were located north-south, which prevented direct sunlight from entering the rooms as much as possible. The set-up ensured the ventilation of the entire site. The gardens between the pavilions had a width of about 25 metres. It became a simple plan due to the insufficient budget. For the time being, air conditioning was not used, although it was taken into account during construction. The hospital opened on January 10, 1940 in the presence of Theo Taen. The hospital later underwent numerous expansions. Almost all original buildings have now been replaced by new ones. As a reminder, the old main building was kept with the small *porte cochère* in front of the original entrance.

Makassar, main entrance of the Stella Maris Hospital in 1940 CFC

81 | 1940 **Jakarta: Canisius College (extension)**

CITY: Jakarta
ADDRESS: Menteng 40/Jl. Menteng Raya No. 64
ARCHITECT: Th. Taen, F. Dicke
YEAR: 1940
CLIENT: 'Strada Vereeniging'
CURRENT SITUATION: Chapel SMA Kanisius
SOURCES: *De Indische Courant*, July 8, 1939; *Bataviaasch Nieuwsblad*, August 15, 1940; *Bataviaasch Nieuwsblad*, December 9, 1940

In July 1939, the Canisius College purchased an adjoining plot to extend their school with a new assembly hall and chapel. Fermont-Cuypers were commissioned to design it. This extension was taken into account in the design of the 1929 school. On 15 August 1940 when the new buildings were completed, Theo Taen spoke on behalf of Fermont Cuypers. In his speech, Taen looked back to the creation of the plans in 1926: 'We did not enhance the visibility from the road. On the contrary, the modest old buildings along Menteng have been camouflaged for years. Only in the last few months have the renovations come to the forefront with the construction of the boarding school'. Theo Taen told his audience how the school complex had grown and how it could further develop through the purchase of plots 44 and 46 on Menteng. 'The most recent addition was deliberately three-storeyed to leave as much space as possible for a sports field. As far as the interior of the chapel is concerned', according to Taen, 'we have tried to achieve something with simple means'. 'The spatial effect has been increased by the high arches of the side corridors, while the high windows in the middle section ensure that light enters the area uniformly. It was taken into account that the interior could later be modified and enriched. 'Some stained-glass windows of the priest's choir are being replaced by a stained-glass representation from the Gospel of Christ's Miraculous Multiplication of Loaves and Fish at the Lake of Gennesaret'. That was Robert Deppe's creation. *Het Bataviaasch Nieuwsblad* showed the result of Deppe's work on December 9, 1940, as can still be seen in the chapel now.

Jakarta, photo made in 1940 of the chapel at Canisius College CNJ

Jakarta, the chapel in 2014 CVN

82 | 1940 **Jakarta: Mater Dolorosa Chapel**

CITY: Jakarta
ADDRESS: Pasarstraat 122/Jl. Jantinegara Barat Raya No. 122
ARCHITECT: Th. Taen, F. Dicke
YEAR: 1939
CLIENT: Sisters of the Good Shepherd from Leiderdorp (the Netherlands)
CURRENT USE: Chapel SD Santa Maria Fatima
SOURCES: *Het Nieuws van den Dag voor Nederlandsch-Indië*, November 16, 1939; *Bataviaasch Nieuwsblad*, March 13, 1940; Vletter (1997), p. 67; Beekhuis (2009), p. 50

In the first plans that Fermont-Cuypers made for The Good Shepherd order in around 1930, the chapel was positioned centrally in the middle of all new buildings on the large sloping plot. For reasons described earlier, the church had to be located closer tothe nearby road. When the foundation stone was laid on November 15, 1939, a certificate was signed as usual which, together with a few coins, was placed into a copper cylinder behind the masonry as a message for later. Four months later, the classic-looking white chapel with tent roof and roof turret with bell was ready. From the outside, the attached apse and the arched windows are clearly visible. The arches connect with the arches in the arcade of the main building, creating unity in architecture from the street. Mgr. P.J. Willekens S.J., the Apostolic Vicar of Jakarta, dedicated the church in a simple manner on March 13, 1940. The monsignor walked, dressed in mantle and mitre, to the entrance of the chapel, where the 'Asperges me' was sung. After the outside of the chapel was sprinkled with holy water, the 'Asperges me' sounded again.

During the Japanese occupation, the complex, including the chapel, served as a camp hospital. Only 34 nurses cared for about 13,000 sick people. Many died. From May 1945, about 1,000 men and older boys from various men's camps were received, many of whom also succumbed. The chapel is still there.

Jakarta, the back of the new chapel of the Mater Dolorosa convent in 1940 on Pasarstraat (now: Jl. Jantinegera Barat Raya) CFC

Jakarta, the chapel in 2014 CVN

83 | 1940 Semarang: Business school (extension)

CITY: Semarang
ADDRESS: Koningin Emmalaan 6/Jl. Dr. Sutomo No. 6
ARCHITECT: Th. Taen, F. Dicke
YEAR: 1940
CLIENT: Brothers from Maastricht (the Netherlands)
CURRENT SITUATION: SMP PL Domenico Savio
SOURCES: *Bataviaasch Nieuwsblad*, February 4, 1936; *De Indische Courant*, October 8, 1936; *De Indische Courant*, August 5, 1938; Christinus (1940), pp. 253, 302, 305; Archive of Brothers from Maastricht

At the beginning of February 1936, Fermont-Cuypers heard that they had missed out on a major commission. The Brothers from Maastricht decided on the architect J.Th. van Oyen for the construction of a Brother's house, a school complex and a new church at Randoesari in Semarang. Someone who was involved in that decision later wrote: 'The architects Fermont-Cuypers and Van Oyen were invited to deliver a proposal. Van Oyen's plan was deemed the most efficient and the least expensive'. Shortly afterwards, Van Oyen's plan began to take shape and the school was completed in August 1936 and the Brother house in October of that year. The church was consecrated at the end of July 1937. Van Oyen had even moved to Semarang again especially for this project. It must have surprised Fermont-Cuypers then that at the beginning of 1939 they were commissioned for new buildings for the Trade school. In March they submitted the construction drawings for this building, which was to be built next to the Brother house. Both buildings were orientated to the public road. The architecture of the Brother house, with its small vertical windows, shutters and turret, is reminiscent of the style that was promoted in the Netherlands by Professor Granpré Molière in Delft. The thought of working in a similar style may have played a role. In the end, Taen and Dicke from the firm reinforced the autonomous character of the school building by making it strictly symmetrical, horizontal and giving it a modern look with horizontal window strips.

Semarang 2016, the name of the firm amidst painted river boulders CVN

By placing the classrooms behind the open loggias and galleries, there was no direct sunlight and they remained cool. In the damp course of the building the architects incorporated river pebbles, as Van Oyen had in the Brother house, which emphasised the relation between the buildings. The Fermont-Cuypers name was introduced between the pebbles. The inauguration took place on August 1, 1940.

Semarang, on the left the brother house designed by J.Th van Oyen and the new business school in 1940 CFC

Semarang 1940, the back of the business school, shortly after the completion of the building CFC

84 | 1940 Jakarta: Tanjung Priok harbour establishment

CITY: Jakarta Tanjung Priok
ADDRESS: Ambonkade/Jl. Ambon
ARCHITECT: Th. Taen, F. Dicke
YEAR: 1940
CLIENT: 'N.V. Nederlandsch-Indische Scheepvaart-Etablissementen'
CURRENT SITUATION: office premises in the container port
SOURCES: *Het Nieuws van den Dag voor Nederlandsch-Indië*, February 16, 1940; *Bataviaasch Nieuwsblad*, February 16, 1940; *Soerabaijasch Handelsblad*, February 17, 1940; *Haagsche Courant*, February 16, 1940; *De Indische Courant*, October 22, 1940; CMM Rotterdam, various photos

On February 16, 1940, it became known that work had begun on the harbour establishment in Tandjung Priok, on behalf of the 'N.V. Nederlandsch-Indische Scheepvaart-Etablissementen'. This involved new office premises and a reception area at the top of the Ambonkade for two partner companies: the 'Rotterdamsche Lloyd and Scheepvaart Maatschappij Nederland'. Fermont-Cuypers created a scale model for the project in advance, a photograph of which appeared in a few newspapers. 'The existing office of the Rotterdam Lloyd will be placed there when this building has been completed,' one of the newspapers reported. 'Those who come to pick up or drop off passengers will have an open view of the sea from this building. A comfortable seating area for those waiting is planned, consisting of a semi-circular hall on the ground floor with large plate-glass on all sides and spacious terraces are located on the first and second floors. The building is flanked by a tower that will be visible from a very large distance from the sea'. In August 1940 the opening took place without any publicity. The high expectations were fulfilled. The glazed hall was located below in a semi-circular extension. Above, an awning and a floor with a further protruding continuous awning with a ribbon window below, also offers a terrace overlooking the sea. The building appeared similar to the cabin of a modern ship. The extension has a pronounced horizontal character, the square tower to the right of it with the vertical slit window stands in contrast. With an intermediary, the extension was connected to a broad warehouse with a slight roof slope. 'A lot of care has been devoted to the interior of the reception room', a newspaper noted. 'Tiling is everywhere. There are mosaic reliefs on the walls, while in the hall on the first floor a mosaic tableau of the Port of Rotterdam can be seen. These last works have been executed according to design in the Robert Deppe studios'. Shortly after completion, the building underwent a visible change as a result of the outbreak of the Second World War. All buildings in the port area were painted using camouflage colour, masking the fresh white. The building resumed service in the years 1945-1957, and was a beacon at sea, both on arrival and at the final departure of the last Dutch citizens in 1957.
The building still exists. It stands on the closed harbour site and stripped of its once proud towers, it functions now as an office building.

Jakarta, scale model made by Fermont-Cuypers of the cruise terminal in Tanjung Priok CFC

Jakarta, view from the water of the passenger terminal with tower in the fifties VLETTER (1997) P. 136

Jakarta, the harbor establishment viewed from the water in the late 1940s PHOTO CAREL BLASER CMM

85 | 1941 **Surabaya: Offices of 'De Nederlanden van 1845'**

CITY: Surabaya
ADDRESS: Paradestraat 1/Jl. Veteran No. 37
ARCHITECT: Th. Taen, F. Dicke
YEAR: 1941
CLIENT: Dutch insurance comnpany: N.V. Assurantie Mij. 'De Nederlanden van 1845'
CURRENT SITUATION: Office Jiwasraya
SOURCES: *d'Oriënt*, December 25, 1939, p. 31; *Soerabaijasch Handelsblad*, March 4, 1940; *d'Oriënt*, January 11, 1941

'The corner, formed by Sociëteitstraat (now: Jl. Veteran) and Paradeplein (Jl. Sikatan) , is hidden from view by a high fence. There is a large and beautifully executed sign announcing that the new office building of the 'De Nederlanden van 1845' will be built here. Looking over the fence, you see only a very high iron tripod and below that the pile driver thumps the solid heads of the concrete piles. Next to the entrance to the building site it is written that 'access is forbidden here'. We were, however, too curious, hesitated only for a moment and entered. Immediately we were struck by the activity in this area of 2,200 m² where there is nothing as yet, while the work has already been going on for 3 months. In the building supervisor's office, we found a few hundred drawings, maps, tables and Mr. Ad. Kip from the Architects and Engineering Firm Fermont-Cuypers, which has provided the design for this project and also supervises the construction work.' according to *Het Soerabaijasch Handelsblad* of March 4, 1940.
The building was opened on January 4, 1941. At the opening, the Governor of East Java expressed his admiration of the initiators, architects, engineers and builders who had assembled the building materials for such a large project during this difficult time. 'The construction of this office signifies Dutch courage at a difficult time'. The director of the Hollandsche Beton Maatschappij considered it a privilege to be able to build something in a time when much is being broken down. He expressed the hope that 'when the centenary of the 'De Nederlanden van 1845' is celebrated in a few years, this may also be celebrated in the Netherlands under an orange sun above the Kingdom of the Netherlands of 1945'.

The complex has a U-shaped layout with a 17-metre-wide courtyard, ensuring sufficient daylight and air. One side of the building is on the Sociëteitstraat and a long façade is on the Paradeplein. The corner on the two streets is positioned further back and protrudes slightly above the two façades with a staggered structure. Vertical windows are defining here. In the streets on either side, long, continuous awnings give the façades a predominantly horizontal character. Unlike the Borsumij building of the architect C. Citroen on the other side of the Sociëteitstraat, which was completed six years earlier, the firm opted to place the windows in the façade and not recessed behind it, as often happened. 'This benefits the overall image', says Theo Taen in his speech at the opening. This is much more pleasant for passers-by than what is basically a completely closed façade. 'However, the windows on the ground floor have been placed high above the pavement level so that one can view the street from the office without the opposite being possible'. Another special feature was the direct ventilation and lighting of the corridors, the latter partly due to the use of glass building blocks in the ceiling. The position of the main entrance, the central hall and the stairwell ensure that the building lends itself well to multiple tenants. At the opening of the building, the firm 'De Nederlanden van 1845' was housed on the ground floor and in the basement. The Tiedeman and Kerchem companies used the first floor. The stained-glass windows in the hall on the ground floor and in the stairwell come from the studio of Robert Deppe.

Surabaya, the building in 2013 CON

Surabaya, the offices of 'De Nederlanden van 1845' shortly after the opening in 1941 *D'ORIËNT* JANUARY 11, 1941

Surabaya, a postcard from the early 1950s, the offices of 'De Nederlanden van 1845' on the right and the Borsumij building on the left CON

Surabaya, one could take out insurance here against all accidents. Stained glass from Robert Deppe studio CON

Surabaya, one could take out a life insurance. Soon the war would also break out in Asia.
Stained glass from Robert Deppe studio CON

86 | 1954 **Jakarta: Bank of China**

CITY: Jakarta Kota
ADDRESS: Stadhuisplein, Kali Besar oost/Fatahillah Square, Jl. Kali Besar Timur No. 5
ARCHITECT: K. Mekel
YEAR: 1954
CLIENT: Bank of China, Beijing China
CURRENT SITUATION: Bank Mandiri (re-use)
SOURCES: *De Indische Courant*, November 14, 1938; *De Sumatra Post*, November 7, 1941; Archive of Fermont-Cuypers. Ballast-Nedam Collection

After 'Scheepvaart Maatschappij Nederland' finally abandoned its pre-war intention of establishing its headquarters at this location in the old town, the Bank of China declared itself ready to settle here. Karel Mekel filled almost the entire, rectangular plot, which covered an area from the square to the Kali Besar. The first drawings were based on a smaller building volume. The final plan contained three storeys for the total structure. Photomontages were made by Fermont-Cuypers to persuade the officials that the building was not out of place in this area. The main building along Fatahillah Square was approximately 36 by 36 metres. Along the Kali Besar, the building had an L-shaped building mass of 48 by 36 metres, which left room for a small, elongated courtyard. Both buildings were linked by a narrow staircase with an extra entrance on the Stadhuisstraat (now: Jl. Kali Besar Tim. No. 5). This layout allowed separate leasing of the floors. On the side of Fatahillah Square there was the public hall with a main staircase and a lift. In accordance with the building regulations - in place since the beginning of the century - the Kali Besar has a covered gallery on the ground floor. There is also an entrance, including the courtyard, which bordered on one side of the 'Coenmuseum' (now: Museum Wayang). In the spirit of post-war modernism, Mekel worked with assembly and prefab elements. The N.V. Nedam took care of the construction. After completion, the building appeared closed. This was partly because on the Fatahillah Square and on the Kali Besar, there is a façade to exclude direct sunlight. This consists of concrete supports with horizontal awnings in front of small, concealed vertical windows, ensuring a pleasant indoor climate and subdued daylight. A normal façade was sufficient on the shady narrow Jl. Kali Besar Tim. No. 5, although the windows were also recessed there. The outer façades adjacent to the courtyard are less closed. There are open galleries with iron fences. The building was opened in 1955 without much ceremony and has since contributed to the cityscape in the Kota of Jakarta. The owner is considering a new purpose for the building.

Jakarta, the former Bank of China on the Fatahillah square in the Old Town district (Kota Tua) in 2015 CON

Jakarta, the building of the Bank of China close to completion in 1954 PHOTO: JOS VAN MEURS CFC

Jakarta, the former Bank of China seen from Kali Besar Tim. in 2018 PHOTO: MARSAD

Jakarta, the building seen from Fatahillah square in 2015 CON

Jakarta, Bank of China on the Kali Besar in 1954, designed by Fermont-Cuypers, in the background 'Internatio' designed by Ed. Cuypers and Hulswit from 1913 PHOTO: JOS VAN MEURS CFC

87 | 1954 Jakarta: Housing at Percetakan Kebayoran printing works

CITY: Jakarta
ADDRESS: Jl. Trunoyo, Jl. Sunan Kalijaga
ARCHITECT: K. Mekel
YEAR: 1954
CLIENT: Joh. Enschedé from Haarlem (the Netherlands)
CURRENT SITUATION: housing at Peruri Percetakan Uang printing works
SOURCES: *Het Nieuwsblad voor Sumatra*, August 15, 1955; *Javabode*, August 15, 1955; Model by Studio Nico Zomer; Photo of the model, M.A.J. van Bommel from Utrecht (the Netherlands); Archive of Joh. Enschedé Haarlem, Aan de Amstel Architects, Amsterdam.

A new housing regulation of the young Republic of Indonesia stipulated that a foreign employee returning from a vacation abroad lost his rights to his former rented house. This caused a boom in the construction of so-called instant housing by companies. Joh. Enschedé was also forced to build homes for the Dutch staff. Increased land prices meant that as well as a row of houses on the Jl. Sunan Kalijaga, some apartments also had to be built, consisting of two-storey houses, with a generous roof, suitable for four households. These accommodation units were accessed via a porch and a communal staircase, as was customary in post-war Netherlands. It is suspected that the houses may have been designed in the Netherlands, in consultation with Karel Mekel, perhaps by the architecture firm 'Eduard Cuypers' in Amsterdam. In the small archive that this agency left behind, many photographs of these houses were found. To convince the Board of Joh. Enschedé that a beautiful ensemble of a factory with residences could be created, Nico Zomer Studio was asked to make a scale model. A photographer took photos of this model which accompanied the building application in Indonesia. On May 15, 1953, the houses on Jl. Sunan Kalijaga were completed. The houses on Jl. Trunoyo and the Director's residence were completed in July 1954. It was, as the photo from 1956 shows, a quiet street. The management of Joh. Enschedé decided in that year not to build more houses, which explains why the side along Jl. Panglima Polin Raya remained undeveloped for a long time.

Jakarta, the former residence of the director in 2017 CON

Jakarta, in the foreground the director's home and some two-storey houses. Behind it the printing works completed in 1955 CJE

Jakarta, the two-storey houses on Jl. Trunoyo next to the printing works in 1956 CJE

88 | 1955 Jakarta: Ruznar and Go residences

CITY: Jakarta
ADDRESS: Kebayoran Block C-1 No. 308 and Block F2
ARCHITECT: H. Roebbers
YEAR: 1955
CLIENT: Mr. Ruznar and Mr. Go
CURRENT SITUATION: unknown
SOURCES: *Bouwkundig Weekblad* 77 (1959), p. 129

Mr. Ruznar's house in Kebayoran Baru Block C-1 No.308, is an example of what was later referred to in Indonesia as the Jenki style. The house had to be ready quickly for someone who, presumably from abroad, had to live in it. There was a boom in the construction of this kind of relatively simply built housing, as a result of a housing regulation that had been introduced shortly before. It stipulated that a foreign employee lost his rights to his rented house if he went abroad for a few months on leave. Mr. Ruznar had a house built for himself, where he could return to after a period of absence. It did not need to be an expensive and solid home, but it was required to be cool and innovative. Henk Roebbers opted for an open loft design with a large gable roof including a roof overhang and small windows with raised concrete edges to block direct sunlight. He introduced the ventilation openings in the outer walls subtly and artfully. The foundation and jambs consisted of concrete blocks. The first floor was of reinforced concrete, the other floors were finished with tiles. The damp course was of batu-lempeng, a natural stone slab that was often used in this building style and was also suitable as floor covering for terraces. Wooden shingle was used on the roof. The contractor was 'N.V. Djakarta Aannemingsbedrijf' under the direction of Mr. F. Soeterik, which was established on March 15, 1953. That is also illustrative for the 1950s in Jakarta, Dutch people who set up Indonesian companies had to be able to continue working.

Mr. Go's house situated in Kebayoran Baru Block F2, was modest in size. The house had a sitting room, a dining room, a small kitchen and a bathroom, as well as three bedrooms. The most open side of the house was on the north. The other facades were relatively closed. The small window openings, framed in a concrete raised edge, did not allow direct sunlight. There was a kind of carport at the house. On the desk roof there were ironwood slates (sirappen). For the foundation, split quartz was used with a concrete anti-earthquake window. On it came brick walls, contained in a light concrete skeleton. Tiles in different colours lay on the floors. The walls were treated with 'PC splashing' except in places where aluminium sheets were applied. Whether the house still exists could not be determined.

Jakarta 1955, Mr. Ruznar's residence, designed by Henk Roebbers of Fermont-Cuypers CRF

Jakarta 1955, side façade of Mr. Ruznar's residence, from another angle CFC

Side elevations of Mr. Go's home on Kebayoran Baru, designed by Henk Roebbers *BOUWKUNDIG WEEKBLAD* MARCH 14, 1959

89 | 1955 Jakarta: Percetakan Kebayoran printing works

CITY: Jakarta
ADDRESS: Jl. Falatehan I No. 4
ARCHITECT: K. Mekel
YEAR: 1955
CLIENT: Joh. Enschedé from Haarlem (the Netherlands)
CURRENT USE: Peruri Percetakan Uang printing plant
SOURCES: *Het Nieuwsblad voor Sumatra*, August 15, 1955; *De Tijd*, June 5, 1953; *Javabode*, August 15, 1955; Model, Studio Nico Zomer; photos model, M.A.J. van Bommel from Utrecht, Archive of Joh. Enschedé Haarlem, Archive of Aan de Amstel Architects, Amsterdam

After Joh. Enschedé & Sons were requested by the Indonesian government to build a large printing plant in Jakarta, the firm turned to Fermont-Cuypers for a design. The first building plans date from April 23, 1951 and must have been drawn up in close collaboration with the client in the Netherlands, with the help of Arthur Fermont. The construction of a banknote printing factory required, more than any other project, insight into production processes and maximum security. The first sketch shows a totally enclosed area with extensive premises of approximately 100 by 50 metres. The terrain is accessed from one entrance gate with porter houses on either side, the main building in between, and several industrial halls behind. The architecture of the main building was in line with the tradition of Indonesian Art Deco. Within a prefab framework, figurative open building blocks were used that ensured ventilation in the building. A sketch, also dated April 23, shows that the intended main building, in terms of architecture, responds to the Indonesian identity. For example, the roof has the well-known ventilation slot and the outer walls are slightly recessed. Fermont-Cuypers may have wanted to prove that, after more than 25 years, they knew what building in the tropics meant. As the months passed, the plans were not only modified, but the project also increased in size. Not only the main building but also the location because of the construction of staff accommodation. A sketch map shows the plot in Kebayoran with dimensions of 215 by 225 metres. The business premises were positioned almost centrally, with room for expansion possibilities. Work began on July 8, 1952 with the construction of a number of houses. In March 1953, N.V. Nedam started the construction of the business premises. The construction company assumed a budget for the expenses of Rp. 8,500,000. Due to a number of estimates, including the iron construction, the glass building blocks, etc., this amount increased to Rp. 20,000,000.-
At the end of March 1955, the first banknotes rolled off the presses in denominations of 1 Rupiah. Printing equipment here was more advanced than the presses at the parent company in Haarlem. On August 11, 1955, the official opening of one of the largest and most modern printing factories in the world took place. Mrs. Hatta, the wife of the Vice Prime Minister of Indonesia, unveiled the plaque.

Jakarta, the printing works in 2017 CON

Jakarta 1955, the completed building of the Pertjetakan Kebajoran printing works CJE

Jakarta 1955, clearly visible are the façade elements in the vertical windows around the main entrance CJE

90 | 1956 Ambon: Bank Indonesia

CITY: Ambon
ADDRESS: Jl. Pattimura No. 7
ARCHITECT: K. Mekel
YEAR: 1956
CLIENT: Bank Indonesia
CURRENT USE: bank (unrecognisably rebuilt)
SOURCES: Archive of Fermont-Cuypers; *Preangerbode,* March 20, 1956

On Saturday, March 17, 1956, the Governor of Bank Indonesia, Mr. Sjafruddin Prawiranegara, opened the branch office of Bank Indonesia in Ambon. It thus became its 16th branch. 'The opening ceremony was attended by the Director of Bank Indonesia, Mr. Lukman Hakim, who flew in from Jakarta to Ambon, as well as the Secretaries-General of the Ministries of Economic Affairs and Connections, resp. Sumarno and Mutalib Danuningrat, President of Bank Rakjat Indonesia, Durjaatmadja, Treasurer General, Mr. Sugiarto, Director of Bank Industri Negara, Sukasno, and Mr. Tahija of the Caltex Pacific. According to plan, the outgoing First Deputy Prime Minister Djanuismadi, as well as the outgoing Ministers of Finance and Economic Affairs would also be present, but due to political developments in the capital, that intention was abandoned,' according to the Preangerbode, 'The branch office of Bank Indonesia Ambon is now housed in the most beautiful building in the city.'

The building was designed by Karel Mekel (1920-1997), employed by Fermont-Cuypers in Jakarta. In terms of typology and architecture, the building is very similar to striking buildings from the Indonesian past. With this choice, the architecture firm wanted to contribute to the strengthening of Bank Indonesia's own identity, which came into existence in July 1953 through the acquisition of the Javasche Bank.

Ambon, opening of Bank Indonesia, Henk Roebbers, representing Fermont-Cuypers, in the middle CRF

Ambon, the building of Bank Indonesia from 1956 CON

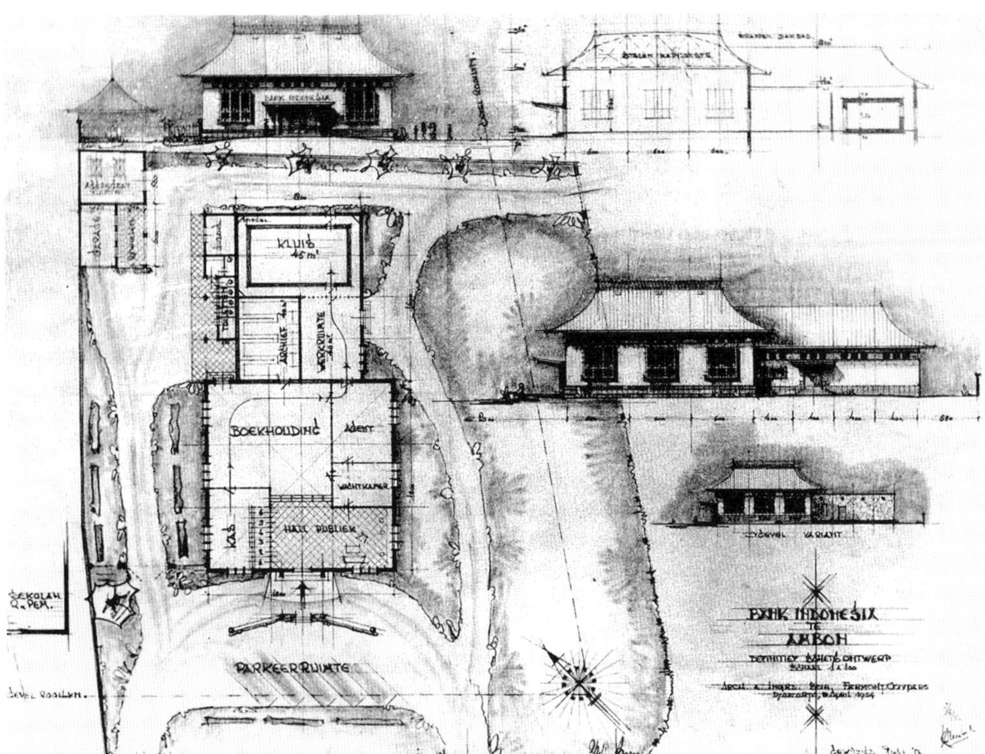

Ambon, the sketch made by Karel Mekel for the bank building in 1954 CFC

91 | 1956 **Jakarta: Essence Indonesia**

CITY: Jakarta
ADDRESS: Jl. Otto Iskandardinata No. 74
ARCHITECT: H. Roebbers
YEAR: 1956
CLIENT: Polak and Schwarz N.V. from Zaandam (the Netherlands)
CURRENT SITUATION: N.V. Essence Indonesia
SOURCES: *Bouwkundig Weekblad* 77 (1959) pp. 125-127

This commercial building contains everything that later would become known as the Jenki style. The company name refers to an Indonesian company, while the client was a Dutch company, namely Polak and Schwarz N.V. from Zaandam. This company commissioned two business premises, which were favourably exposed to or shielded from the sun, namely north-south. The construction consists of a concrete skeleton with brick walls. The design has an angular and playful character. The building has two floors with a roof and has a very simple layout. Terrazzo tiles and PVC tiles are used on the floors. On the ground floor, slightly recessed from the first floor, is the storage area of goods, flexible, sub-divisible office spaces are above and a gallery along the entire length. The square window in the side façade is slightly recessed due to sunlight. The large upright concrete frame around the window is typical of this style. This also applies to the use of light materials, which give the impression that the building is of a temporary nature. The woodwork came from Indonesia. The frames are from teak (*jati*). In addition, there is also use made of what was called cyanised Borneo wild wood. On the roof there are wooden shingles (*siraps*), the walls are clad in *batu-lempeng* (stone slabs). The concrete construction and the end façades were painted light grey, the intermediate fillings were off-white. A simple workshop was built behind the main building. The contractor was an Indonesian company, partly arising from more or less mandatory takeovers of a few Dutch companies under the name BIWEG.

Jakarta, rear of the N.V. Essence Indonesia building in 2013 INTERNET

Jakarta, photographs of the very expressive façades of Essence Indonesia built on behalf of Polak & Schwarz CFC

Jakarta, the east elevation of the Essence Indonesia premises in 1956 CFC

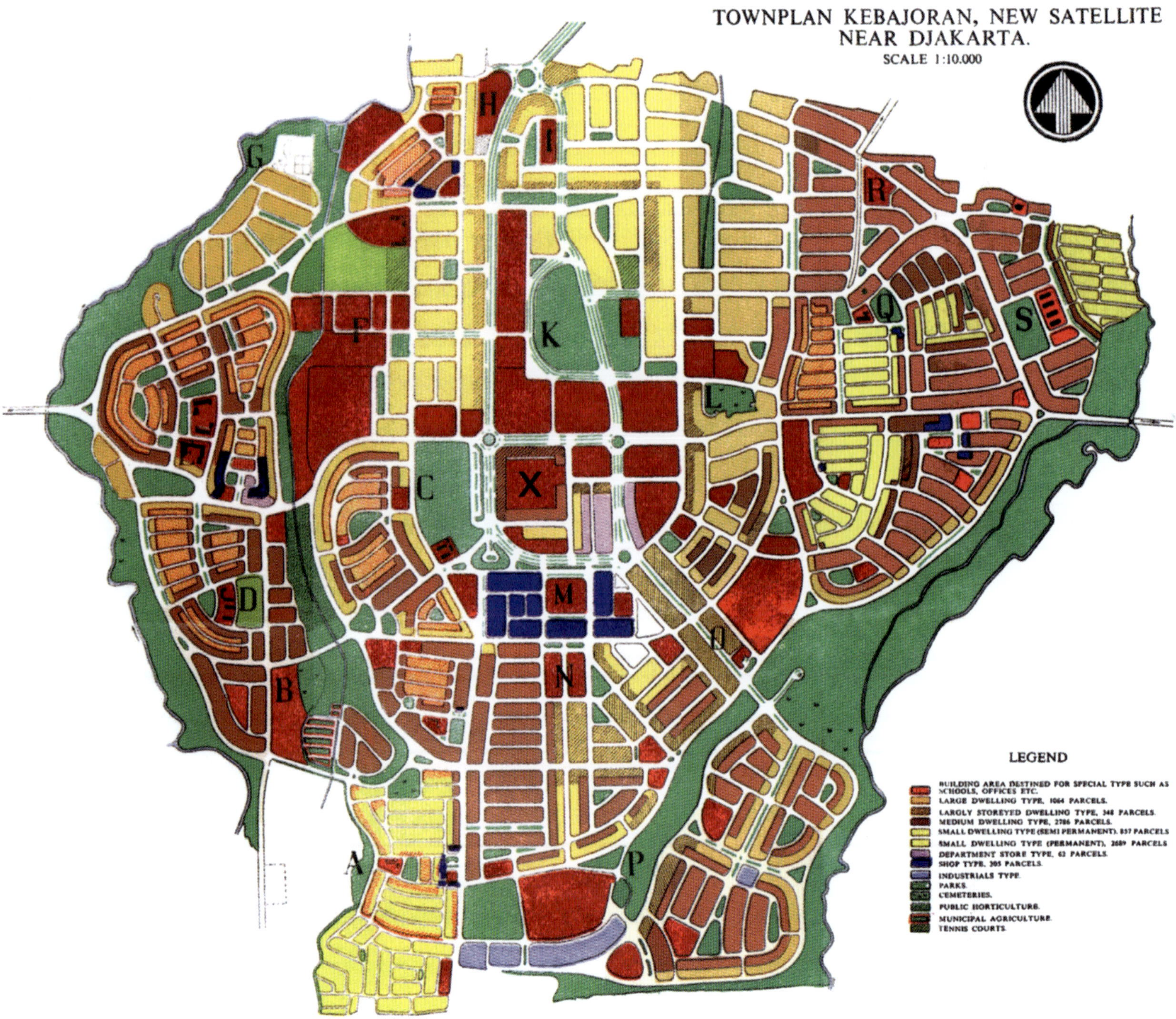

Jakarta, map of the Kebayoran district from the 1950s. Basic design by M. Soesilo. The printing works were built in the center (X) PASSCHIER (2016) P. 237

6 THE ARCHITECTS

Freek Dicke (1909-1985)

Employed by the firm from 1937-1941, as architect and civil engineer

1909 Dordrecht: born on December 19, 1909
1920 Dordrecht: H.B.S.
1932 Delft: Architectural engineer
1933 Dordrecht: married Geertje. L. van Nes
1933 Travelled to the Dutch East Indies in September
1933 Bandung: teacher of drawing and art history at Christian Lyceum
1937 Employed by Fermont-Cuypers
1938 Bandung: bank vault of Javasche Bank (now: Bank Indonesia), Jl. Braga No. 23
1938 Jakarta: Kolff printing works, Jl. Pecenongan/-
1939 Makassar: Brother school (now: SMP Frater, Jl. Thamrin No.3)
1940 Lived on the Lombokweg 8 (now: Jl. Lombok)
1940 Jakarta: Canisius College (extension), Jl. Menteng Raya No. 64
1940 Jakarta: Mater Dolorosa Chapel, Jl. Jatinegara Barat Raya No. 122
1940 Semarang: Business School (extension), Jl. Dr. Sutomo No. 6
1940 Jakarta: Sea Port emplacement, Tanjung Priok
1941 Surabaja: Office of 'De Nederlanden van 1845', now: Jl. Veteran No. 37
1941 Jakarta: still employed at Fermont-Cuypers (according to Registry of European Residents 1941)
1942 Jakarta: National Buildings Agency (*Landsgebouwendienst*)
1942-1945 Japanese internment camp
1946 Jakarta: employed at the National Buildings Agency
1949 Jakarta: Head of the National Buildings Agency
1949 Bogor: restoration of Bogor Palace
1950 Bandung: temporary professor at Institut Teknologi Bandung (ITB)
1951 Bandung: board member of Christian Lyceum
1951 Bandung: board member of Institut Teknologi Bandung (ITB)
1955 Bandung: farewell as a professor and travelled to the Netherlands
1955 Rotterdam: employed at Kraaijevanger architecture firm
1960 Rotterdam: associated with Prof. H.T. Zwiers
1985 Velsen: Freek Dicke died on September 24

Arnold Dikstaal (1903-1968)

Employed by the firm from 1929-1935 as aspiring architect and site foreman

1903 Hilversum: born on February 14, 1903
1927 Utrecht: Secondary Technical School (Department of Architecture)
1928 Hilversum: employed as draftsman by the famous architect W.M.Dudok
1929 Hilversum: married Harmina Reinouw Maria Velt (Mientje)
1929 Jakarta: arrival of Arnold Dikstaal and his wife
1929-1936 Jakarta, lived on Leonilaan 10 (now: Jl. Bekasi Timur IV No. 4)
1929-1936 Jakarta: employed as a draftsman-designer at Fermont-Cuypers
1930 Semarang: British American Tobacco factory (Gedung Sampoera)
1930 Jakarta: Theresia church (design)

1931 Semarang: British American Tobacco factory, Jl. Manisharjo Raya/-
1932 Jakarta: Hotel des Galeries, Jl. Hayam Wuruk No. 1/
1933 Ambarawa: Saint Louis Chapel, Jl. Mgr Sugiyapranata No. 191
1934 Semarang: site foreman for Javasche Bank project (now: Bank Jateng) Jl. Pemuda No. 3
1934 Jakarta: lived on Salembaplein 3 (now: Jl. Kramata 6)
1934 Jakarta: Tan villa/Italian Consulate (now: India House), Jl. Taman Suropati No. 6
1935 Jakarta: Pek villa, Jl. Diponegoro No.51
1935 Leaves Fermont-Cuypers, sailed to Amsterdam
1937 Medan: Head draftsman at Water Authority (*'s Lands Waterstaat*)
1938 Bandung: lived on the Julianalaan (now: Jl. Pudak)
1939 Bandung: passes the architect exam
1942-1945 Japanese internment camp
1942-1945 Dikstaal's wife was interned with their child in a camp in Ambarawa
1946 Return to the Netherlands
1948-1960 Architect at the municipality of Amsterdam
1968 Laren: Arnold Dikstaal died on March 24

Arthur Fermont (1882-1967)

Employed by the firm in the Dutch East Indies/Indonesia from 1915-1957 as director

1882 Terneuzen: born on June 3
1906 Middelburg: apprentice engineer and foreman at the Water Authority (*Waterstaat*)
1906 Terneuzen: married Maria Johanna Bowbyes on December 11
1907 Jakarta: 3rd-class foreman at the Water Authority of the Governor-General
1907 Bandah Aceh: worked as foreman in the government of Aceh
1909 Bogor: honourable dismissal from Water Authority and Public Works
1909-1914 Jakarta: own contracting company
1914 Padang: Dunlop shop, Pasar Ambatjang/-
1914 Jakarta: school (now: National Gallery of Indonesia), Jl. Medan Merdeka Tim. No. 14
1915 Jakarta: construction of Dunlop Shop, Rijswijkstraat/-
1915 Jakarta: Savelkoul Shop, Rijswijk/Jl. Veteran/-
1915 Amsterdam: sailed to the Netherlands. Visited Eduard Cuypers, became a partner
1916 Jakarta: returned to the Dutch East Indies with his wife and four children
1922 Malang: opening of the Javasche Bank (now: Bank Indonesia)
1923 Pematang Siantar: opening of the Javasche Bank (now: Bank Indonesia)
1925 Padang: opening of the Javasche Bank (now: Bank Indonesia)
1926 The Hague: sails with wife and children to the Netherlands (Raamweg 13, The Hague)
1927 Jakarta: lived on Molenvliet W 4/5 (now: Jl. Gajah Mada)
1927 Medan: opening of offices of Handelsvereeniging Amsterdam
1928 Pontianak: opening of Javasche Bank
1928 Medan: opening of the Escomptobank (now Bank Mandiri)
1929 Kediri: opening of Javasche Bank (now: Bank Indonesia)
1930 Jakarta: opening of Canisius College
1930 Madiun: opening of the town hall and theatre
1930-1931 on leave in Europe
1930 Colonial Exhibition Antwerp
1931 Colonial Exhibition Paris
1933 Ambarawa: consecration of Saint Louis chapel
1933 Jakarta: opening Dutch Chinese School on Prinsenlaan (now: Jl. Raya Mangga Besar)
1933 The Hague: long leave in the Netherlands
1935 Jakarta: returns to Dutch East Indies from Europe
1935 Semarang: opening of Javasche Bank (now: Bank Jateng)
1936 The Hague: on leave in the Netherlands
1936 The Hague: attends funeral of Director of the Javasche Bank
1937 Jakarta: opening of Javasche Bank (now: Museum Bank Indonesia)
1937 Padang: first stone laid of the Charitas hospital in Palembang
1937 The Hague: sailed to the Netherlands from Medan
1937 Amsterdam: consultations about Java Textiel in Tegal
1938 Jakarta: arrived in the Dutch East Indies
1938 Palembang: Escomptobank and Volkscredietbank, Tenkoeroekkade/Jl. Bumi Sari/-
1939 Medan: sailed to Europe on May 9
1940 Amsterdam: Dutch capitulation after German occupation
1946 The Hague: based in the Netherlands, worked for the firm Fermont-Cuypers in Jakarta
1946 Youngest son Cyril Fermont left for Jakarta, worked for the firm
1950 Awarded Knight in the order of St. Gregory the Great (granted by the Pope)

1955 The Hague: mediated in the build of Pertjetakan Kebayoran printing works in Jakarta
1967 Rijsbergen: Arthur Fermont died on November 17
1967 The Hague: he is buried in the St. Petrus Banden cemetery

Willem Jaski (1868-1958)

Employed by the firm in the Dutch East Indies from 1909-1928 as contractor and branch manager

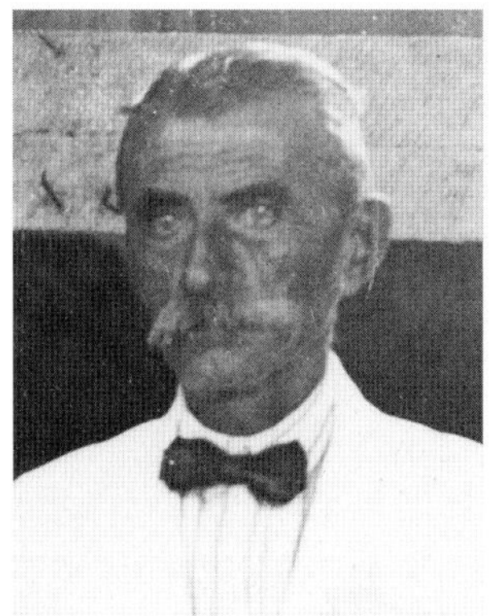

1876 Amsterdam: born on July 27
1896 Johannesburg: employed at the South African Railway Company
1901 Singkep: worked on this island in the tin-ore processing industry
1902 Medan: worked as a contractor
1902 Medan: married Johanna Kasteleyn
1904 Medan: Enkelaar & Jaski engineers and contractors
1904 Medan: construction and design of Roman Catholic Church in gothic style
1908 Medan: completed build of town hall, Jl. Balai Kota No. 2 (designed by Ch. Boon architect)
1909 Medan: built Javasche bank (now: Bank Indonesia) Jl. Balai Kota No. 4
1909 Medan: meeting with Eduard Cuypers
1910 Makassar: project managed the Javasche Bank, Pasarstraat/-
1911 Makassar: project managed offices of Nederlandsche Handel Maatschappij, Pasarstraat/-
1916 Manado: project managed Javasche Bank (now: Bank Indonesia, Jl. 17 August No.56)
1917 Bandah Aceh: project managed Javasche Bank (now: Bank Indonesia, Jl. Cut Meutia No. 15)
1922 Medan: Fully-authorised branch manager at Fermont-Cuypers
1923 Pematang Siantar: project managed Javasche Bank (Bank Rakyat Indonesia), Jl. Merdeka No. 145
1924 Surabaya: acting branch manager Fermont-Cuypers
1925 Surabaya: executor at the 'Handelsvereeniging Amsterdam' building, Jl. Merak No.
1925 Medan: represents Fermont-Cuypers
1926 Medan: design and construction of Catholic Girls' boarding school, Jl. Pemuda No. 1
1927 Medan: town councillor
1927 Bandah Aceh: construction of the Catholic Church, Jl. Jenderal Ahmad Yani
1927 Medan: site manager on 'Handelsvereeniging Amsterdam' building, Jl. Letjen Suprapto No. 2.
1927 Belawan: built 'Rotterdamsche Lloyd', Oceaankade/-
1928 Medan: construction of the Escomptobank, Jl. Jend. Ahmad Yani No. 109
1928 Amsterdam: wife and daughter in the Netherlands
1928 Medan: retires as a town councillor
1928 Amsterdam: treated for eye disease
1929 Ungaran: given a building plot as a pension where he built his own house
1942-1945 He survived Japanese occupation in internment camp
1946 Velp (the Netherlands)
1958 Velp: Willem Jaski died on April 1

Han de Jongh (1886-1965)

Employed by the firm in the Dutch East Indies from 1921-1937 as civil engineer

1886 Hilversum: born on July 4 (during parents' leave)
1886 Pandang: childhood
1888 Muntok: childhood
1890 Jakarta: H.B.S.
1910 Delft: Polytechnic School
1913 Medan: apprentice engineer at Public Works
1919 Medan: engineer Port Works Belawan/Medan
1919 Medan: married J.H.J Grijzen (July 7, 1919)
1922 Jakarta: authorised signatory at Hulswit-Fermont-Ed. Cuypers
1922 Amsterdam: six months' leave in the Netherlands
1927 Medan/Belawan: involved with warehouses on Belawan docks, Oceaankade/-
1928 's Hertogenbosch: six months' leave to the Netherlands
1931 Banjarmasin: Escomptobank Jl. Lambung Mangkurat/-
1931 Padang: opening of the Escomptobank (now: Bank Mandiri)
1931 Semarang: British American Tobacco factory, Jl. Manisharjo Raya/-
1932 Pangkal Pinang: attended opening of boarding school
1932 Belinyu: attended opening of sister house and school
1932 Muntok: visited building site of mission post
1933 Jakarta: reappointment as director on November 25
1934 Semarang: first stone laid for the Javasche Bank (now: Bank Jateng), Jl. Pemuda No. 3

1935 's-Hertogenbosch: six months' leave in the Netherlands
1936 Jakarta: returned to the Dutch East Indies
1937 Tegal: Textile factory, Jl. Pala Raya/-
1937 Jakarta: tenders resignation and returns finally to the Netherlands
1949-1956 The architecture firm in the Netherlands: De Jongh, Taen, Nix.
Projects include:
- 1951 Bakkum, Maria ten Hemelopneming (Assumption) Church
- 1952 Nijmegen, Dominicus Church
- 1952 Doorneburg, St. Martinus Church
- 1953 Eindhoven, St Catharina lyceum (Maerlantlyceum)

1957 Rotterdam, Heilige Nikolaas Church
1965 Driebergen: Han de Jongh died on October 19

Matthias Kaptijn (1890-1963)

Employed by the firm in the Dutch East Indies from 1921-1946 as project manager

1890 Hoofddorp: born in the Haarlemmermeer
1918 married Anthonia Cornelia Medenblik on May 15
1921 Jakarta: employed by Hulswit-Fermont
1927 Jakarta: lived at Koningsplein-oost 16 (now: Medan Merdeka Tim.)
1930 Jakarta: resigned as a city councillor
1930 Jakarta: produced designs to improve the Catholic Social Union building
1931 Jakarta: led visitors around the Hotel des Galeries, Jl. Hayam Wuruk No. 1
1931 Jakarta: first stone laid of Carolus hospital chapel, Jl. Raya Salemba No. 41
1934 Bengkulu: opening of Catholic school and mission post, Jl. Todak No. 119
1934 Surabaya: opening the Vincentius hospital, Jl. Raya Diponegoro No. 51
1936 Tegal: attended the start of the Textile Factory construction, Jl. Pala Raya/-
1937 Jakarta: compiled Commemorative book of the Javasche Bank (now: Bank Indonesia)
1938 Jakarta: opening of children's pavilion of the Carolus hospital, Jl. Salemba Raya No. 41/-
1942-1945 Japanese internment camp
1947 Jakarta: lived at Laan de Riemer 10 (now: Jl. Tanah Abang No. 3)
1949 resigned from Fermont-Cuypers and returned to the Netherlands
1963 Haarlem: Matthias Kaptijn died on April 6

Laurent Logemann (1898-1954)

Employed by the firm in the Dutch East Indies from 1926 -1931 as architect

1898 Rotterdam: born on August 23
1898 Rotterdam: son of city architect Dirk Burghard Logemann (1872-1964)
1921 The Hague: resigned from the City Development Department
1922 Rotterdam: worked for the municipality of Rotterdam as building site foreman
1924 Amsterdam: Diploma of Architecture Supervisor
1926 The Hague: married Cornelia Helena Maria Hakker
1926 Sailed from Amsterdam to Jakarta
1926 Jakarta: lived on Molenvliet Oost and worked at Hulswit-Fermont-Cuypers
1927 Jakarta: produced drawing for main building of Hotel des Indes
1928 Tanjung Karang: Catholic Church, Stationsavenue/ Jl. Dipo/-
1929 Subang: The Clubhouse, Jl. Ade Irma Suryani Nasution No. 2, with Th. Taen
1929 Kediri: Javasche Bank (now: Bank Indonesia) and residence, Jl. Brawijaya No. 2
1929 Surabaya: Catholic Church Ketabang (design)
1930 Jakarta: Duo Passenger terminal (now Ministry), Medan Merdeka Barat No. 3
1930 Jakarta: produced design for Javasche Bank (now: Bank Jateng) in Semarang
1930 Madiun: Town Hall, Jl. Pahlawan No. 37
1930 Madiun: Theatre and cinema, Jl. Pahlawan-Jl. Kalimantan/-
1930 Jakarta: bird's-eye view drawing of Vincentius Hospital in Surabaya
1930 Ambarawa: Saint Louis institute, Jl. Mgr Sugiyapranata No. 191
1931 Pangkal Pinang: Boarding school, Jl. Budi Mulia No. 107
1932 Jakarta: worked for the Municipality of Jakarta
1934 Jakarta: married M.A. van Lith on May 1

1934 Jakarta: became head of the City Development Department after reorganisation
1935 Jakarta: became involved in fraud cases within his department/lawsuit
1937 sailed from Jakarta to Belawan Deli with his wife
1937 sailed from Jakarta to Amsterdam on June 13
1938 sailed from Amsterdam to Jakarta
1939 Jakarta: involved in air protection exercise
1942-1945 Japanese internment camps
1947 Jakarta: married Selma Spanjaard on July 18
1954 The Hague: Laurent Logemann died on February 19

Advertisement Fermont-Cuypers in 1934 SCHLÖMER 1934

Karel Mekel (1920-1997)

Employed by the firm in Indonesia from 1952 -1956 as architect

1920 Roermond: born on January 4, 1920
1951 married Catarina (Kitty) Paffen on November 17, 1951
1952 Jakarta: lived at the office address (Jl. Hajam Wuruk No. 30)
1952 Jakarta: design for Pertjetakan Kebajoran printing works and associated houses
1953 Jakarta: design for Bank of China , Jl. Kali Besar Timur No. 5
1954 Ambon: design for the Bank Indonesia building
1958 Waalwijk (the Netherlands): starts own office
1959-1969 various construction and renovation projects in Waalwijk and the surrounding area
1997 Waalwijk: Karel Mekel died on July 23

Thomas Nix (1904-1998)

Employed by the firm in the Dutch East Indies from 1930-1941 as architect

1904 Bandung: born on December 21
1904 Bandung: son of the director of the Publisher A.C. Nix & Co
1920 Amsterdam: Grammar School
1929 The Hague: married Elisabeth Hermine, Hendrika, Petronella van der Waals (1902-1987)
1930 Delft: architectural engineer
1930 Jakarta: arrival with wife by ship
1930 Jakarta: employed at Fermont-Cuypers
1930 Jakarta: lived on the Theresiakerkweg (now: Jl. H. Agus Salim)
1931 Solo: Javanese Catholic Church and presbytery (design)
1932 Semarang: School (now: SMP Maria Goretti), Jl. Imam Bonjol No. 198
1932 Muntok: Sister's house, church, school, Jl. Basuki Rahmat No. 208
1932 Jakarta: Hotel des Galeries, Jl. Hayam Wuruk No.1/

1933 Jakarta: Sancta Maria school (now: Jl. Lap. Banteng Utara, Jl. Pos No. 2)
1933 Purworejo: Catholic church, Jl. K.H. Wahid Hasyim No. 1
1933 Palembang: Boarding school, Jl. Jantinegara Barat Raya No. 122
1934 Jakarta: Tan villa/Italian Consulate (now: India House, Jl. Taman Suropati No. 6)
1934 Jakarta: secretary of the Artists' Association
1934 Jakarta: Brothers' home, Koningsplein-Oost /Medan Merdeka Tim./-
1934 Surabaya: Vincentius hospital, Jl. Raya Diponegoro No. 51
1934 Bandung: Pandu church, Jl. Pandu No. 4
1935 Jakarta: Pek villa, Jl. Diponegoro No. 51
1935 Pekalongan: Catholic Church, Jl. Blimbing 1/-, with Th. Taen
1936 Bandung: Schools, Sister House, 'Maria Sterre der Zee', Jl. Kebon Jati No. 209.
1937 Jakarta: front building of Javasche Bank (now: Museum Bank Indonesia Jl. Lada No. 3)
1938 Jakarta: Kolff printing works, Jl. Pecenongan/-
1938 Semarang: Bataafsche Petroleum Mij., (now: Pertamina), Jl. Pemuda No. 114
1938 Jakarta: 'De Koloniale' (now: Departemen Energi), Jl. Medan Merdeka Sel. No. 18
1938 Jakarta: Bataafsche Petroleum Mij. (now: Pertamina), Jl. Medan Merdeka Tim. 1A
1938 Jakarta: Dutch East Indies Tourist Office (Nitour), Jl. Majapahit No. 2A
1938 Jakarta: Departure for Europe in December
1939 Paris: visited in June
1940 Jakarta, Medan, Bogor: painting exhibitions
1941 Bandung: lived on Jan Steenstraat 17 (now: Jl. Raden Pagergunung)
1941 Bandung: worked at the Technical Department of the municipality of Bandung
1941 Bandung: designed office for Military Aviation and Topographic Service
1942 Bandung: separated from wife and children who are interned in camps
1942 Bandung: worked under the Japanese for the former Dutch Indies Railroad Me. (NIS)
1943 Cilacap: designed railway station, Gg. Surya V No. 53
1946 Sailed to the Netherlands (youngest son died on board from the effects of war)
1946 Rotterdam: employee at the Rotterdam construction office
1946 Utrecht: Bureau Nix Van Hasselt
1947 Rotterdam: worked for the Bataafsche Petroleum Maatschappij (Balikpapan and Plaju)
1949 Delft: PhD dissertation: 'Urban design in Indonesia'
1949-1965 Nijmegen: The architecture firm in the Netherlands: De Jongh, Taen, Nix.

Projects include:

- 1951 Bakkum, Maria ten Hemelopneming (Assumption) Church
- 1952 Nijmegen, Dominicus Church
- 1952 Doorneburg, St. Martinus Church
- 1953 Eindhoven, St. Catharina lyceum (Maerlantlyceum)
- 1957 Rotterdam, St. Nikolaas Church
- 1957 Cuijk town hall
- 1959 The Hague, Pius X church in Bouwlust
- 1960 Utrecht, St Bonifatius Lyceum
- 1961 Geleen, St. Michel Lyceum
- 1962 Nagele, St. Isidorus Church
- 1963 The Hague, plan for Mariahoeve shopping centre with Zwolsman
- 1965 Amsterdam, St. Lucas-church
- 1965 Malaga (Spain), develops a project where he later lived

1998: Albala Romaine (France): Thomas Nix died on July 9

Henk Roebbers (1923-1999)

Employed by the firm in Indonesia from 1954-1957 as architect

1923 Deventer: born on September 28
1953 Delft: Architectural engineering
1953 Deventer: married D.M. van Eekelen
1954 Flew to Jakarta on March 3
1954 Mrs. Roebbers sailed on the Willem Ruys on June 9 to Indonesia (arrival June 30)
1954 Jakarta: lived on Djalan Tosari 92
1954-1957 employed by Fermont-Cuypers
1955 Jakarta: Mr. Ruznar's house in Kebayoran
1955 Jakarta: Mr. Go's house in Kebayoran
1956 Jakarta: NV Essence Indonesia
1956 Ambon: attended opening of Bank Indonesia premises
1956 Jakarta: Mrs. Roebbers sailed back to the Netherlands with her children
1957 Roebbers flew back to the Netherlands
1957 Deventer: independent architect
1957-1987 numerous projects in the north and east of the Netherlands
1999 Deventer: Henk Roebbers died on December 4

Theo J. Taen (1889-1970)

Employed by the firm in the Dutch East Indies from 1921-1942 as architect and manager

1889 Berlin: born December 12
1897 Berlin: moves to Roermond due to his grandfather P.J.H. Cuypers
1898 Roermond: Boarding school
1915 Aachen (Germany): Baugewerbeschule (construction college)
1917 Utrecht: works for H. Bijlard, architect in Utrecht
1917 Amsterdam: married Elisabeth Bernadina de Sain (1896-1983) on January 2
1918 Amsterdam: lived in Eduard Cuyper building, Jan Luykenstraat 2
1919 Amsterdam: employed at Ed. Cuypers' office
1918 Eindhoven: St. Joriscollege (design 1919, opened 1924)
1920 Valkenswaard: town hall (design 1920, opened 1927)
1921 Goirle: town hall (design 1920, opened 1928)
1921 departed for the Dutch East Indies (May 28)
1921 Jakarta: head of architect department at Fermont-Cuypers
1922 Semarang: visited the Congress for Public Housing
1923 Yogyakarta: Hospital Dr. Yap, Jl. Cik Di Tiro no. 5
1923 Jakarta: member of the NIAK (Nederlandsch-Indische Architecten Kring)
1923 Jakarta: Chapel at Great monastery, Jl. Ir.H. Juanda No. 29, with Ed. Cuypers
1923 Pematang Siantar: Javasche Bank (now: Bank Rakyat Indonesia), with Ed. Cuypers
1923 Jakarta: Borneo Company Ltd. business premises, Jl. Malaka No. 7-9
1923 Banjarmasin: Javasche Bank, with Ed. Cuypers
1924 Ambarawa: St Joseph church, Jl. Mgr. Soegijapranata No. 56. with Ed. Cuypers
1924 Cirebon: British American Tobacco, Jl.Pasketan with Ed. Cuypers
1924 Jakarta: Escompto Bank (now: Bank Mandiri) Jl. Ir. H. Juanda No. 24
1925 Padang: Javasche Bank (now: Bank Indonesia) Jl. Batang Arau No. 66, with Ed. Cuypers
1926 Yogyakarta: St. Anthonius church, Jl. Abubakar Ali No. 1, with Ed. Cuypers
1927 Jakarta: Theresia school, Jl. H. Agus Salim No. 75, with Ed. Cuypers
1927 Sukabumi: Ursuline schools, with Ed. Cuypers
1927 Bandung: Jozeph pavilion of Borromeo hospital, Dagoweg 80/Jl. Ir. H.Juanda 100/-
1927 Banda Aceh: Catholic Church, Jl. Jenderal Ahmad Yani
1927 Semarang: Xaverius school, Karreweg 91/Jl. Dr Cipto No. 91/-
1928 Yogyakarta: Seminary, Jl. Ahmad Jazuli No. 2
1928 Pontianak: Javasche Bank, Residentsweg/-
1928 Medan: Escomptobank (now Bank Mandiri), Jl. Jend. Ahmad Yani No. 109
1928 Surabaya: Housing at Petodjo Ice factory, Radersmastraat/Jl. Kidal/-
1928 Cilacap: Harbour office, Nederlandsche Handels. Mij./-
1928 Tanjung Karang: Catholic Church, Stationsavenue/ Jl. Dipo/-
1928 Malang: Towers at the Sacred Heart Church, Jl. Mgr. Sugiyopraneto No. 2
1929 Kediri: Javasche Bank (now: Bank Indonesia) and residence, Jl. Brawijaya No. 2
1929 Subang: Clubhouse, Jl. Ade Irma Suryani Nasution No. 2
1929 Bandung-East: Catholic Church, Jl. Kamuning No. 25
1930 Jakarta: Presbytery, Jl. Gereja Theresia No. 2
1930 Jakarta: Shop buildings with upstairs dwellings, Jl. Veteran I
1930 Jakarta: Canisius College, Jl. Menteng Raya No. 64
1930 Jakarta: Duo Passenger terminal (now Ministry), Medan Merdeka Barat No. 3
1930 Madiun: Town Hall, Jl. Pahlawan No. 37
1930 Madiun: Theatre and cinema, Jl. Pahlawan-Jl. Kalimantan/-
1930 Purwokerto: Schools, Jl. Jend. Gatot Subroto No. 44
1930 Purwokerto: Catholic Church, Jl. Jend Gatot Subroto/-
1930 Ambarawa: Saint Louis institute, Jl. Mgr Sugiyapranata No. 191
1931 Padang: Escomptobank (now: Bank Mandiri) Jl. Batang Arau No. 42
1931 Belinyu: Sister house and school, Jl. Mayor Syahrrie Rakhman No. 103
1931 Pangkal Pinang: Boarding school, Jl. Budi Mulia No. 107
1931 Jakarta: Carolus hospital main building, chapel, Jl. Raya Salemba No. 41
1931 Banjarmasin: Escomptobank, Jl. Lambung Mangkurat/-
1931 Jakarta: Boarding school, Jl. Jantinegara Barat Raya No. 122
1932 Muntok: Church, school, Sister house, Jl. Basuki Rachmad No. 208
1932 Semarang: Franciscan sisters' school, Jl. Imam Bonjol No. 198
1932 Jakarta: Van Lidtschool with chapel, Jl. Gunung Sahari Raya No. 91

1932 Pekalongan: Primary school and Fröbel school, Jl. Progo No. 16
1932 Jakarta: Sancta Ursula convent, Jl. Pos No. 2
1932 Rangkasbetung: Regency building of Lebak, Jl. Alun Alun Selatam No. 2
1933 Rangkasbetung: Hospital, Jl. Multatuli No. 41
1933 Jakarta: Dutch-Chinese Primary school, Jl. Mangga Besar Raya No. 135/-
1933 Jakarta: Sancta Maria School, Jl. Lap. Banteng Utara or Jl. Pos No. 2
1933 Ambarawa: Chapel at Saint Louis institute, Jl. Mgr. Sugiyapranata No. 191
1933 Purworejo: Catholic Church, Jl. KH Wahid Hasyim No. 1
1933 Palembang: Boarding School and Fröbel school, Jl. Kol. Atmo 132/-
1934 Jakarta: 'Mater Dei' vocational school, Jl. Ir. H. Juanda No. 29/-
1934 Bengkulu: Schools, Sister house, chapel, Jl. Todak No. 119
1934 Surabaya: Vincentius hospital, Jl. Raya Diponegoro No. 51
1934 Yogyakarta: Seminary (extension), Jl. Ahmad Jazuli No. 2
1935 Cirebon: Dutch-Chinese Primary school, Jl. Sisingamangaraja No. 22
1935 Jakarta: Pek villa, Oranjeboulevard 51/Jl. Diponegoro 51
1935 Jakarta: Bank vault of Javasche Bank (now: Bank Indonesia), Jl. Lada No. 3/-
1935 Jakarta: Tarcisius Primary school, Jl. KH. Hasyim Ashari No. 26
1935 Semarang: Javasche Bank (now: Bank Jateng), Jl. Pemuda No. 3
1935 Pekalongan: Catholic Church, Jl. Blimbing 1/-
1936 Bandung: Schools, Sister house, 'Maria Sterre der Zee', Jl. Kebon Jati No. 209
1937 Tegal: Ursuline schools, Jl. Kapt. Ismail 120
1937 Jakarta: Front building Javasche Bank (now: Museum Bank Indonesia), Jl. Lada No. 3
1938 Palembang: Charitas hospital, Jl. Jendral Sudirman No. 1054
1938 Jakarta: Children's pavilion of Carolus hospital, Jl. Salemba Raya No. 41/-
1938 Sungailiat: Brother school, Jl. Maria Goretti No. 7
1939 Wonosobo: Institute for the deaf and mute, Jl. Mangli No. 10
1939 Lahat: Schools and monastery, Jl. Sekolah No. 13
1939 Bandung: Ciumbuleuit villas
1939 Makassar: Brother school (now: SMP Frater), Jl. Balaikota No. 3
1939 Makassar: 'Stella Maris' hospital, Jl. Somba OPU No. 273
1940 Jakarta: Canisius college (extension), Jl. Menteng Raya No. 64
1940 Jakarta: 'Mater Dolorosa' chapel, Jl. Jantinegara Barat Raya No. 122
1940 Semarang: Business school (extension), Jl. Dr. Sutomo No. 6
1940 Jakarta: Sea port emplacement, Tanjung Priok
1941 Surabaja: 'De Nederlanden van 1845' building, Jl. Veteran No. 37
1941 Jakarta: employed for 20 years at Fermont-Cuypers
1942-1945: Japanese internment camps
1945 Amsterdam: returned to the Netherlands
1949-1961 Nijmegen: The architecture firm in the Netherlands: De Jongh, Taen, Nix.

Projects include:

1951: Bakkum, Maria ten Hemelopneming (Assumption) Church
1952 Nijmegen, Dominicus Church
1952 Doorneburg, St. Martinus Church
1953 Eindhoven, St. Catharina lyceum (Maerlantlyceum)
1957 Rotterdam, St. Nikolaas Church
1957 Cuijk town hall
1959 The Hague, Pius X church in Bouwlust
1960 Utrecht, St Bonifatius Lyceum
1961 Geleen, St. Michel Lyceum
1962 Nagele, St. Isidorus Church

1970 Boxtel: Theo Taen died on October 30

File for specifications of a construction plan CFC

7 BIBLIOGRAFIE

Adriaenssens, W. (1996), *Art deco Architectuur (Brussel 1920-1930)*, Brussel

Akihary, H. (1990), *Architectuur & Stedebouw in Indonesië* (1870-1970), Zutphen

Akihary, H. (1996), *ir. F.J.L. Ghijsels Architect in Indonesia (1910-1929)*, Utrecht

Algra, A. (1967). *De Gereformeerde Kerken in Nederlands-Indië (1877-1961)*. Franeker: Wever

Bakker, C. (2014), *Zusters in de Zorg (Een Geschiedenis van de Franciscanessen van Charitas)*, Zutphen

Barbieri, U. (1987). *J.J.P. Oud*. Rotterdam: Uitgeverij 010 Rotterdam

Bartetzko, D. (2012). *Illusionen in Stein*. Berlin: Zentralverlag

Bayer, P. (1992). *Art Deco Architecture*. London: Thames & Hudson

Beekhuis, H. (2009). *Geillustreerde Atlas van de Bersiapkampen in Nederlands-Indië 1945-1947*. Bedum: Profiel BV

Beekman, D. A. (1932). *De Goede Herder*. Nijmegen: Dekker van de Vegt

Beekum, R. v. (2007). *Cornelis van de Linde (Bouwer voor de Nederlandsche Handel-Maatschappij)*. KNOB: koninklijke Nederlandse Oudheidkundige Bond, 263-271

Bergeijk, H. v. (1995). *Willem Marinus Dudok*. Naarden: V+K Publishing

Bergeijk, H. v. (2008). *Amerikaanse Dromen (Frank Lloyd Wright en Nederland)*. Rotterdam: 010 publishers

Bergson, H. (1925). *De Scheppende Evolutie*. Amsterdam: Maatschappij voor Goede en Goedkoope Lectuur

Berlage, H. (1931). *Mijn Indische Reis*. Rotterdam: W.L. & J. Brusse's Uitgeversmaatschappij

Beusekom, H. v. (1944). *Woningbouw Problemen en Perspectieven*. Amsterdam: A.J.G. Strengholt

Bezemer, T. (1921). *Beknopte Encyclopedie van Nederlandsch- Indië*. 's-Gravenhage: Martinus Nijhof

Bijlard, H. (1928). Bij de reproducties van werken van wijlen Eduard Cuypers, architect te Amsterdam. *Het Nederlandsche en Ned. Indische Huis Oud en Nieuw*, 5-27, 35-48, 51-61

Blijdenstijn, R. (1994). *Bouwstijlen in Nederland*. Utrecht: Kosmos

Bloembergen, M. (2002). *De Koloniale Vertoning (Nederland en Nederlands Indië op wereldtentoonstellingen)*. Amsterdam: Wereldbibliotheek

Blom, A. v. (1997). *Nederlandse Schilderkunst*. Alphen aan den Rijn: Atrium

Bodenschatz, H. (2011). *Städtebau für Mussolini*. Berlin: DOM publishers

Boeyinga, B. (1923). De Nationale Bouwkunst-tentoonstelling 1898-1923. *De Socialistische Gids*, pp. 1024-1036

Borsi, F. (1987). *The Monumental Era (European Architecture and Design 1929-1939)*. New York: Rizzoli

Bossenbroek, M. (1996). *Holland op zijn breedst*. Amsterdam: Bert Bakker

Bree, L. d. (1928). *Gedenkboek van De Javasche Bank 1828 - 24 Januari-1928 Deel 2*. Weltevreden: G. Kolf & Co

Breuning, H. (1954). *Het voormalige Batavia* (Heemschutreeks). Amsterdam: Allert de Lange

Broekhuizen, D. (1995). *Het Shell-gebouw van J.J.P. Oud*. Rotterdam : NAi

Broekhuizen, D. (2000). *De Stijl toen / J.J.P. Oud nu*. Rotterdam: NAi

Broeshart, A. (1995). *Soerabaja Beeld van een Stad*. Purmerend: Asia Maior

Brommer, B. (1988). *Het Indische Bouwen*. Catalogus, Helmond

Brommer, B. (1995). *Semarang beeld van een stad*. Purmerend: Asia Maior

Bruggen, M. (1998). *Djokja Solo Beelden van Vorstensteden*. Purmerend: Asia Maior

Buys, L. (1934). De Nieuwe Theresia-Kerk in Batavia. *Berichten uit Nederlandsch-Oost Indië*, 95-101.

Christiansen, B. (1931). *Het Aspect Van Onzen Tijd*. Arnhem: N.V. Van loghum Slaterius Uitgeversmaatschappij

Christinus, B. (1940). *Ons Missiewerk op Java 1920-1940 Congregatie der Broeders van de Onbevlekte Ontvangenis*. Djokjakata : Eigen beheer

Colombijn, F. (2010). *Under Construction. The Politics of Urban Space and Housing during the Decolonization of Indonesia, 1930-1960*. Leiden: KITLV Press

Coolhaas, W. D. (1946). *Insulinde Mensch en Maatschappij*. Deventer: Van Hoeve

Coté, J. (2017). *The life and work of Thomas Karsten*, Amsterdam

Dawson, B. (1994). *De traditionele bouwkunst van Indonesië*. Bussum: Thoth

Delprat, D. (1930). *De Koloniale Roeping van Nederland.* 's-Gravenhage: N.V. Nederlandsch-Engelsche Uitgeversmaatschappij

Diessen, J. v. (1989). *Jakarta/Batavia Kunstreisgids.* De Bilt: Cantecleer

Diessen, J. v. (1998). *Stedenatlas Nederlands-Indië.* Purmerend: Asia Maior

Diessen, J. v. (2003). *Grote Atlas van Nederlands Oost-Indië.* Zierikzee: Asia Maior

Diessen, J. v. (2004). *Soerabaja 1900-1950.* Purmerend: Asia Maior

Doel, H. v. (1996). *Het Rijk van Insulinde.* Amsterdam: Prometheus

Doorn, J. v. (1995). *Indische Lessen.* Amsterdam: Bert Bakker

Doorn, J. v. (2013). *De Laatste eeuw van Indië.* Zutphen: de Walburg Pers

Dullemen, C. (2010). *Tropical Modernity. Amsterdam*: SUN

Dulm, J. v. (2000). *Geillustreerde Atlas van de Japanse kampen in Nederlands-Indië 1942-1945.* Purmerend: Asia Maior

Duncan, A. (2009). *Art deco Complete.* London: Thames & Hudson

Duparc, H. (1972). *Trams en Tramlijnen De elektrische stadstrams op Java.* Rotterdam: Uitgevers WYT

Eisenman, P. (2003). *Giuseppe Terragni Transformations Decompositions Critiques.* New York: The Monacelli Press

Embden, J. v. (1930). De geschiedenis van de Kring . In *Jaarboek BSK*, 1930 (Bouwkundige Studiekring Delft).

Ethelbert, W. (1986). *60 jaar missiewerk in Indonesië 1926-1986 (Broeders van Dongen).* Indonesië : Grafische School Desa Putera

Faber, G. (1934). *Nieuw Soerabaia* (10 delen met stadsplattegrond). Soerabaia: Van ingen

Fanelli, G. (1978). *Moderne architectuur in Nederland 1900-1940.* 's-Gravenhage: Staatsuitgeverij

Farrell, N. (2003). *Mussolini Een nieuwe visie.* Kampen: Ten Have

Fasseur, C. (1994). *De Indologen (Ambtenaren voor de Oost 1825-1950).* Amsterdam: Bert Bakker

Fasseur, C. (1995). *De Weg naar het Paradijs.* Amsterdam: Bert Bakker

Fletcher, B. (1975). *A History of Architecture.* London: The Athlone Press

Geest, J. v. (1996). *S.J. van Embden.* Rotterdam: Uitgeverij 010

Gelder, W. v. (1937). *Atlas van Nederlandsch-Indië.* Groningen/Batavia: Wolters

Gelink, J. (1948). *50 Jaren Hotel des Indes Batavia.* Batavia: Unie Studio

Gerlagh, B. (1979). *Ed Cuypers* (doctoraalscriptie UVA). Amsterdam: UVA

Giedion, S. (1954). *Ruimte, Tijd en Bouwkunst* (oorspronkelijk "Space, Time and Architecture" uit 1941). Amsterdam: Wereldbibliotheek

Gill, R. (1994). *De Indische Stad op Java en Madura (Een morfologische studie naar haar ontwikkeling).* Delft: THDelft

Gonggryp, G. (1934). *Geïllustreerde Encyclopedie van Nederlandsch-Indië.* Leiden: N.V. Leidsche Uitgeversmaatschappij.

Gonggrijp, G. (1948). De Economische Ontwikkeling van Nederlands-Indië. In *F. B. Blokland, 50 Jaren* (pp. 445-467). Amsterdam: Scheltens & Giltay

Gorris, G. (1937). *Liefdezusters v.d.h.Carolus Borromeus 1837-1937.* Maastricht: Onder de Bogen

Goumans, J. (1935). *Gedenkboek van de Religieuzen Ursulinen der Rom. Unie op Java.* Bandoeng: Kleijne & Co

Graaf, H. (1949). *Geschiedenis van Indonesië.* 'sGravenhage/Bandung: W.van Hoeve

Graaff, B. d. (1997). *Kalm te midden van woedende golven (ministerie van Koloniën).* 's-Gravenhage: SDU

Granpré-Molière, M. (1949). *Woorden en Werken van Prof. ir Granpré Molière.* Heemstede: De Toorts

Groenen, P. M. (1940). *Jaarboek 1940 (Katholieke Missie in Nederlands-Indië).* Batavia: Centraal Missie Bureau

Groeneveld de Kater, J. (1934). *N.V. Nederlandsche Aanneming Maatschappij.* 's-Gravenhage: N.V. Zuid-Hollandse Boek-Handelsdrukkerij

Haasse, H. (2010). *Het dieptelood van de herinnering.* Amsterdam: EM. Querido's Uitgeverij BV

Hagen, P. (2018). *Koloniale oorlogen in Indonesië.* Amsterdam/ Antwerpen

Hall, C. D. (1942). *Insulinde werk en welvaart.* Naarden: In den Toren

Helsdingen, W. v. (1941). *Daar wèrd wat groots verricht...* Amsterdam: Elsevier

Heuken, A. (1983). *Historical Sites of Jakarta.* Jakarta: Cipta Loka Caraka

Hitchcock, H. (1958). *Architecture Nineteenth and Twentieth Centuries.* London: Pelican

Hoof van, A. (1934). *Chronologisch Overzicht van de Werkzaamheid der Jezuïeten in de Missie van Nederlandsch-O.-Indië.* Bandoeng: A.C. Nix & Co

Hoytema, J. van (1946, januari-april). *De Tropisch-Nederlandsche Bouwkunst in Indië.* Cultureel Indië, pp. 9-24

Huizinga, J. (1950). *Verzamelde Werken VII In de Schaduwen van Morgen.* Haarlem: H.D. Tjeenk Willink & Zoon N.V.

Hüsken, F. (2004). De ingenieurs en de koloniale erfenis. In W. Ravesteijn, *Bouwen in de Archipel* (pp. 191-295). Zutphen: Walburg Pers

Iongh, D. d. (1941). De Indische Stad. In W. v. Helsdingen, *Daar werd wat groots verricht* (pp. 125-137). Amsterdam: Elsevier

Jessup, H. (1988). *Netherlands Architecture in Indonesia 1900-1942.* London : Courtauld Institute of Art

Jong, J. d. (1998). *De Waaier van het Fortuin.* Den Haag: SDU uitgevers

Jong, L. d. (1969). *Het Koninkrijk der Nederlanden in de Tweede Wereldoorlog Deel 2 Neutraal.* 's-Gravenhage : Staatsuitgeverij

Jong, L. d. (1984). *Het Koninkrijk der Nederlanden in de Tweede wereldoorlog Deel 11a Nederland-Indië 1. eerste helft.* 's-Gravenhage: Staatsuitgeverij

Jong, L. d. (1984). *Het Koninkrijk der Nederlanden in de Tweede Wereldoorlog Deel 11a Nederlands-Indië 1. tweede helft.* 's-Gravenhage: Staatsuitgeverij

Jongejans, J. (1937). *Land en Volk van Atjeh Vroeger en Nu*. Baarn: Hollandia

Kaptijn, M (1937). *De Javasche Bank*, Batavia

Katam, S. (2007) *Preserving an Architectural Heritage*, Jakarta

Katam, S. (2013) *Gedung Bank Indonesia Bandung Dari Masake Masa*, Bandung

Kerchman, J. (1930). *25 Jaren Decentralisatie in Nederlandsch Indië . Weltevreden*. Kolff & Co

Kleijn, K. (1995). *Nederlandse Bouwkunst een geschiedenis van tien eeuwen architectuur*. Alphen aan den Rijn: Icob

Klein, D. (1987). *Art Deco*. Alphen aan den Rijn: Atrium

Klemann, H. (2002). *Nederland 1938-1948 Economie en samenleving in jaren van oorlog en bezetting*. Amsterdam: Boom

Knaud, J. (1980). *Herinneringen aan Soekaboemi*. Den Haag: Moeson

Kok, R. (2010). *Koloniale Oorlog van Indië tot Indonesië 1945-1949*. Amsterdam: Uitgeverij Carrera

Koopmanschap, J.(1996) *De Broeders van Liefde in de Missie van Java vanaf 1929*. CEK

Kunto, H. (1986). *Semerbak Bunga di Bandung Raya*. Bandung

Kurniawan, K.R. (2014) *The Hybrid Architecture of Colonial Tin Mining Town of Muntok*, Jakarta

Kusno, A. (2000). *Behind the Postcolonial (Architecture, urban space in Indonesia)*. London & New York: Routledge

Kusno, A. (2006). The Afterlife of the Empire Style. In P. Nas, *The Past in the Present* (pp. 131-146). Rotterdam: NAi

Kusno, A. (2010). *The Appearances of Memory*. Durham/Lodon: Duke University Press

Lampugnani, V. (2008). *Lexicon van de architectuur van de twintigste eeuw*. Amsterdam: SUN

Langeveld, H. (1998). *Hendrikus Colijn 1869-1944 Deel 1 Dit leven van krachtig handelen*. Amsterdam: Balans

Langeveld, H. (2004). *Hendrikus Colijn 1869-1944 Deel 2 Schipper naast God*. Amsterdam: Balans

Leerdam, B. v. (1988). *Henri Maclaine Pont (architect tussen twee werelden)*. Delft: DUP

Leidelmeijer, F. (1983). *Art Nouveau en Art Deco in Nederland (verzamelobjecten uit de vernieuwingen in de kunstnijverheid van 1890-1940)*. Amsterdam: Meulenhof

Leushuis, E. (2011). *Gids historische stadswandelingen Indonesië*. Leiden: KIT publishers

Linden, J. v. (1981). *Donum Desursum: de Broeders van Maastricht in Indonesia, 1920-1980*. Salatiga: Provinciaal bestuur van Indonesia

Lintum, C. t. (1923). *Nederland en de Indiën in de laatste kwart eeuw*. Zutphen: W.J. Theme & Co

Loderichs, M. (1997). Medan beeld van een stad. Purmerend: Asia Maior.

Loghem, J. van. (1934). *Balans 1934 . De 8 en Opbouw*, 189-195

Luckman, T. (1996). *The History of Medan (in the olden times)*. Medan: Perwira

Maes, A. (2010). *175 jaar Goede Werken (een fotoverhaal van de Broeders van O.L.Vrouw v.Lourdes)*. Oostakker: Uitgeverij O.L. Vrouw van Lourdes

Mansvelt, D. (1924). *Gedenkboek der Nederlandsche Handel-Maatschappij*. 's-Gravenhage : Mouton & Co

Mattie, E. (1999). *Wereldtentoonstellingen*. Blaricum: V+K

Merrillees, S. (2010). *Groeten uit Jakarta*. Alphen aan den Rijn: Icob B.V.

Merrillees, S. (2015). *Jakarta portraits of a Capital 1950-1980*. Jakarta

Meulen, D. v. (1990). *E. du Perron*. 's-Gravenhage: SDU

Molema, J. (2010). *Moderniteit in een behoudende omgeving - Jan Arbarda en De Groep van Delft*. Heijningen: Jap Sam Books

Molenaar, J. (2012). *Brinkman & Van der Vlugt Architecten*. Rotterdam: NAI010

Nix, C. (1949). *Stedebouw in Indonesië en de Stedebouwkundige Vormgeving*. Bandoeng: Nix-Bandoeng

Nix, C. (1989). *Massa Ruimte & Verblijf*. Antwerpen: HAIR

Oostindie, G. (2010). *Postkoloniaal Nederland Vijfenzestig jaar vergeten, herdenken, verdringen*. Amsterdam: Bert Bakker

Oud, J. (ca 1962). *Ter Wille van een Levende Bouwkunst*. 's-Gravenhage: Nijgh & Van Ditmar

Passchier, C. (1988). Bandung (Groei en ontwikkeling van een stad; 1900-1942). in: H.M. van den Berg, *De Stenen droom (Opstellen over Bouwkunst en Monumentenzorg)* (pp. 94-102). Zutphen: De Walburg Pers

Passchier, C. (2006). Colonial Architecture in Indonesia. In P. Nas, *The Past in the Present* (pp. 97-112). Rotterdam: NAi Publishers

Passchier, C. (2008). *The quest for the ultimate architecture Indonesia in the late colonial period*, (pp. 1-14)

Passchier, C. (2016). *Bouwen in Indonesië*. Volendam: LM Publishers

Pehnt, W. (1998). *Die Architektur des Expressionismus*. Ostfildern: Hatje

Perron, E. d. (1956). *Verzameld Werk: De Man van Lebak*. Amsterdam: Van Oorschot

Perron, E. d. (1981). *Brieven VII*. Amsterdam: Van Oorschot

Perron, E. d. (1984). *Brieven VIII*. Amsterdam : Van Oorschot

Perron, E. d. (1990). *Brieven IX*. Amsterdam : Van Oorschot

Pisani, E. (2014). *Indonesia Exploring the Improbable Nation*. London: Granta

Polman, Z. (1935). *Deus providebit: de Congregatie van Heythuysen, 1835-1935, gedenkboek*. Eigen beheer

Pratihari-Kubontubuh, C. (2011). *Guidelines For Managing Post-Disaster Conservation of Heritage Buildings Padang*. Jakarta: BPPI

Ravesteijn, W. (1997). *De Zegenrijke Heeren der Wateren*. Delft: Delft University Pers

Ravesteijn, W. (2004). *Bouwen in de Archipel*. Zutphen: Walburg Pers

Reitsma, S. (1941). De Overwinning op den Afstand. In W.H. van Helsdingen, *Daar wèrd wat groots verricht (Nederlands Indië in de twintigste eeuw)* (pp. 250-263). 's-Gravenhage: Elsevier

Rijckevorsel, L. (1929). Vanuit Ambarawa's Kerktoren. *Berichten uit Nederlandsch-Oost Indië van de Claverbond*, 68-76

Roosmalen, P. v. (2004). Ontstaan van een stedenbouwkundige discipline . In W. Ravesteijn, *Bouwen in de Archipel* (pp. 176-199). Zutphen: De Walburg Pers

Roosmalen, P. v. (2008). *Ontwerpen aan de stad (stedenbouw in Nederlands-Indie en Indonesië 1905-1950).* Delft: DUP

Sain, L. d. (1968). *Er ging een ster mee naar het oosten (50 jaar missiearbeid in Indonesië).* Nijmegen: Thoben

Schaik, A. v. (1996). *Malang beeld van een stad.* Purmerend: Asia Maior

Schlömer, J. (1934). *400 Jaren Missie in Nederlandsch Indië.* Batavia: Maandblad Sociaal Leven

Scholten, B. (1988). *Rotterdamsche Lloyd.* Houten: Unieboek

Segaar-Höweler, D. (1988). A.F.Aalbers Architect van het “Nieuwe Bouwen” in Bandung. In H. M. van den Berg, *De Stenen Droom (Opstellen over Bouwkunst en Monumentenzotg)* (pp. 103-112). Zutphen: De Walburg Pers

Segaar-Höweler, D. (1998). *J.M.Groenewegen.* Rotterdam: BONAS

Segaar-Höweler, D. (2000). *A.F. Aalbers.* Rotterdam: BONAS.

Smits, A.P en Linde, C. v.d., ‘Kantoorgebouw der Nederlandsche Handel-Maatschappij NV Factorij Batavia’ in *Bouwkundig weekblad* 55 (1934), pp. 125-130

Stern, R. (1988). *Modern Classicisme.* London: Thames and Hudson

Stroomberg, D. J. (1930). *Handbook of the Netherlands East-Indies.* Batavia: Kolff & Co

Sumalyo, Y. (1993) *Arsitektur kolonial Belanda di Indonesia mengetengahkan arsitek dan biro arsitek Maclaine Pont, Thomas Karsten, C.P. Wolff Schoemaker, W. Lemei, C. Citroen, Ed. Cuypers & Hulswit, Batavia Algemeene Ingenieurs Architecten*, Yogyakarta.

Taselaar, A. (1998). *De Nederlandse Koloniale Lobby (Ondernemers politiek 1914-1940).* Leiden: Leidse Universiteit

Taverne, E. (2001). *J.J.P. Oud.* Rotterdam : NAI Uitgevers

Temminck Groll, P. C. (2002). *The Dutch Overseas Architectural Survey.* Zwolle: Waanders

Terweij, S. (1948). *Door Tyd en Vlyt. Gedenkboek uitgegeven ter gelegenheid van het honderdjarig bestaan van de N.V. Koninklijke Boekhandel en Drukkerij G. Kolff & Co.*, 1948. Djakarta : Kolff

Thoor, M. v. (1998). *Het Gebouw van Nederland.* Zutphen: Walburg Pers

Tichelman, G. (1948). *Wordend Indonesië.* Haarlem: Drukkerij Spaarnestad

Vletter, M.E. (1997). *Batavia, Djakarta, Jakarta (Beeld van een metamorfose).* Purmerend

Vletter, M. (2007). Tradition and Modernity in the Netherlands East Indies . In P. Nas, *The Past in the Present* (pp. 113-122). Rotterdam: NAI Publishers

Voorneman, E. (1937). *Batavia als Handel-, Industrie- en Woonstad.* Batavia: Kolff&Co

Voskuil, R. (1989). *Batavia, Beeld van een Stad.* Houten : Fibula

Voskuil, R. (1996). *Bandoeng Beeld van een Stad.* Purmerend: Asia Maior

Vriend, J. (1938). *De Bouwkunst van ons Land.* Amsterdam: Scheltema & Holkema

Vries, D. d. (1946). *Gordel van Smaragd.* Amsterdam: Contact

Vries, G. d. (2009). *Henri Maclaine Pont (architect, constructeur, archeoloog).* Rotterdam : BONAS

Wagenvoort, M. (1911). Zoeklichten over Insulinde . In H.Colijn, *Neerlans Indië (Land en Volk Geschiedenis en Bestuur Bedrijf en Samenleving) Deel 1* (pp. 54-101). Amsterdam: 1911

Wal, S. v. (1968). *Herinneringen van Jhr. Mr. B.C. de Jonge. Met brieven uit zijn nalatenschap.* Utrecht: Historisch Genootschap

Watkin, D. (1994). *De Westerse Architectuur Een geschiedenis.* Nijmegen : SUN

Witte, J. (1976). *J.B.van Heutsz (leven en legende).* Bussum: Unieboek

Wolff-Schoemaker, C. (1923). Indische bouwkunst en de ontwikkelingsmogelijkheid van een Indo-Europeesche Architectuur stijl. *Indisch Bouwkundig Tijdschrift* 26, 188-194

Woud, A. v. (2008). *Sterrenstof Honderd jaar mythologie in de Nederlandse architectuur.* Rotterdam: Uitgeverij 010

Zandvliet, K. (2002). *De Nederlandse Ontmoeting met Azië (1600-1950).* Zwolle: Waanders

Zeijlstra, H. (1931). *Nederland te Parijs 1931 Gedenkboek van de Nederlandsche deelneming aan de Internationale Koloniale Tentoonstelling.* Deventer: De IJsel

Zwaan, J. (1980). *Nederlands-Indië 1940-1946 Gouvernementeel Intermezzo 1940-1942.* Den Haag: Uitgeverij Omniboek

8 INDEX

Aalbers, A.F. 51-52, 71, 75
Bataafsche Petroleum Maatschappij (Shell) 45, 47, 52, 78, 226-229, 234-239, 286
Beeke-Heijnneman, E.E.P. ter 10, 28, 35, 62, 64
Beelen, H.G. 36, 62, 64, 178, 208, 222
Bel, G.J. 62
Berghoef, J.F. 71
Bergson, H. 16, 71-72, 289
Berlage, H.P. 20, 26, 28, 31, 40, 47, 71-73, 75
Bernhard, Prince of the Netherlands 42, 45-48
Blankenberg, J.F.L. 51, 71, 74-75
Boeken, A. 71
Boeyinga, B.T. 71
Bogtman, firm 210
Boon, Ch. W. 283
Bos, K.H.G. 62
Bowbyes, M.J. 282
Braak. M. ter 42
Breuning, H.A. 52, 74, 230, 232, 234
Brinkman, F.W. 62, 291
Britten, B. 68
Bruyn, J.J.J. de 73
Burhoven Jaspers, N.E. 118
Buttingha Wichers, G.G. 38, 73, 194
Cancellotti, C. 73
Canton, firm de 210
Cenzi, L. 38, 73, 186
Chamberlain, N. 49, 52
Chirico, G. de 58
Christiansen, B. 16, 31, 71-72
Citroen, C. 71, 74, 262
Colijn, H. 8, 38, 40, 42, 45, 49, 56
Corbusier, Le 16, 66, 71-72, 74
Cornelisse-Van Eedenburg, J.S. 226
Cramer, B.J.K. 71
Cuypers, E.H.G.H. 7, 10-11, 13, 15-17, 20, 22, 26, 31, 34, 36, 38, 42, 45, 47, 63, 68-69, 71-72, 74-75, 90, 92, 107-108, 118, 177, 190, 210, 216, 226, 240, 256, 269-270, 282-283, 287
Cuypers, P.J.H. 10-11, 287
Daladier, E. 49, 52
Deppe, B.W.J. 31, 47, 57, 62, 75, 144, 210, 216, 226, 230-231, 234, 236, 240, 256, 260, 262, 264-265
Dicke, F. 10, 31, 36, 49, 56, 60, 71, 73, 75, 220-221, 253, 256-258, 260, 262, 281
Dijkmans SJ 160
Dikstaal, A.S. 10-11, 20, 25-26, 28-29, 33, 36-38, 40, 71-74, 108, 134, 148, 170-171, 186, 193, 200, 281-282
Dikstaal-van der Bijl, M. 73, 170
Dudok, W.M. 10-11, 26, 29, 33, 72, 148, 281
Duiker, J. 72, 74
Dupuis, T. 236
Edison, A. 13, 71
Eekelen, D.M. van 286
Einstein, A. 71
Elsässer, M. 72
Embden, S.J. van 71, 73
Essen, H. von 71
Estourgie, H.L.J.M. 106
Evers, H. 71
Fasseur, C. 9, 11, 72, 74-75, 290
Fermont, A.A. 10-12, 15, 18-19, 21, 25-26, 30-31, 35-36, 38, 40, 42-43, 45, 47, 51-52, 55, 62-64, 66, 69-70, 73-75, 88, 92, 94, 110-111, 144, 166, 170, 178, 186, 195-196, 208, 222, 234, 240, 246-247, 250, 254, 256, 274, 282-283
Fermont, C. 63-64, 69, 75
Fischer, H. 62-64, 66
Ford, H. 71
Friedhoff, G. 71
Gendt, J. van 62
Gerber, I.J. 71
Gerlagh, B. 10-11
Ghijsels, F.J.L. 71, 118-119
Graeff, A.C. de 31
Granpré Molière, M.J. 10, 16, 36, 71, 75, 204, 258
Grijzen, J.H.J. 283
Groenewegen, J.M. 15, 19, 71
Grünberg, A. 19, 71, 99
Haase, H. 9, 73
Hakker, C.H.M. 284
Hatta, M. 13, 68-69, 73, 118, 274
Hendriks, G. 52, 62
Heutsz, J.B. van 7, 12-13, 33, 38, 71, 187
Hitchcock, H.R. 31
Hitler, A. 19, 26, 31, 33-34, 38, 47, 49, 52, 55-56, 60, 73
Hollandsche Beton Maatschappij 10, 45, 60, 97, 100, 108, 134, 176, 200, 212, 230, 262
Hoog, firm A. de 212
Hoytema, J.F. van 290
Huizinga, J. 40-41, 73
Hulswit, M.J. 7, 10, 13, 15-16, 18-19, 99, 170, 269, 292
Jaski, W. 15, 19, 71, 84, 88, 94, 283
Job & Sprey (architecture firm) 71, 73-74
Johnson, Ph. 31
Jonge, Jhr. B.C. de 31, 45
Jongh, A.A. de 72
Jongh, J.I. de 10, 12, 15, 28-29, 35-36, 38, 40, 49, 62, 72, 74, 88, 130-132, 134, 140, 154, 162, 194, 200, 208, 283-284, 286, 288
Juliana, Princess of the Netherlands 12-13, 42, 45-48, 168
Kalken SJ, pastoor Van 154, 170
Kannegieter, H. 71

Kaptijn, M. 10, 12, 15, 25, 28, 31, 34, 36, 38, 45, 47, 51-52, 55-56, 62, 72-74, 136, 144, 178, 180, 211-212, 284
Karsten, H.Th. 11, 21, 33, 47, 49, 52, 62, 71, 73, 134, 216
Kasteleyn, J. 283
Kip, A. 262
Koch SJ, H. 146
Koene, R. 75
Koninklijke Pakketvaart Maatschappij 26, 88, 152
Kreisler, A. 16, 71, 84-85, 107, 118-119
Kunstkring, De 58, 68, 71
Kurris SJ 110
Laan, H. van der 71
Lansdorp, N. 31, 36, 72-73
Lemei, W. 62
Lidth de Jeude, Jhr. I.M. van 220
Lie, firma Sin Hap 240
Lindbergh, Ch. 71
Linde, C. van de 73
Linden, J. van der 128
Lint, firma De 210
Lith, M.A. van 284
Lith SJ, F. van 158
Logemann, D.B. 71, 284
Logemann, L.C. 10, 12, 15-16, 20--24, 28, 36, 39, 71, 80, 98, 100, 102, 106, 108, 114, 118-120, 124, 128, 132, 180, 200, 202, 284-285
Loghem, J.B. van 72, 74
Maclaine Pont, H. 71
Manuel, M.E.J. 19, 25, 124
Marconi, G. 13, 71
Medenblik, A.C. 284
Mekel, K. 64, 66-68, 266, 270, 274, 276-277, 285
Mesman Schultz, firm 210, 240
Meubelindustrie Andriesse 210
Meyroos, A. 110
Mieras, J.P. 71
Montuori, E. 73
Moojen, P.A.J. 20, 26, 28, 71-72, 190
Mook, J.H. 208
Mourik, W.G.J. 71
Multatuli 34, 162, 164, 288
Mussert, A. 38, 40, 60
Mussolini, B. 13, 19, 49, 52, 71-73, 186, 289-290
Nedam NV (contracting company) 66, 68, 96, 194, 226, 234
Nederlandsche Handel-Maatschappij 15, 17, 34, 42, 73, 77, 97, 194, 240-241
Nederlandsche Koloniale Petroleum Maatschappij 45
Nederlandsch Indische Architecten Kring (N.I.A.K.) 52
Nes, G.L. van 281
Nix, C.Th. 10, 19, 25, 28, 30-31, 35-37, 40, 42-45, 47, 51, 54-56, 58, 62-63, 69, 71, 73-76, 104, 108, 146-148, 152, 154, 156, 168, 172-173, 176, 180, 186, 190-191, 193-196, 204, 206-207, 210, 221, 226-227, 230-231, 234, 237, 242, 284-286, 288, 290-291
Noordaa, L. van der 33, 47, 226, 230-231, 233, 236
Oud, J.J.P. 16, 31, 49, 71-72
Oyen, J.Th. van 26, 35-36, 40, 45, 62, 72, 74, 107-108, 146, 154, 196, 240-241, 258-259
Pears, P. 68
Perron, E. du 34, 42, 55, 72-74, 162
Philips, firm 13
Picasso, P. 45
Piccinato, L. 73
Ravesteyn, S. van 31, 72-73
Rijksen, R. 62, 106
Roebbers, H. 10, 66, 68-69, 272-273, 276, 278, 286
Roo, E.H. de 52, 62
Roosenburg, D.P. 71, 73
Rooy OSC, pastor De 196
Rotterdamsche Lloyd 7, 21, 26, 47, 51, 55-57, 59, 68, 88, 114, 116-117, 260, 283
Sain, E.B. de 287
Sain, L. de 36, 178, 250
Sandrock, Th. Chr. 94
Schedler, E. 12, 15, 28, 35, 45, 71, 206
Schoemaker, R.L.A. 62
Schotman, R.A. 71, 120
Selle & De Bruyn, architecture firm 194, 208
Sjahrir, S. 55, 73
Smits, A.P. 73
Snuyf, S. 62, 75
Soeterik, F. 272
Spanjaard, S. 285
Spitsbergen, Mr. 141
Stalin, J. 19, 38, 72
Stoomvaart Maatschappij Nederland 21, 51, 55-56, 60, 64, 88, 114, 116-117
Sukarno, A. 10, 13, 22, 31, 64, 68-69, 71-73, 118
Sutardjo, K. 60
Taen, Th. 10-12, 15, 25, 28, 30, 35-36, 38, 40, 45, 51-52, 55-56, 60, 62, 69, 71, 74, 80, 84, 86, 90, 92, 94, 96-98, 100, 102, 104, 107-110, 114, 120, 124-126, 128, 130-132, 136, 140, 144, 152, 154, 158-160, 162, 164, 166, 168, 170, 176-178, 180, 184, 186, 192, 194-195, 200, 204, 206, 208-210, 222, 246-248, 250, 252-258, 260, 262, 284, 286-288
Tan Tjoan Hong 252
Tan Tjoan Keng 36-38, 186, 252
Terragni, G. 21
Thamrin, M.H. 25, 56, 60-61, 75
Tideman, M.B. 21, 71
Tjarda van Starkenborgh Stachouwer, A.W.L. 45, 246
Treub, M. 216
Trip, L.J.A. 42, 74
Vegter, J.J.M. 71
Velt, H.R.M. 281
Vlugt, L.C. van der 11
Volkers, NV contracting company 222, 240
Waals, E. van der 285
Welter, C.J.I.M. 55
Westmaas, W. 62
Wiener, firm 210
Wijdeveld, H.Th. 22, 72
Wijsman, Ph. 12, 15, 28, 35, 71, 136
Wilhelmina, Queen of the Netherlands 12-13, 23, 54-55, 102, 162, 236
Willekens SJ, P.J. 257
Willink, A.C. 55, 58
Wolff Schoemaker, C.P. 61, 71, 75
Zeilinga, E.A. 13
Zomer, studio Nico 270, 274
Zweedijk, W.J.G. 71-72
Zwiers, H.T. 281

9 ABBREVIATIONS

AIA Algemeen Ingenieurs- en Architectenbureau (General Engineering and Architectural Office)
BOW Burgerlijke Openbare Werken (Civil Public Works)
CAA Collection Architectenbureau 'Aan de Amstel', Amsterdam
CBM Collection 'Brothers from Maastricht'
CBN Ballast Nedam collection, Nieuwegein
CCR Collection Sisters of Charitas in Roosendaal
CDJ Collection Nanette de Jong
CEK Collection Erfgoed Kloosterleven (Heritage Monastic life) St. Agatha
CEM Collection Erik Mattie
CFC Fermont-Cuypers collection
CFL Collection Logemann Family
CFN Collection Nix Family
CFR Collection Franciscan' Sisters of Roosendaal
CFT Collection Taen Family
CJE Collection Joh. Enschedé, Haarlem
CJW Collection Joep Walter, Deventer
CMB Collection Museum Bank Indonesia
CMM Collection Maritime Museum, Rotterdam
CNJ Collection Jesuits European Low Countries Kadoc, Leuven (B)
COF Unknown photographer, internet
COH Collection Sisters of the Sacred Heart, Tilburg
CON Collection Obbe H. Norbruis, Amsterdam
CPD Collection Palmboom Division
CRF Collection Roebbers Family
CSL Collection Sander Lugtenburg
CTM Collection Tropen Museum (Royal Institute for the Tropics), Amsterdam
CVN Collection Van Nes Family
CWH Collection Watse Heringa, Bloemendaal
HNI Het Nieuwe Instituut (The New Institute), Rotterdam
KDC Collection of the Catholic Documentation Center, Nijmegen
KITLV Koninklijk Instituut voor Taal-, Land- en Volkenkunde, Leiden
NA Nationaal Archief (National Archives), The Hague
NIOD Nederlands Instituut voor Oorlogsdocumentatie (Institute for War, Holocaust and Genocide Studies)

Magazines

HH *Het Huis* (1903,1904)
HHON *Het Huis Oud & Nieuw* (1905-1926)
HNIHON *Het Nederlandsch-Indische Huis Oud & Nieuw* (1913-1916)
HNNIHON *Het Nederlandsche en Nederlandsch Indische Huis Oud & Nieuw* (1928-1930)
IBT *Indisch Bouwkundig Tijdschrift*
NION *Nederlandsch-Indië Oud & Nieuw* (1916-1930)

LM Publishers
Parallelweg 37
1131 dm Volendam
0031 85 8772397
info@lmpublishers.nl
www.lmpublishers.nl

TEKST Obbe H. Norbruis
EDITING Radboud van Beekum, Gerrit Vermeer
TRANSLATION Aileen Stronge
DESIGN Ad van Helmond
PRINTING Hightrade bv

DUTCH EDITION *Architectuur met vlag en wimpel*, 2018
COVER PHOTO FRONT Stairs in the former B.P.M. building, now Pertamina, in Jakarta. Photo: Joep Walter.
COVER PHOTOS BACK Architects of Fermont-Cuypers in 1936 / Buildings designed by Fermont-Cuypers / Stairs in the former B.P.M. building, now Pertamina, in Semarang.

THIS PUBLICATION WAS MADE POSSIBLE IN PART BY FINANCIAL CONTRIBUTIONS FROM:
Partners in Equity, Brussels; Corts Foundation (www.cortsfoundation.org/nl); Marinus Plantema Foundation (www.marinusplantemafoundation.nl); Dutch Culture (www.dutchculture.nl); a/d Amstel architects Amsterdam (www.adamstel.nl); Pusat Dokumentasi Arsitektur, Jakarta (www.pda.or.id); Hulswit-Fermont-Cuypers Foundation (www.stichtinghulswitfermontcuypers.nl)

Also available:
Landmarks from a bygone era
Life and Work of Ed.Cuypers & Hulswit-Fermont
in the Indonesian Archipelago
1897-1927

Pages 320
ISBN 978-94-6022-015-9

LMpublishers.nl

Hulswit-Fermont-Cuypers
Foundation for Indonesian-Dutch Milestones in Architecture

DutchCulture | Shared Cultural Heritage

Corts Foundation

Marinus Plantema Foundation

Partners in Equity

Pusat Dokumentasi Arsitektur Indonesia

a/d amstel architecten